The Patissier's Art

Professional Breads, Cakes, Pies, Pastries, and Puddings

George Karousos
Bradley J. Ware
Theodore H. Karousos

John Wiley & Sons, Inc.
New York   Chichester   Brisbane   Toronto   Singapore

Publisher: Margaret K. Burns
Senior Editor: Claire Thompson
Associate Managing Editor: Jacqueline A. Martin
Editorial Production: Michelle Neil/Editorial Services of New England, Inc.
Photography: Ron Manville

This text is printed on acid-free paper.

Library of Congress Cataloging-in-Publication Data:
Karousos, George
    The patissier's art: professional breads, cakes, pies, pastries, and puddings / George
Karousos, Bradley J. Ware, Theodore H. Karousos.
        p.   cm.
    Includes index.
    ISBN 0-471-59716-3 (alk. paper)
    1. Pastry. 2. Desserts.   I. Ware, Bradley J. (Bradley John), 1953-   .
II. Karousos, Theodore H.   III. Title.
TX773.K327   1993
641.8'6—dc20

                                                                              93-40222
                                                                                  CIP

Printed in the United States of America
10   9   8   7   6   5   4   3   2   1

Contents

Foreword   v

Preface   vii

1   **The Art of Pastry**   1

2   **French Pastry and Vienna Pastry**   11

3   **Petits Fours and Fancy Cakes**   61

4   **Puddings, Sweets, and Sauces**   119

5   **Cakes, Pies, Muffins, and Griddle Cakes**   175

6   **Ice Creams, Water Ices, and Sherbets**   235

7   **Bread and Rolls**   281

Glossary   299

Index   307

Foreword

The *Patissier's Art* is designed to assist the pastry chef who is responsible for planning pastry and dessert production in hotels and restaurants. This collection of recipes and formulas reflects the practical and creative thinking of many professionals and will serve as a valuable and reliable resource for food service personnel.

The perfect dessert is a work of art. It leaves a sense of satisfaction not easily forgotten. It gives joy both to the chef and to the customer. Its creation and presentation require knowledge, thought, imagination, and attention to detail.

You may follow the recipes in this book or change them about. Add your special touch to a torte, a tasty sauce, or a particular bread. Make your creation yours alone and a treat your customer will not forget. The finishing touch is your personal signature and the one element that will make you stand out as a pastry chef.

Lars Johansson, C.E.P.C., C.C.E.
Johnson & Wales University
College of Culinary Arts
International Baking and Pastry Institute

Preface

When pastry first made its appearance on our tables, it was a simple accessory to the dinner. Instead of playing a secondary part, as in the past, dessert now stands side by side with *l'art de la cuisine,* given equal and legitimate rights and pretensions.

Modern cuisine could not do without an auxiliary so strong and so rich in its proper merits and in the beauty and splendor of its ornamentation. The great and multitudinous variety of its design renders the study of this art a complicated and difficult process. To succeed, one must be enthusiastic and ambitious to attain, with the fire and perseverance of the artist, whom nothing can turn aside in the search and efforts to penetrate the secrets of any given art or science.

Sculpture and architecture are the sources of inspiration to the pastry chef—flowers, fruits, bronzes, statuary, and numberless other works of art and nature showing the beauty and grace of line.

This book is based on the work of K. Camille Den Dooven, *The Hotel and Restaurant Dessert Book,* published in 1927. The original work is a treasury of classic pâtisserie.

To those who are capable of judging the progress of pâtisserie, it is evident that it is still progressing. It is a science not without prestige, and it has its souvenirs and traditions. The present edition maintains the rich traditions that are the backbone of the original, while bringing a fresh look at ingredients, preparation, and, perhaps most importantly, presentation.

Included are new recipes, nutritional information, and ideas that trace the progress of the art of pastry. Many of the new recipes are for brownies, cookies, and muffins—items suited to the quick and casual lifestyle of the 1990s. Which is not to say that today's chefs do not continue to focus on the elegant side of the industry. In a more formal setting, the pastry chef's creativity is challenged today more than ever. Chefs are expected to balance color, texture, flavor, and freshness, meet a desire for richness, while offering concessions to the public's awareness of and need for lighter, lower fat desserts. The modern chef may prepare the same rich dessert for a main item, but will serve a smaller portion, complemented by a crisp, elegant cookie and a fresh, colorful fruit sauce, thereby meeting the varied and somewhat contrary requirements of today's customers.

To see the artists at their work, one would imagine they were laboring for posterity, and still they know that their productions, of undeniable merit, are short-lasting and ephemeral. In practice, the art of pâtisserie is very minute in detail and claims the entire attention and solicitude of an expert, for here everything is calculated, everything methodical—the weights, quantities, numbers, etc. are observed according to exact laws and rules. Metric conversions are included in the current edition to ensure precise calculations. To achieve commendable results, a pâtissier must possess intelligence and cleverness and give the work complete attention. The patissier also must possess the fine and delicate taste that is the essential and indispensable attribute of an artist.

Acknowledgments

We would like to thank the following professionals, whose work has made this book a reality:

> Jean-Luc Derron: Metric Conversions
> Jon Manville: Photography
> Louise R. Phaneuf: Maunuscript Development and Preparation
> Nancy Thomas-Garnett, M.S., R.D.: Nutritional Information

A special note of thanks is due to Lars Johansson, C.E.P.C., C.C.E., Director of the International Baking & Pastry Institute of Johnson & Whales University. Chef Johansson brought his extensive experience and concentrated efforts to ensuring the accuracy and professionalism of the formulas, yields, charts, and photographs.

1

The Art of Pastry

❦ The Pastry Chef

A pastry chef must work well with ice cream, confections, sugar artistry, and decoration, as well as be a pastry baker, and above all a good organizer. In some of the large hotels, the pastry and bake shops are separate departments, under different supervisory heads or chefs, i.e., the pastry chef and master baker (or chef baker). However, in most hotels and restaurants, pastry and bread are in one department and are under the supervision of the pastry chef.

The pastry chef supervises the production and service of the desserts, pastries, salted nuts, and patties or *vol-au-vents* and in some hotels also supervises the stewed fruits, waffles, and griddle cakes. The pastry chef personally prepares all artistic decorations, such as wedding and birthday cakes, sugar baskets, and the fancy pieces for table decoration, as well as doing the clerical work necessary in the operation of the department—making a list of the fresh fruits, milk, and cream needed in the preparation of desserts so that the steward will be able to properly arrange the ordering, deliver goods in time for preparation, and avoid any unnecessary waste to the hotel. The chef also makes a requisition in the evening for all other materials needed from the storeroom to be delivered the next morning and posts on the pastry shop bulletin board (in the morning of the day before) a copy of the menu for the succeeding day, with the explanation of all fancy desserts and copies of all banquet menus.

At 11:30 A.M., the chef makes the rounds and sees that all desserts are ready and that the pastry is satisfactory. The chef also personally supervises the service from the department, seeing that the wait staff is served in a proper manner and with as little delay as possible. After the rush hour (about 2:00 or 2:30 P.M.), the chef reviews the entire department, seeing that there is enough of all necessary articles on hand for the afternoon *à la carte* service and that the cakes and pastries are prepared for the tea room.

At 5:30 P.M., the first duty is to look over all orders for the evening service, such as special orders for Baked Alaska, soufflés, or fruits served with ice cream, seeing that all silver platters and covers are cleaned and prepared (soufflé dishes with folded napkins, etc.) and that there are memoranda slips on all platters of proper size denoting number of portions and kind of dessert to be served on each. The chef also ensures that bowls are placed on platters with napkins for all fruits served with ice cream and that all *friandise* and *petits fours* for small *à la carte* parties are prepared and ready to be served in sugar baskets or other fancy containers. Dinner service is supervised in the same manner as luncheon. The bill of fare and storeroom requisitions are prepared for the next day, the ice cream or whatever dessert is to be served for banquet parties is readied, and all *friandise, petit fours,* and salted nuts are prepared, ready to serve half an hour prior to the start of the banquet.

🍎 Equipment

The equipment found in pastry and bake shops will depend on the particular establishments. Items found may include the following:

Storage: Refrigerators, freezers, a variety of cans and bins, shelves and cabinets, and pan racks

Scaling: Floor and table scales and liquid and dry measuring equipment

Preparation: Work benches, tables, mixing bowls, cookie machine, dough divider, proof box, flour sifter, steam kettles, and knives

Baking: Stoves, ovens, doughnut fryer, pots, pans, and cooling racks

Finishing: Decorating table, portioning tools, spatulas, sinks, display case, and pastry bags

🍎 Management Skills

The most difficult aspect of the pastry chef's work lies in making up a proper menu, estimating the amount of each *du jour* (or special for the day) dish and each *à la carte* dessert that must be made in order to ensure service to everyone. Unavoidably, a certain amount of pastry and desserts will be left over after each meal, and while these are served in the officer's dining hall and are not entirely wasted, they still bring no profit to the firm. The pastry chef must therefore see that enough desserts are made to fill all orders and at the same time cut the surplus to a minimum.

Increasing demand and the need for efficiency in every hotel department make it doubly important for the pastry chef to exercise close food control throughout the pastry department, cutting waste to the minimum, directing the crew in such a manner as to make each person 100 percent efficient, and arranging the schedule so as to have no waste of time and no confusion. It is also a help toward greater efficiency to have all employees specialists in their lines.

Another condition upon which successful baking depends is the proper management of the pastry department. One of the most important points is the necessary clearing up as you go along. Contrast, for instance, a well-ordered pastry department, in which the tables and equipment are kept clean, all utensils are in their proper places, and all personnel are proceeding quietly and efficiently about their work, with a badly managed department at that trying moment known as the service hour, or *l'heure de service*. In the latter you will find the helpers with flushed faces and a hurried, nervous manner, surrounded by a chaos of dirty pans, basins, and knives congregated on sloppy, uncleared tables, all excited and arguing irritably with the wait staff. As a consequence, the correct service to the guests is delayed and the nervous tension and ill humor gradually spread until they reach the guests. The results are sometimes even more far reaching than the production of a general spirit of disorder, discord, and dissatisfaction. Such disorder can lead to loss of business to the hotel because a dissatisfied guest may not wait for the order to be complete or may refuse to pay for it, which involves not only a lost sale but also waste of good material, and the guest may at least hesitate to return to the establishment.

It is also important that the chef and helpers do not argue with the wait staff, a very common occurrence in hotels, particularly when the staff presents an order for something a little unusual or a special preparation. The chef must understand that in this case the server represents the guest's wishes and is simply communicating the order and manner of serving that the guest desires and is willing to pay for. To refuse or delay an order of this kind is the same as refusing the guest. In this connection, it is well to remember that "the guest is always right" in the hotel business, no matter what the employee's private opinion of the order may be.

In the hotel or restaurant business, the chef and staff, though indirectly, are a vital and important part of the sales staff and should recognize the importance of the use of sales methods in their department. Remember that the dessert course that is delayed or improperly served in any way may spoil the entire meal and leave in the guest's mind the impression of poor service throughout. If, on the other hand, the first part of the meal is unsatisfactory for any reason, a well-served and attractive dessert will often entirely erase the memory of that which preceded it and leave in the guest's mind a pleasant impression of "all's well that ends well."

Ninety-nine percent of the complaints that go to the manager's office could be avoided by following the preceding suggestions.

❦ Food Values

People often ask about the nutritional values of certain ingredients or formulas. They are, for example, always very interested in knowing the amount of protein, carbohydrates, and calories contained in a cake or dessert. The study of the comparative food values is a necessary part of every chef's education. Table 1.1 is a useful reference on the composition and comparative values of the materials with which you are working, as well as a guide to producing more nutritious desserts.

TABLE 1.1   Nutrient Composition of Common Bakeshop Ingredients

One Ounce	Carbo-hydrates (g)	Protein (g)	Fat (g)	Saturated Fat (g)	Cholesterol (mg)	Fiber (g)	Sodium (mg)
Butter, salted	0	0.2	23.0	14.2	62	0	234
unsalted	0	0.2	23.0	14.2	62	0	3
Chocolate, baking	8.2	3.0	15.1	8.4	0	4.37	1
bittersweet	15.7	1.9	9.8	5.9	0	0.89	2
dark, sweet	16.0	1.0	10.0	5.9	0	0.90	5
milk	16.2	2.2	9.2	5.1	6	0.79	27
Cornmeal	5.3	0.6	0.1	0	0	0.49	0
Cornstarch	25.9	0	0	0	0	0.28	4
Corn syrup, dark	30.7	0	0	0	0	0	28
light	30.7	0	0	0	0	0	28
Cream, half & half	1.2	0.8	3.3	2.0	10	0	12
heavy	0.8	0.6	10.6	6.6	39	0	11
sour	1.2	0.9	5.9	3.7	13	0	11
Eggs, fresh, large	0.3	3.6	2.9	0.9	122	0	36
whites	0.3	3.0	0	0	0	0	47
yolks	0.5	4.8	8.7	2.7	361	0	12
Flour, bread	21.2	3.3	0.3	0	0	0.08	1
cake	22.1	2.3	0.2	0	0	0.79	1
rye	22.0	2.7	0.5	0.1	0	4.15	1
white	21.7	2.9	0.3	0	0	0.77	0
whole wheat	20.7	3.9	0.5	0.1	0	3.59	1
Fruit							
Apple, fresh	4.4	0.1	0.1	0	0	0.63	0
Apricot, dry	6.3	0.4	0	0	0	0.78	1
Dates, fresh	20.8	0.6	0.1	0	0	2.32	1
Figs, fresh	5.5	0.2	0.1	0	0	1.07	1
Fillings	7.1	0.1	0	0	0	0.38	8
Grapes, fresh	5.1	0.2	0.2	0.1	0	0.20	1
Jams/preserves	19.9	0.2	0	0	0	0.26	2
Lemons, fresh	2.7	0.3	0.1	0	0	0.59	0
juice	2.0	0.1	0.1	0	0	0.09	6
Orange, fresh	3.3	0.3	0	0	0	0.68	0
Pear, fresh	4.3	0.1	0.1	0	0	0.75	0
Raisins	22.5	0.9	0.1	0	0	1.67	3
Raspberries, fresh	3.3	0.3	0.2	0	0	1.78	0
Strawberries, fresh	2.0	0.2	0.1	0	0	0.74	0
Margarine	0.1	0.2	22.7	3.9	0	0	306
Milk, evaporated, skim	3.6	2.4	0.1	0	1	0	37
evaporated, whole	3.2	2.1	2.4	1.4	9	0	33
low fat, 1%	1.5	1.0	0.3	0.2	1	0	15
low fat, 2%	1.5	1.0	0.6	0.4	2	0	15
nonfat milk solids	14.9	10	0.2	0.1	5	0	156
whole milk	1.4	1.0	1.0	0.6	4	0	15
Nuts							
Almonds	5.3	5.8	15.0	1.4	0	3.21	3
Brazil	3.6	4.0	18.5	4.5	0	2.50	0
Coconut, flaked	13.7	0.9	9.3	8.2	0	3.78	74
Filberts/hazelnuts	4.3	3.7	17.8	1.3	0	1.83	1
Peanuts, unsalted	6.1	6.7	14.1	2.0	0	2.50	2
Pecans, unsalted	6.3	2.3	18.3	1.5	0	1.84	0
Walnuts	5.2	4.1	17.6	1.6	0	1.37	3
Rice, white	22.7	2.0	0.2	0	0	0.34	1
Sugar, brown	27.6	0	0	0	0	0	9
confectioner's	28.5	0	0	0	0	0	0
granulated	28.5	0	0	0	0	0	0
Tapioca	25.1	0.1	0	0	0	0.31	0

Most of the recipes contained in this book can be easily reduced to smaller quantities for home cooking by using Table 1.2.

TABLE 1.2   Equivalent Weights and Measures

Volume	Weight
3 teaspoons	1 tablespoon
4 tablespoons	$^{1}/_{4}$ cup
6 teaspoons baking powder	1 ounce
4 teaspoons fine salt	1 ounce
2 tablespoons butter	1 ounce
2 tablespoons granulated sugar	1 ounce
4 tablespoons flour	1 ounce
1 cup liquid	8 ounces
2 cups liquid	1 pint
4 cups liquid	1 quart
2 cups butter, solid	1 pound
2 cups lard or compound	1 pound
2 cups granulated sugar	1 pound
$2^{1}/_{2}$ cups confectioner's 4× sugar	1 pound
1 cup salt	9 ounces
1 cup molasses	12 ounces
1 cup cornstarch	6 ounces
3 cups raisins	1 pound
2 cups rice	1 pound
4 cups flour	1 pound
10 eggs	1 pint
16 egg whites	1 pint
26 egg yolks	1 pint
5 eggs	1 cup
8 egg whites	1 cup
13 egg yolks	1 cup
24 lemons, juice of	1 quart
6 lemons, juice of	1 cup
14 oranges, juice of	1 quart
$3^{1}/_{2}$ oranges, juice of	1 cup

Always sift flour before measuring
Always use level measurements

🐝 Items Used in Baking and Confectionery

Acetic acid   A clear liquid having a strong acid taste and peculiar sharp smell; it is a major component of vinegar. Acetic acid is used in sugar cookery.

Agar-agar   A seaweed-based gelatinous substance obtained from Japan; it comes in long, narrow, whitish strips that swell slightly in cold water and considerably in boiling water before dissolving. Without odor or flavor, agar-agar is very strong as a gelatin and is used in jellies, jams, nougat, etc.

Albumen The white viscous material found in egg whites. Obtained by drying egg whites, albumen is used in confectionery cooking.

Allspice Seasoning derived from a small, dry, globular berry that is the fruit of an evergreen tree common in the West Indies.

Arrowroot A starch obtained from the roots of several species of West Indian plants and used, like starch, for binding sauces and puddings.

Bicarbonate of soda (baking soda) Used commercially in the baking trade in connection with cream of tartar as a leavener for cakes, biscuits, etc. In connection with sour milk or molasses, however, it may be used alone.

Cacao The bean or seed of a small evergreen tree grown in tropical countries, from which cocoa and chocolate are prepared.

Cassia An aromatic bark, also known as Chinese cinnamon. Since it is cheaper to produce, it is often used as a substitute for true cinnamon.

Chocolate A product derived from the dried, roasted, and ground seeds of the cacao tree.

Cinnamon Derived from the bark of the cinnamon tree, a native of Ceylon; it is used in both stick and powder form.

Citric acid Obtained principally from lemons, it also can be abstracted from various other fruits. It is used to make lemonade, as well as orange and lemon syrups.

Cloves The flower buds of a tropical evergreen tree, which are picked by hand and then dried in the sun; used as a seasoning.

Cocoa See cacao.

Cocoa butter A product derived from the cacao bean and used in chocolate coatings, buttercreams, and confections.

Coconut butter Used principally in the preparation of salted nuts and in chocolates; also used as a substitute for cocoa butter in chocolates.

Cornstarch A white, corn-based thickening agent.

Corn syrup A thick, yellowish liquid that does not crystallize easily; it is used in confectionery cooking.

Cream of tartar A slightly acidic, fine white powder; it is a component of baking powder.

Eggs, frozen During preparation, the egg is removed from the shell and is then quickly frozen and held at a temperature of approximately 0°F, thus retaining all its natural goodness.

Gelatin A substance found in animal bones, tissues, and membranes which, when dissolved in hot water and then cooled, forms a jelly. Gelatin is used in ice creams, desserts, candies, icings, and fillings.

Ginger The scraped and dried root of a pungent aromatic plant that is cultivated in almost all tropical countries; used as a flavoring agent.

Glucose A sugar naturally found in many fruits. Since it does not crystallize, glucose is used commercially in confectionery cooking.

Gum An adhesive substance that originates from the stems of certain plants. Several kinds of gums are used in baking, confections, ornamental table decorations, etc.

Malt Used in baked goods primarily because of the attractive appearance and golden crust its use produces in breads and rolls. Pleasing flavor, fine texture, and better keeping qualities are obtained by its use.

Milk products Several types of milk products are used in baking to achieve various degrees of flavor, color, and texture. These include whole milk, 2% milk, 1% milk, skim milk, nonfat milk solids, evaporated milk, and condensed milk. Types of cream used include half & half, light, medium, and heavy whipping cream.

Mint An aromatic plant yielding a pungent essential oil. Mint extract is obtained by distillation and is used in confections and beverages.

Nutmeg The interior kernel of a fruit resembling a small pear grown in the East Indies; used as a flavoring agent.

Paraffin A white, translucent substance obtained from the distillation of petroleum. In its solid form, it is used for sealing preserves. As a liquid, it is used to make chocolate keep well by preventing rancidity.

Pepper Black and white pepper are the fruit of the pepper plant, *Piper nigrum*, a climbing perennial shrub. While black pepper is ground from the dried, unripe fruit, white pepper is ground when the berries are almost ripe. Cayenne, or red pepper, is ground from the dried pod of the *Capsicum frutescens* plant.

Rice A grain grown in most tropical countries. It is generally used as a vegetable in place of potatoes and in desserts, puddings, etc.

Rice flour Dried rice ground to a very fine powder; it is used in cakes, puddings, etc.

Tapioca A farinaceous food grown in Brazil and tropical countries and obtained from the roots of the cassava plant.

Truffle A species of fungus that grows several inches underground and is much esteemed as a table delicacy.

Vanilla Vanilla beans are derived from a tropical plant native of Mexico. It is a climbing plant, with thick, sharply pointed leaves, and large and attractive, though odorless, flowers. From these flowers spring long, brown, heavily ribbed pods or beans containing thousands of small black specks, which give the vanilla its wonderful and delicate flavor.

✌ Fruits and Nuts

Almonds Elliptically shaped light brown nuts used in baking or ground to make almond nut butter. Two principal varieties used in commercial production are Harpareil and Yordanolo.

Brazil nuts Fruit of the *Bertholettia excelsa*, a tree that grows in Latin America. The white nut is encased in a dark brown shell with three sharp sides.

Cashews Nuts that grow in the tropics. They are kidney-shaped, about an inch long, and grow on the end of a pear-shaped fruit, enclosed in a double shell. The whole nuts are used principally for salting.

Coconuts Fruits of the coconut palm tree. Coconut is used for pies, cakes, fillings, cookies, and candies.

Dates Fruits of the date palm tree. There are two types of dates, hard and soft. While soft dates are considered preferable, both are high in nutritional value.

Evaporated fruits (dried fruits) Any fruit dried by the sun or by artificial heat.

Figs Fruits of the fig tree, which originated in southern Arabia. There are three types of figs, white, purple, and red. The commonly imported dried fig is the smyrna.

Filberts (hazelnuts) Nuts produced by the filbert tree, which is a variety of the common hazel tree.

Peanuts Not really nuts, but rather legumes that grow in soft shells beneath the ground. Highly nutritious, they are used raw or roasted and can be pressed for their flavorful oil.

Pecans Grown chiefly throughout the southern United States, these light brown and oval-shaped nuts are popular with confectioners and bakers.

Pineapple The fruit of a tropical plant, resembling a pine cone in shape. It is juicy and sweet, used for jams, fillings of pies and cakes, and in confections, as well as for a dessert or breakfast dish.

Pistachios Seeds of the small tree, *Pistacia vera.* These reddish nuts have a light green meat and are used for their flavor as well as for decorative purposes.

Plums The edible fruits of plum trees, *Prunus rosaceae.* They are dark purple in color and are used for tarts and pies, are candied, and also are served as a stewed fruit.

Prunes Dried plums, derived from a species of plum tree. Most dried prunes are cooked or stewed before being used.

Walnuts The fruits of the European walnut tree. There are many varieties of walnuts, from the golden-shelled English walnut to the dark-shelled black walnut.

❦ Flours

Bread making is a very difficult and complex operation for many reasons. One of the foremost is the great differences encountered in the chemical compositions of various flours. As the yeast plant acts on different flour compounds, many intricate chemical reactions take place that must be controlled but are usually very little understood. If the fermentation process is not properly controlled, acid and other compounds are formed that check the activity of the alcoholic ferments and produce a poor quality of bread. Poor bread can also result from a lack of skill on the part of the bread baker or from poor yeast, as well as from poor flour. The best-quality bread, however, and the most valuable commercially is produced from fully matured hard wheat flour.

Several fundamental and important rules must be observed in the use of flour if the baker wishes to achieve really satisfactory results. The first rule is that flour must always be sifted. Sifting incorporates air into the flour and also removes foreign particles and impurities.

The storage temperature of the flour is also important. Flour stored in a cold storeroom or closet does not produce good results, because cold checks fermentation and is frequently the cause of poor bread. If the flour is too warm, the effect on fermentation is also unfavorable.

When flours low in gluten are used in bread making, it is advisable to also use skimmed milk in the preparation in order to increase the protein content, since the composition of bread depends mainly on the flour used in it and its quality. Of course, when milk and butter are also used in making the dough, their nutrients are added to those of the flour, but when simply flour and water are used, the nutrients of the bread are only those contained in the flour.

❦ Salt

The most familiar salt is common table salt, sodium chloride. Salt is found in seawater, rock salt, and brines. (Seawater contains about 4 percent salt.) Rock salt deposits are found in the ground, and the salt is mined and purified. While salt is added to food products as a flavoring or preservative, consistent overuse is considered nutritionally unhealthy.

❦ Baking Powder

Very good baking powder is available commercially. However, good baking powder, which produces most satisfactory results, can be made by the baker if desired. The following formula makes a long-keeping powder:

4 lb baking soda

3 lb corn starch

8 lb cream of tartar

If a quick-acting powder is desired, use only 1 lb of corn starch. All materials should be thoroughly dry before mixing, and the soda and starch should be mixed first by thoroughly shaking together in a large can or container. Then add the cream of tartar and shake again. It is very important to mix the ingredients thoroughly to produce good results.

❦ Yeast and Fermentation

Yeast is a plant of very simple structure, consisting of chains of small round or oval cells or single cells that grow and multiply by the thousands under the proper conditions, that is, if properly nourished or fed, especially by a warm liquid containing sugar in some form.

Yeast of the fungus variety multiplies by budding; that is to say, the mother cell produces several buds, which in turn break away as new plants and cells and constantly repeat the same process, which continues so rapidly that in a short time millions of these cells are formed.

The action of yeast is especially interesting. As the yeast cells multiply, they break up the sugar and form alcohol and carbon dioxide gas, which in turn forces its way between and becomes entangled in the tenacious particles of the gluten, which prevents the gas from escaping too quickly. In this way the dough rises and becomes porous.

❦ Sugar

The sugars generally used in confectionery and baking are cane sugar and beet sugar. When equally refined, these two sugars are identical in every respect, and there is also no difference in their chemical composition. Sugars are graded according to the size of the granule, color, and the general appearance of the crystals.

2

French Pastry and Vienna Pastry

❧ The Plated Dessert

Attractive presentation is the secret to producing a superb dessert that customers just cannot resist. Variety and creativity in appearance enhance the appeal of plated desserts. Create a great dessert, and offer it on a nicely decorated plate.

Today, tastes are more sophisticated than ever, and customers are more health conscious as well. Even the most traditional of chefs is adopting new strategies in preparation and presentation. Reduce sugar content and use a variety of flavored yogurts as a base. Experiment with items such as poached fruit, which adds both color and flavor.

Strive to know and meet dietary trends. Knowledgeable pastry chefs and bakers who pay close attention to patrons' tastes will deliver customer satisfaction. Keep your plated desserts current and exciting!

❧ Puff Pastry

French pastry is made from puff paste, short paste, sponge cake, jams, jellies, creams, and the chef's choice of various other components. Puff paste was invented in 1620 by a young artist named Claude Gelée, also known by the name *Le Lorrain*, who was born in Château de Champagne, France, in the year 1600, and who died in Rome in 1682. He deserted his painting and became a pastry cook in 1620, and he became so interested in this work that he continued in this line until 1639. He then went to Rome and started a school of painting. His principal and best known paintings are *Sacre de David, Le Debarquement de Cleopatre, La Fête Villageoise, La Vue d'un Port de Mer au Soleil Couchant,* and *La Madre Dolorata.*

The procedures indicated in the recipe for puff paste should be observed carefully in order to obtain the best results.

Puff Paste (Pâte Feuilletée)

YIELD:
10 lb, 1 oz (4 kg, 568 g)

	U.S.	Metric
Bread flour	*4 lb*	*1 kg, 800 g*
Salt	*1 oz*	*28 g*
Salted butter	*4 lb*	*1 kg, 800 g*
Cold water	*1 qt*	*9.4 dl (approx.)*

1. Scale the flour into a bowl. Add salt, 1 lb (450 g) of butter, and about 1 qt (9.4 dl) of cold water.
2. Work all ingredients together into a smooth paste, and let stand overnight covered with a wet cloth.
3. When ready, wash 3 lb (1 kg, 350 g) of butter in ice water and shape into a flat square.
4. Cut across the paste with a sharp knife, and pull down the four corners.
5. Roll out the paste, following the direction of the four corners and leaving the center somewhat thicker. Place the butter in the center of the paste, fold in the four corners to completely envelop the butter, and then roll out very gently in one direction only.
6. Fold in three, and roll out again, but in the other direction; then fold in three again. Cover with a damp cloth, and let stand in the refrigerator for 2 hours. Repeat rolling as before. This is called the *fourth turn,* and the paste will keep this way from 2 to 4 days on ice if well covered with a damp cloth. Before using, however, give it two more turns, always following the same direction as for the first two turns. Any leftover from the puff paste should be given one turn before being used, since it will not spring properly otherwise.

Margarine or puff pastry shortening may be used instead of butter or may be mixed half and half with butter, but do not use cream of tartar, lemon juice, or eggs, since puff paste should rise on its own merits.

In warm weather the puff paste should be rolled in a cool place and kept there until ready for the oven. In rolling, great care should be taken to see that every part is chilled evenly, and the pans on which the puff paste is to be baked must be wet. To prevent shrinking, puff paste should always be allowed to rest for awhile in a cool place before baking.

To obtain a nice glaze when the cakes are baked, dust 4× sugar on top and return to a very hot oven until the sugar is melted and of a nice brown, shiny color.

FRENCH PASTRIES MADE WITH PUFF PASTE

■ Allumettes

Roll out a piece of prepared puff paste about $\frac{1}{6}$ inch (4 mm) thick, cut into strips 4 inches (10 cm) wide, and place on top a layer of royal icing (made without any acid or lemon juice). Cut these strips into bars $1\frac{1}{2}$ inches (4 cm) wide, place on wet pans and bake at 400°F (204°C) until puffed, and then reduce heat to 325°F (163°C) and bake until done. When baked, cut in two lengthwise and fill with pastry cream.

■ Apricot Mignon

Roll out a piece of prepared puff paste about $\frac{1}{8}$ inch (3 mm) thick, and cut into 3-inch (8-cm) squares; wash the top with egg, place half an apricot in the center, and let stand for 15 minutes. Then bake at 410°F (210°C) until puffed, and then reduce heat to 350°F (180°C) and bake until done. When baked, cut in two and fill with boiled custard cream. Glaze the top with a hot apricot jelly, and sprinkle a few chopped pistachio nuts on top.

■ Bande au Pomme

Roll out a piece of prepared puff paste, and then cut into long strips, the length of the pan by 4 inches (10 cm) wide. Wash the borders with water about $\frac{1}{4}$ inch (6 mm) wide. Fill the center with a well-reduced apple sauce, and then place some sliced apples on top. Bake at 400°F (210°C) until puffed, and then reduce heat to 350°F (180°C) and bake until done. When baked, cover the top with a well-reduced hot apricot jelly and cut into bars.

■ Cheese Sticks

Give two turns to 1 lb of puff paste using 2 oz of grated Swiss or Gruyère cheese mixed with a little salt and pepper for dusting between the folds, and roll this out about $\frac{1}{6}$ inch (4 mm) thick. Cut into strips 5 inches (12 cm) wide, and then cut into small bars and roll these into twisted sticks. Place on wet pans and let rest a while before baking. These are often made without twisting, by washing the strips with egg wash, sprinkling with grated cheese, and cutting into strips $\frac{1}{2}$ inch (1 cm) wide. Bake at 425°F (220°C).

■ Coronet à la Crème (Cream Horns)

Roll out some scraps of puff paste very thin, cut into strips about ¾ inch (20 mm) wide and 12 inches (30 cm) long, and then wash with water and roll on cone-shaped tins. Place on clean pans, wash with egg, and bake at 390°F (200°C). When cold, fill with pastry cream or whipped cream.

■ Cream or Jelly Envelopes

Roll out a piece of prepared puff paste about ⅙ inch (6 mm) thick, and cut into 4-inch (10-cm) squares. Fill the center with pastry cream or jelly. Wash the border with water, and fold the paste over the filling by bringing two points together. Wash the top with egg, place on wet pans, and bake at 400°F (205°C) until puffed; then reduce heat to 370°F (190°C), and bake until done. Then glaze the top with sugar.

■ Dartois

Roll out a piece of prepared puff paste the length of the baking pan, cut into strips about 4 inches (10 cm) wide, and place frangipane in the center. Wash the borders with water, and place another strip of puff paste on top, pressing the borders with your fingers to make the two strips stick together. Then wash the top with egg, make fancy decorative cuts on top with a sharp knife, and bake at 400°F (205°C) until puffed; then reduce heat to 350°F (180°C) and bake until done. When cold, glaze the top with a hot apricot jelly and cut the strips into bars about 1½ inch (4 cm) wide.

■ Fruit Tartlets

Roll out a puff paste about ⅛ inch (3 mm) thick, and cut out with a fancy cutter a little larger than the mold to be used. Place in the tins, and press the sides up with your fingers. Then fill them the same way as the large French fruit tarts. Bake at 390°F (200°C) until puffed; then reduce heat to 350°F (180°C). When baked, remove from the molds and glaze with jelly, the same as fruit tarts.

■ Joconde

Bake two sheets of puff paste, the same as for a Napoleon, and place some custard cream on top of one sheet. Place a layer of sponge cake on top, and cover with another layer of custard cream. Place the second sheet of Napoleon cake on top, and frost all over with a vanilla fondant. Cut into squares.

Macaroon Tartlets

Line some tartlet tins with scraps of puff paste, and then fill with the following soft macaroon mixture.

YIELD:
2 lb, 10 oz (1 kg, 180 g)

	U.S.	Metric
Almond paste	1 lb	450 g
Granulated sugar	1½ lb	675 g
Bread flour	2 oz	56 g
Egg whites	To make a soft mixture	

1. Make crosses of puff paste, and place one on each tartlet.
2. Moisten the tops, and bake at 390°F (200°C).
3. When baked, turn tartlets over and set to cool.

Merliton

Line some tartlet tins with puff paste, same as for the Fruit Tartlets, and fill about three-fourths full with a mixture made as follows:

YIELD:
1 lb, 7 oz (620 g)

	U.S.	Metric
Almond paste	3 oz	84 g
Granulated sugar	12 oz	336 g
Eggs	7 oz	200 g

1. Mix well until very smooth.
2. Add 1 Tbsp of heavy cream.
3. Dust the top with plenty of 4× sugar.
4. Place a half-almond on top.
5. Bake at 390°F (200°C).

■ Millefeuilles

Roll out a piece of prepared puff paste, and cut into long strips about $4\frac{1}{2}$ inches (12 cm) wide. Place on a wet baking pan, and dock all over, then bake at 400°F (205°C) until puffed; then reduce heat to 300°F (180°C) and bake until done. When cold, cover one strip with whipped cream $\frac{1}{2}$ inch (1 cm) thick, and place another strip on top and cover in the same way. Then cut another strip into bars 1 inch (3 cm) wide, place these bars on top of the cream, and dust all over with 4× sugar. Cut the strips through with a sharp knife.

■ Moscovites

Moscovites are made the same way as Religieux, only fill the center with a frangipane and, when baked, cover with a well-reduced apricot sauce and sprinkle chopped pistachio nuts on top.

■ Napoleon

Roll out some scraps of puff paste very thin, the size of the baking pan. Place on a pan, let rest for awhile, and then dock all over to prevent blistering when baking. Bake at 400°F (205°C); then reduce heat and bake at 350°F (180°C). When baked, cut into three strips and then put them together with a vanilla-flavored custard cream. Frost on top with fondant of one or more flavors, and when the fondant is dry, cut into bars about 4 inches (10 cm) long and 2 inches (5 cm) wide.

■ Palmyre Leaves

Take a puff paste that is ready on four turns and give it two more turns by rolling into fine granulated sugar. Then roll into a long strip. Fold the sides to the middle so that the ends meet in the center, press well together with a rolling pin, and fold one side on top of the other. Now cut the leaves from this strip with a sharp knife, place them cut side down on clean pans, and bake at 380°F (195°C). When half baked, turn them over with a palette knife and finish baking to a nice golden brown color. For this, it is better to use scraps of puff paste and let stand for 30 minutes before baking.

■ Palmyre Leaves Fourrés

When palmyre leaves are baked and cold, place two leaves together with apricot jam, custard cream, or whipped cream.

◼ Papillon (Butterfly)

Take a puff paste that is ready on four turns and give it two more turns by rolling into fine granulated sugar. Roll out about $\frac{1}{8}$ inch (3 mm) thick, and cut into long strips about 3 inches (8 cm) wide. Place three of the strips on top of each other, press down in the center with a small dowel, and then cut them with a sharp knife into strips about $\frac{1}{3}$ inch (8 mm) wide. Twist the strips in the center, place on a greased pan, and bake quickly at 380°F (195°C) until a nice golden brown color is obtained. Remove the cakes from the pan as soon as they are taken from the oven, and place them on a table or rack to cool.

◼ Papillon Chantilly

Make some papillons a little smaller than the usual size. Place two together with an apricot jam, and glaze the top with a hot apricot jelly.

◼ Patty Shells

Roll out a six-turn puff paste about $\frac{1}{6}$ inch (4 mm) thick, and then cut out with a round fancy cutter. Place on wet pans, and wash with water. Then cut another piece of the same size and thickness, cut a hole in the center with a small cutter, and place the ring on top of the washed part. Wash the ring with egg and let stand for 10 to 20 minutes before baking. Bake at 410°F (210°C).

◼ Pattyhouse (Vol-au-Vent)

A pattyhouse is a large patty shell that is made the same way as the patty shell but somewhat thicker in proportion to the size.

◼ Praline Bars

Roll out a piece of scrap from the puff paste about $\frac{1}{6}$ inch (4 mm) thick, and cut into long strips. Wash the top with egg, and sprinkle on top a praline made from two parts sugar and one part sliced nuts rubbed together with a little egg white to moisten the mixture. Cut into bars 4 inches (10 cm) long by 2 inches (5 cm) wide. Place on wet pans, and bake at 400°F (205°C) until puffed; then reduce heat to 350°F (180°C) and bake until done. When baked, fill with custard cream and dust the top with 4× sugar.

■ Puits d'Amoures

Bake some tartlet shells from pie crust or French puff paste, and when cold, fill them with vanilla custard cream. Put a little sugar on top, and brown the top using a propane torch.

■ Religieux

Roll out a piece of the prepared puff paste 4 inches (10 cm) wide and ½ inch (1 cm) thick. Place on a wet baking pan, fill the center with vanilla custard cream, and place small strips of puff paste on top of the cream to form a latticework pattern. Wash with egg, and place long strips all around the border; wash again, and sprinkle chopped almonds on top. Bake at 390°F (200°C). When baked and cold, cut into bars.

■ Turinos

Line some round flat tins with a short crust paste, put a little red currant jelly in the bottom, and fill with a frangipane. Bake at 390°F (200°C). When cold, place a small cream puff on top, and frost all over with coffee icing.

■ Turnovers

Roll out a piece of six-turn puff paste about ⅙ inch (4 mm) thick. Cut out with a round fancy cutter, and then fill in the center with finely chopped apples mixed with apple sauce and sultana raisins. Wash the border with egg wash, fold the paste over the filling, and press well together with your fingers. Place on a wet pan, wash the top with egg wash, and bake at 400°F (205°C) until puffed; then reduce heat to 375°F (190°C) and bake until done. When baked, dust all over with powdered sugar, and expose to a flash heat until the sugar is melted to a golden brown color. This is called *glacéed in the oven.*

❦ Cream Puff Paste

Cream puff paste, or *choux paste*, is used to create classical and always impressive cream puffs, éclairs, and profiteroles. It is quickly and easily prepared on the stove top, then piped onto baking sheets. Once baked, it stores well and may be frozen for assembly at time of service. The wide variety of fillings, garnishes, sizes, and shapes employed for cream puff paste items account for the perennial popularity of these products.

Cream Puff Paste

YIELD:
5 lb, 9¹/₄ oz (2 kg, 560 g)

	U.S.	Metric
Whole milk	1 qt	9.5 dl
Salted butter	1 lb	450 g
Granulated sugar	1 oz	28 g
Salt	¹/₄ oz	7 g
Bread flour, sifted	1 lb	450 g
Eggs	1¹/₂ lb	675 g (approx.)

1. Place the milk, butter, sugar, and salt in a pan, and bring to a boil over high heat.
2. Be sure that all the butter has melted; then add the flour. Stir briskly until the paste is smooth and dry. (If the paste is removed from the heat too soon, the puffs or éclairs may not spring properly during the baking process.)
3. After removing from heat, mix the paste at medium speed, adding the eggs a little at a time. If mixed with a spatula, work well each time before adding more eggs, and continue adding enough eggs to produce a smooth and medium-soft paste. (If the mixture is too stiff, the puffs or éclairs will be heavy and small.)
4. When ready, dress with a bag through a medium-sized plain tube in finger shape or any desired shape, wash the top with egg wash, and bake at about 400°F (205°C).

CREAM PUFFS AND ÉCLAIRS

◼ Chocolate Cream Puffs

Drop cream puff mixture on clean pans, wash the top with egg, and bake in a 400°F (205°C) oven. When cold, fill with a vanilla-flavored custard cream, and frost all over with chocolate icing. Decorate the top with an aganasse cream through a star tube.

◼ Coffee Cream Puffs

Drop cream puff paste on a clean pan, wash the top with egg, and bake in a 400°F (205°C) oven. When cold, fill the puff with a coffee custard cream, and frost with coffee icing.

◼ Chocolate Éclairs

Dress the cream puff mixture through a bag and round tube into long finger shapes on clean pans. Wash the top with egg, and bake in a 400°F (205°C) oven. When cold, fill with a vanilla-flavored custard cream. Dip into chocolate icing, or ice the éclair all over with chocolate fondant.

◼ Coffee Éclairs

Treat the same as for chocolate éclairs, but fill with coffee cream and dip into coffee icing.

◼ Vanilla Éclairs

Treat the same as for chocolate éclairs, but fill with a vanilla-flavored custard cream and dip into vanilla fondant.

◼ Barquette Melba

Line some barquette tins with a short crust paste, put a little red currant jelly on the bottom, and then fill through a star tube with a mixture of three parts cream puff paste and one part custard cream. Wash the top with egg, and sprinkle a few sliced nuts on top. Bake at 390°F (200°C), and when cold, fill with apricot jam or custard cream and dust all over with 4× sugar.

■ Choux Chantilly

Bake a round cream puff, and when cold, cut the top off with a sharp knife. Fill the puff about 1 inch (3 cm) higher than the cream puff with vanilla-flavored whipped cream. Place the top of the cream puff on the whipped cream, and dust all over with 4× sugar.

■ Divorson

Bake an oval cream puff, and fill it with a praline custard cream. Frost half and half with coffee fondant and chocolate fondant. Decorate the center where the icing joins with three half pistachio nuts.

■ Pains à la Meque

Make cream puffs the shape of small Vienna rolls, wash the tops with egg, and sprinkle a few sliced nuts on top. Bake at 390°F (200°C). When cold, cut them open in the center, fill with whipped cream through a star tube, and dust with 6× sugar.

■ Polka

Roll and cut out small bottoms of short crust paste, and place on wet pans. Place a ring on each from the cream puff paste through a small tube, and bake at 390°F (200°C). When cold, dust all over with 4× sugar, fill up the center with a vanilla-flavored custard cream, place a little granulated sugar in the center, and burn to a nice brown color with a propane torch.

■ Pontneuf

Line some tartlet molds with a short crust paste, fill with the same mixture as for the Barquette Melba, place small strips of short crust paste on top to form a cross, and bake at 390°F (200°C). When cold, fill with vanilla-flavored custard cream and dust all over with 4× sugar.

■ Saint Honoré

Prepare the same as for Polka, and when cold, frost the ring with chocolate icing. Fill the center with vanilla-flavored whipped cream through a star tube, and place a cherry half on top.

❦ Sponge Cakes

There are many formulas for sponge cakes, and all are made with the same intention of obtaining a light and, at the same time, rich cake. Some (genoises) are made by the hot process, while others (chiffon sponges) are made by the cold process, and since the results of both processes are good, it is a matter of personal opinion as to which is better. Some pastry chefs believe that if a sponge is to be sold plain, the hot process is better, but if it is to be filled and coated with buttercream or mocha cream, then the cold process is preferable, since by this process the yield is greater and the cakes are lighter and do not dry so rapidly.

Flour *always* should be well sifted before mixing in the sponges. Butter always should be added last, and then very carefully mixed, so that the mixture will not drop down and become heavy.

When pans are filled, they should not stand but should be placed in a preheated oven as quickly as possible, and when a sponge is baked, it always should be turned over immediately to prevent it from shrinking.

Hot-process sponge is made by beating the eggs and sugar over heat until warm and then removing from the range and beating again until cold; after this, the flour is folded in by hand, and lastly, the butter.

Cold-process sponge is made by beating the yolks and part of the sugar cold, while the whites are beaten separately to a meringue with the rest of the sugar and mixed lightly with the yolk mixture; then the flour is mixed in, and lastly, the butter.

Never stir in flour in cake mixtures; always mix in or fold in. Stirring breaks down the air cells formed during the beating process and will render a mixture heavy. The yield will be less also, and the cake will be heavy when baked.

Almond Sponge Cake (Genoise)

YIELD:
5 lb, 4 oz (2 kg, 345 g)

	U.S.	Metric
Eggs	1½ lb	675 g
Egg yolks	11½ oz	320 g
Granulated sugar	1 lb	450 g
Almond powder	½ lb	225 g
Bread flour	1 lb	450 g
Sweet butter, melted	½ lb	225 g

1. Beat the eggs and egg yolks together with the sugar in a pan over low heat until warm; then beat again until cold.
2. Mix in the almond powder and flour and then the melted butter.
3. Bake in square or round cake pans at 350°F (180°C).

Butter Sponge Cake

YIELD:
7 lb (3 kg, 245 g)

	U.S.	Metric
Eggs	2 lb	900 g
Egg yolks	11½ oz	320 g
Granulated sugar	2 lb	900 g
Bread flour	2 lb	900 g
Sweet butter, melted	½ lb	225 g

1. Beat the eggs and egg yolks together with the sugar in a pan over low heat until warm and quite stiff, remove from heat, and continue to beat until cold.
2. Mix in the bread flour and then the melted butter.
3. Bake in square or round cake pans at 390 to 400°F (200 to 205°C).

Chocolate Sponge Cake (Cold Process)

YIELD:
21 lb, ½ oz (9 kg, 464 g)

	U.S.	Metric
Egg yolks	3 lb	1 kg, 350 g
Granulated sugar	4 lb	1 kg, 800 g
Bitter chocolate	1½ lb	675 g
Sweet butter	1½ lb	675 g
Egg whites	7 lb	3 kg, 150 g
Almond powder, roasted	2 lb	900 g
Bread flour	2 lb	900 g
Cinnamon	½ oz	14 g

1. In a mixer, beat the egg yolks and half the sugar.
2. Melt together the bitter chocolate and the butter.
3. Beat the egg whites with the remaining sugar until very stiff.
4. Mix the egg white and egg yolk mixtures lightly.
5. Mix in the roasted almond powder, flour, cinnamon, and lastly, the butter and chocolate.
6. Bake at 350°F (180°C).

Coffee Sponge Cake (Cold Process)

YIELD:
17 lb, 8 oz (7 kg, 875 g)

	U.S.	Metric
Egg yolks	3 lb	1 kg, 350 g
Granulated sugar	3½ lb	1 kg, 575 g
Coffee extract	½ pt	225 g
Egg whites	6 lb	2 kg, 700 g
Almond powder, roasted	2 lb	900 g
Bread flour	2 lb	900 g
Sweet butter, melted	½ lb	225 g

1. Beat the egg yolks with 2 lb of sugar and the extract in a mixer.
2. In a separate bowl, beat the egg whites and the remaining sugar very stiff.
3. Mix the egg white and egg yolk mixtures lightly.
4. Mix in the roasted almond powder, flour, and lastly, the melted butter.
5. Bake at 380°F (195°C).

Lemon Sponge Cake (Genoise)

YIELD:
7 lb, 4 oz (3 kg, 262 g)

	U.S.	Metric
Eggs	3 lb	1 kg, 350 g
Granulated sugar	2 lb	900 g
Rinds of lemons, grated	12	112 g
Bread flour	1½ lb	675 g
Sweet butter, melted	½ lb	225 g

1. Beat the eggs and sugar in a pan over low heat until warm; remove from heat and continue to beat until cold.
2. Mix in the lemon rind, flour, and then the melted butter.
3. Bake in square or round cake pans at 380°F (195°C).

Plain Hot-Process Sponge Cake (Genoise)

YIELD:
6 lb, 8 oz (2 kg, 925 g)

	U.S.	Metric
Eggs	2 lb	900 g
Granulated sugar	2 lb	900 g
Bread flour	2 lb	900 g
Sweet butter	½ lb	225 g

1. Beat the eggs and sugar over low heat until slightly warm; then remove from heat and continue to beat until cold.
2. Mix in very lightly the flour and then the butter.
3. Bake in cake pans at 380°F (195°C).

Plain Cold-Process Sponge Cake (Chiffon)

YIELD:
18 lb (8 kg, 100 g)

	U.S.	Metric
Egg yolks	3 lb	1 kg, 350 g
Granulated sugar	4 lb	1 kg, 800 g
Egg whites	6 lb	2 kg, 700 g
Bread flour	4 lb	1 kg, 800 g
Sweet butter, melted	1 lb	450 g

1. Beat the egg yolks with 2 lb of the sugar in a mixer.
2. In a separate bowl, beat the egg whites and the remaining sugar until very stiff.
3. Mix the egg yolk and egg white mixtures very lightly.
4. Mix in the flour and then the melted butter.
5. Bake in square or round cake pans at 380°F (195°C).

Savoy Sponge

YIELD:
5 lb, 8 oz (2 kg, 475 g)

	U.S.	Metric
Granulated sugar	2 lb	900 g
Water	1 pt	450 g
Eggs	1 1/2 lb	675 g
Bread flour	1 lb	450 g

1. Boil the sugar with the water to a thick syrup.
2. Beat the eggs, and stir in the syrup.
3. Whisk this over a pan of boiling water until it resembles a thick cream.
4. Add the sifted flour.
5. Pour mixture into a buttered and sugar-coated savoy mold.
6. Bake at 380°F (195°C).

Walnut Sponge Cake (Cold Process)

YIELD:
16 lb, 4 1/2 oz (7 kg, 327 g)

	U.S.	Metric
Egg yolks	2 lb	900 g
Granulated sugar	3 lb	1 kg, 350 g
Egg whites	5 lb	2 kg, 250 g
Bread flour	3 lb	1 kg, 350 g
Ground walnuts	1 1/2 lb	675 g
Cinnamon	1/2 oz	14 g
Sweet butter, melted	1 1/2 lb	675 g
Coffee extract	1/4 lb	113 g

1. Beat the egg yolks with 1 lb of the sugar in a mixer.
2. In a separate bowl, beat the egg whites with the remaining sugar until very stiff.
3. Mix the egg yolk and egg white mixtures together lightly.
4. Add the flour, ground walnuts, cinnamon, coffee extract, and then the melted butter.
5. Bake in square or round cake pans at 380°F (195°C).

DESSERTS MADE WITH SPONGES

■ Altesse

Take a square coffee sponge cake and cut into three layers. Fill with kirsch-flavored buttercream, cut into small diamond shapes, and mask all over with the same buttercream. Then cover with crushed brown nougat, and decorate the top with a rosette of the same buttercream.

■ Arlequins

Cut a square cold-process sponge cake into three layers and fill with coffee buttercream. Cut into long bars, mask the sides with the same buttercream, and dip into praline. Frost the top with chocolate fondant, and decorate the top with pistachio buttercream.

■ Aveline

Cut a square coffee sponge cake into three layers, and fill with praline buttercream. Cut into squares, mask the sides with the same buttercream, and dip into finely chopped roasted filberts. Frost the top with coffee icing, and place a roasted filbert on top.

■ Cardinal

Cut a square cold-process sponge cake into two layers, and fill with a well-reduced apricot jam mixed with crushed pineapple. Cut into squares, and cover with hot red currant jelly. Dip the sides into finely chopped roasted almonds, and decorate the top with candied pineapple glazed with a well-reduced apricot jelly.

■ Castillon

Cut a square walnut sponge cake into three layers, and fill with nougat buttercream. Place in the refrigerator, and when set, cut out with a round cutter. Dress on top a round ball from the same buttercream, and return the cakes to the refrigerator to set. When set, frost all over with coffee fondant and decorate as desired.

■ Courtissan

Prepare a chocolate sponge cake, spread on well-greased paper, and bake at 410 to 420°F (210 to 215°C) and as quickly as possible. When cold, put four of them together with praline buttercream. Cut into long strips about 3 inches (8 cm) wide, and frost with coffee and chocolate fondant. Decorate the center, where the icing joins, using the same buttercream through a star tube. Cut into bars when set.

■ Délices

Cut a square almond sponge cake into three layers, and fill with almond-flavored buttercream. Cut into squares, frost all over with vanilla icing, and decorate the top with a rosette of chocolate buttercream.

■ Espérance

Cut a square lemon sponge cake into three layers, and fill with a well-reduced apricot jam. Cut into triangles, frost all over with pistachio fondant, and decorate the top with candied fruit.

■ Florentine

Cut a square butter sponge cake into three layers, and fill with orange-flavored buttercream. Cut into long strips about 3 inches (8 cm) wide, and mask the sides and top with the same buttercream. Cover the sides with roasted and finely chopped almonds, decorate the top with buttercream, and cut into bars.

■ Lacam

Cut a square chocolate sponge cake into three layers and fill with apricot jam. Cut into squares, and pour all over with chocolate fondant. Decorate the top with a rosette of chocolate buttercream.

■ Marjolaine

Cut a square cold-process sponge cake into three layers, and fill with custard cream. Cut into squares, mask all over with vanilla buttercream, cover all over with cake crumbs, and dust with 4× sugar.

■ Marquisettes

Fill a baked hot-process sponge cake with chocolate mocha cream. Cut into squares, and spread cream on the four sides. Dip the sides into finely chopped and roasted almonds, and decorate the top with chocolate mocha cream pressed through a star tube.

■ Mocha Squares

Cut a square hot-process sponge cake into three layers, and fill with mocha cream. Cut into squares, and spread cream on the four sides. Then dip the sides into finely chopped and roasted almonds, and decorate the top with mocha buttercream pressed through a star tube.

■ Noisetier

Cut a square walnut sponge cake into three layers, and fill with coffee buttercream. Cut into squares, frost all over with a coffee fondant, and place a half walnut on top of each.

■ Nougat Barquette

Line some barquette molds with brown nougat. When cold, fill the molds with hot-process sponge cake and buttercream. Decorate the top with mocha buttercream.

■ Pistachio Squares

Treat the same as for Marquisettes, using pistachio buttercream and placing half a pistachio nut on top of each.

■ Potatoes

Mix all leftovers from mocha squares with rum and a little mocha cream; then mold into the shape of a potato and chill in the refrigerator. When hard, roll in a thinly rolled almond paste, and then roll in chocolate powder or cocoa. Mark by making an impression with any sharp-pointed utensil to create the potato eyes.

■ Roméo

Line some barquette molds with a cookie dough and bake. When cold, place a piece of sponge cake in the mold and fill with strawberry mocha cream. Spread up high in the center, and frost all over with a pink icing. Write *Roméo* with royal icing on the top.

■ Rum Punch Squares

Cut a baked sponge cake crossways, spread one part with apricot jam flavored with rum, and place the other part on top. Cut into squares, and cover all over with a rum-flavored fondant. Decorate with French candied fruits.

■ Sans-Souci

Cut a square walnut sponge cake into three layers, and fill with vanilla buttercream. Cut into small squares, and mask the sides and top with the same buttercream. Cover all over with praline, and dust with powdered sugar.

■ Seville

Cut a square lemon sponge cake into three layers, and fill with apricot jam. Cut into round cakes with a cutter, place half of an apricot on top, and then cover all over with well-reduced apricot jelly. Dip the sides into sliced almonds.

■ Suprême

Cut a square butter sponge cake into three layers, and fill with pistachio buttercream. Cut into round cakes with a cutter, frost all over with pistachio fondant, and decorate the top with a rosette of pistachio buttercream. Place half a pistachio nut on top.

🐦 Filled Rolls

A good variety of filled rolls, made of different sponges, creams, and jellies, are very attractive, and most of them are novel. If properly made, these rolls will bring credit to any baker or pastry chef. Try to make one of them every week for an assortment with French pastry, and watch the result. Jelly rolls are made using the technique in the following recipe, but many rolls are simply made with sponges.

Jelly Roll

YIELD:
13 lb, 4³/₄ oz (5 kg, 983 g)

	U.S.	Metric
Granulated sugar	4 lb	1 kg, 800 g
Salted butter	¹/₂ lb	225 g
Salt	¹/₂ oz	14 g
Lemon flavoring	¹/₄ oz	7 g
Eggs	1¹/₂ lb	675 g
Milk	1 qt	900 g
Bread flour	5 lb	2 kg, 250 g
Baking powder	4 oz	112 g

1. Cream the sugar, butter, salt, and lemon flavoring well.
2. Add the eggs, a little at a time, and then the milk.
3. Sift together the flour and baking powder, and add to the egg mixture.
4. Line jelly roll pans with greased paper, and spread the batter on the pans.
5. Bake at 420°F (215°C).
6. When baked, turn the pan over on a paper dusted with granulated sugar to prevent the cake from sticking, and remove the greased paper.
7. Spread a coat of jelly or jam over the cake, and roll up very tight.
8. Roll the jelly roll in a paper, and let stand with the seam on the bottom until cold.
9. Remove the paper and slice.

NOTE: Jelly rolls also can be made from lady finger mixture or sponge cake mixture.

■ Chocolate Roll

Prepare a chocolate sponge cake, spread on well-greased paper, and bake at 410 to 420°F (210 to 215°C) and as quickly as possible. When cold, spread with a layer of chocolate buttercream, and then roll up and refrigerate. When the cream is stiff, decorate the top and sides of the roll with chocolate buttercream through a star tube and return to the refrigerator to chill. When chilled, slice and place in paper cups. Dip the knife into hot water before cutting.

■ Fédora Roll

Make a chocolate sponge cake, spread on well-greased paper, and bake as above. When cold, spread with a layer of pistachio buttercream. Roll up and place in the refrigerator. When the buttercream is firm, pour pink fondant all over, slice, and place slices in paper cups.

■ Marguerite Roll

Make a walnut sponge cake, spread on well-greased paper, and bake. When cold, spread with a layer of mocha cream, roll up, and refrigerate. When the cream is firm, mask all over with mocha cream, roll in finely chopped walnuts, and dust all over with 6× sugar. Slice and place in paper cups.

■ Marquise Roll

Make a chocolate sponge cake, spread on well-greased paper, and bake. When cold, spread with a thin layer of aganasse cream, roll up, and place in the refrigerator. When stiff, mask all over with aganasse cream, and return to the refrigerator. When chilled, slice and place in paper cups.

■ Mocha Roll

Make a coffee sponge cake, spread on well-greased paper, and bake. When cold, spread with a layer of mocha buttercream, roll up, and chill in the refrigerator. When the cream has stiffened, decorate the top and sides with mocha buttercream pressed through a star tube. Return to the refrigerator to chill. When ready, slice and place in paper cups.

■ Swiss Roll

Prepare a plain cold-process sponge cake, spread on well-greased paper, and bake. When cold, spread with a layer of coffee buttercream, roll up, and refrigerate. When the cream is firm, pour chocolate fondant all over, slice, and place in paper cups.

❦ Vienna Pastry

Vienna pastry, as we know it, is really a Hungarian pastry that originated in Budapest. When properly made, it is by far the richest and best pastry known. All Vienna pastries are very rich in flavor. The sponges are light, and generally, very little flour is used in them. Almond or nut flour is used in place of wheat flour. To make them successfully, particular care must be taken in the baking, on account of the small amount of flour used. The baking must be done in a very slow oven, and the cakes should not be moved during the baking process. When baked, they should be dusted with a little flour and turned over on wire racks. Very satisfactory results should be obtained by following the given formulas and directions carefully.

Vienna Chocolate Sponge

YIELD:
8 lb, 4¼ oz (3 kg, 857 g)

	U.S.	Metric
Eggs, separated	3½ lb	1600 g
Granulated sugar	2 lb	900 g
Salted butter	½ lb	225 g
Bitter chocolate	½ lb	225 g
Flour, made from roasted almonds and hazelnuts	1½ lb	675 g
Bread flour	½ lb	225 g
Cinnamon powder	¼ oz	7 g

1. Beat the yolks of the eggs with half the sugar until very light.
2. Melt the butter and chocolate together.
3. In a separate bowl, beat the whites of the eggs with the remaining sugar until very firm.
4. Mix the egg yolk and egg white mixtures lightly.
5. Sift the flours and the cinnamon together, and fold into the egg mixture.
6. Very carefully mix the melted butter and chocolate into the batter.
7. Line cake pans or rings with greased paper, and fill the pans with the batter.
8. Bake at 340°F (170°C).

NOTE: The nut flour is prepared by roasting lightly 1 lb of almonds and 1 lb of hazelnuts to a nice brown color; when cold, put through a meat chopper until very fine, and then sift through a fine sieve.

Vienna Coffee Sponge

YIELD:
8 lb, 4 oz (3 kg, 850 g)

	U.S.	Metric
Eggs	3½ lb	1600 g
Granulated sugar	1½ lb	675 g
Coffee extract	½ pt	225 g
Almond and hazelnut flour	1 lb	450 g
Bread flour	1 lb	450 g
Salted butter, melted	1 lb	450 g

Treat and bake the same as Vienna chocolate sponge. If desired, 1 lb (450 g) of almond flour and 1 lb (450 g) of hazelnut flour may be used, omitting the bread flour and using 1 lb (450 g) of sugar instead of 1½ lb (625 g).

Vienna Walnut Sponge

YIELD:
4 lb, 8¼ oz (2 kg, 32 g)

	U.S.	Metric
Eggs, separated	2 lb	900 g
Salted butter, melted	½ lb	225 g
Granulated sugar	1 lb	450 g
Roasted walnut flour	½ lb	225 g
Bread flour	½ lb	225 g
Cinnamon powder	¼ oz	7 g

Treat the same as Vienna chocolate sponge.

Vienna Cookie Dough

YIELD:
3 lb, 12 oz (1 kg, 698 g)

	U.S.	Metric
Granulated sugar	14 oz	392 g
Salted butter	1 lb	450 g
Egg yolks	8½ oz	240 g
Bread flour	1 lb, 6 oz	616 g

1. Rub together the sugar and butter.
2. Add the egg yolks.
3. Mix in the flour.
4. Place dough in refrigerator until ready for use.

Almond Slices

YIELD:
9 lb, 10 oz (4 kg, 331 g)

	U.S.	Metric

Line a deep pan with Vienna cookie dough, and bake until about half done. Fill with the following mixture:

	U.S.	Metric
Chopped almonds	4 lb	1 kg, 800 g
Granulated sugar	4 lb	1 kg, 800 g
Bitter chocolate	2 oz	56 g
Egg whites	1½ lb	675 g

1. Combine all ingredients in a pan, and cook until very hot.
2. Pour mixture over prepared cookie dough.
3. Bake at 380°F (195°C).
4. When cold, cut into bars.

NOTE: Almond slices may be made without the chocolate, if desired. Use ¼ oz (7 g) of cinnamon powder instead.

VIENNA PASTRIES

■ Bettina (Coffee Sponge)

Cut a square Vienna coffee sponge cake into three layers. Fill with coffee buttercream, and cut into strips about 3 inches (8 cm) wide. Mask the sides and top with the same cream, and cover the sides with cake crumbs. Decorate the top with coffee buttercream pressed through a cornet or small tube in a latticework pattern. Cut into small bars.

■ Blidak (Chocolate Sponge)

Prepare the same as Bettina, but use Vienna chocolate sponge cake, chocolate buttercream, and chocolate cake crumbs or chocolate shot.

■ Branika (Walnut Sponge)

Cut a square Vienna walnut sponge cake into two layers. Fill with $\frac{1}{2}$ inch (1 cm) of whipped cream mixed with finely ground roasted walnuts. Dust the top with powdered sugar, cut into small square cakes, and place a half walnut on top of each cake.

■ Camargo (Chocolate Sponge)

Cut a Vienna chocolate sponge cake into three layers, and fill with coffee buttercream. Cut into strips about 3 inches (8 cm) wide, mask the sides with buttercream, and dip into finely chopped roasted almonds. Ice the top with a chocolate fondant, decorate the top with coffee buttercream, and then cut into strips.

■ Créole

Line tartlet tins with a cookie dough, fill with frangipane cream, and bake at 375°F (190°C). When cold, ice the top with chocolate fondant. When the fondant is dry, dress a ball of vanilla buttercream on top and sprinkle chopped pistachio nuts all over.

■ Electra (Walnut Sponge)

Cut a square Vienna walnut sponge cake into four layers, and fill with chocolate buttercream. Cut into squares. Frost all over with chocolate icing, decorate the top with a rosette of aganasse cream, and place a candied violet on top.

■ Feria (Cookie Dough)

Roll out Vienna cookie dough into long strips about 4 inches (10 cm) wide and the length of the baking pan. Wash the borders with water, and place ¼ inch (6 mm) of raspberry jam in the center. Place narrow strips of the same dough crosswise to form a latticework pattern over the jam. Place a narrow border of the same dough on the edge, egg wash all over, and sprinkle almonds on top. Bake at 380°F (195°C). When cold, glaze with hot apricot jelly, and cut into bars.

■ Flower Baskets

Line some tartlet molds with cookie dough, and fill about half full with frangipane cream. Bake at 350°F (180°C). When cold, decorate the top with different flavors and colors of buttercream, and place a handle on top made from cookie dough or sweet coating chocolate.

■ Froufrou (Chocolate Sponge and Coffee Sponge)

Cut one layer from a Vienna chocolate sponge cake, and two layers from a Vienna coffee sponge cake. Assemble, placing the chocolate layer in the middle and filling with kirsch buttercream. Cover all over with chocolate icing, and cut into bars. Decorate the top with buttercream and roasted almonds.

■ Glorieux

Line some tartlet pans with a cookie dough, and fill with frangipane. Bake at 350°F (180°C), and when cold, top with chopped candied fruits mixed with hot apricot jelly. Sprinkle a few chopped pistachio nuts over the top.

■ Hortensia

Line some tartlet pans with a cookie dough, fill with frangipane mixed with chopped candied fruit, and bake at 375°F (190°C). When cold, top with a thick coating of chocolate buttercream and sprinkle chopped brown nougat all over.

■ Java (Coffee Sponge)

Cut a square Vienna coffee sponge cake into four layers, and fill with coffee buttercream. Cut into small bars, mask the sides with the same cream, dip into Vienna coffee sponge crumbs, and frost the top with coffee icing. Place a coffee bean made from almond paste on top.

■ Loïe Fuller Truffles (Coffee Sponge)

Mix some scraps of Vienna coffee sponge cake with coffee buttercream. Form balls from the mixture, and chill in the refrigerator. When stiff, mask all over with aganasse cream, and roll into chocolate cake crumbs. Dust all over with sugar and place in paper cups.

■ Marie Antoinette (Walnut Sponge)

Cut a square Vienna walnut sponge cake into three layers, and fill with plain buttercream mixed with chopped strawberries. Frost all over with pink icing, and decorate the top with a strawberry and a green leaf made from almond paste.

■ Merveilleuses (Chocolate Sponge)

Cut a square Vienna chocolate sponge cake into three layers, and fill with coffee buttercream. Cut into small square cakes, mask the top and sides with buttercream, and place four chocolate leaves around the cake to form a square box. The leaves should be $\frac{1}{2}$ inch (1 cm) higher than the height of the cake. Sprinkle a few broken chocolate leaves on top, and dust with 6× sugar.

NOTE: To make the leaves, prepare a sweet chocolate coating in the same way as for the coating of bonbons. Spread the prepared chocolate on paper very thinly, and when dry, cut into desired shapes with a knife and remove from the paper.

■ Metternich (Chocolate Sponge)

Cut a square Vienna chocolate sponge cake into two layers, and fill with $\frac{1}{4}$ inch (6 mm) of chestnut buttercream. Frost the top thickly with chocolate icing. Cut into small bars, and place a piece of chestnut on the top of each cake.

■ Mignon (Coffee Sponge)

Cut a square Vienna coffee sponge cake into three layers, and fill with a nougat buttercream. Cut out with a round cutter, and frost all over with coffee icing. Sprinkle a few broken brown nougats on top before the icing is dry.

Néva Wafers

YIELD:
3 lb, 15 oz (1 kg, 768 g)

	U.S.	*Metric*
Salted butter	*19 oz*	*532 g*
Granulated sugar	*11 oz*	*308 g*
Egg whites	*2 oz*	*60 g*
Almond powder	*12 oz*	*336 g*
Bread flour	*19 oz*	*532 g*

1. Combine all ingredients to make a cookie paste.
2. Chill in the refrigerator overnight.
3. When ready, roll out in two thin sheets and place them on separate pans. Mark one sheet in squares, and bake both at 380°F (195°C).
4. When baked, cut the one that is marked, and spread a well-reduced red currant jelly on top of the other.
5. Place the squares on top of the jelly and cut through.
6. Brush some red currant jelly on top, and sprinkle with a few pistachio nuts.

■ Vienna Galette

Make a paste the same as for Néva wafers, and chill in the refrigerator overnight. Roll out in two thin sheets, and place them on separate pans. Cut one into squares, and bake the two sheets at 380°F (195°C). When baked, decorate the one that is cut with royal icing by drawing straight lines crossways. Return it to the oven to dry the icing. When dry, remove from oven and cut the icing while hot. Spread a well-reduced apricot jam on top of the undecorated layer, place the decorated squares on top, and then cut through.

Vienna Madeleine

YIELD:
4 lb (1 kg, 800 g)

	U.S.	Metric
Salted butter	*1 lb*	*450 g*
Granulated sugar	*1 lb*	*450 g*
Eggs	*1 lb*	*450 g*
Almond flour, unroasted	*1 lb*	*450 g*

1. Cream the butter and sugar well.
2. Gradually add the eggs.
3. Add almond flour.
4. Bake in Madeleine tins.
5. When cold, put two together with aganasse cream, and dust with powdered sugar.

LARGE VIENNA CAKES

Bohemian Cake

YIELD:
5 lb (2 kg, 250 g)

	U.S.	Metric
Egg whites	2 lb	900 g
Granulated sugar	1 lb	450 g
Chocolate powder	1 lb	450 g
Cinnamon	To taste	
Powdered roasted walnuts	1 lb	450 g

1. Beat egg whites with sugar until very stiff.
2. Fold egg whites into the powdered roasted walnuts, chocolate powder, and cinnamon.
3. Grease and dust baking pans, and spread round cakes ¼ inch (6 mm) thick onto pans.
4. Bake in 360 to 380°F (180 to 195°C) oven.
5. When cold, assemble four layers with praline buttercream. Trim the sides, and frost all over with chocolate fondant.
6. Decorate the top with aganasse cream.

Crème d'Or Cake

YIELD:
6 lb, 8 oz (2 kg, 925 g)

	U.S.	Metric
Sweet butter	1 lb	450 g
Granulated sugar	1 lb	450 g
Almond paste	1 lb	450 g
Eggs	1 lb	450 g
Egg whites	1½ lb	675 g
Bread flour	1 lb	450 g

1. Cream the butter, sugar, and almond paste well.
2. Gradually add the eggs.
3. In a separate bowl, beat the egg whites.
4. Fold the butter mixture into the egg whites.
5. Fold the flour into the batter.
6. Spread batter in round shapes about ¼ inch (6 mm) thick.
7. Bake at 350°F (175°C).
8. When baked, assemble three layers with raspberry jam, trim the sides, and pour all over with pink fondant.
9. Decorate the top with assorted candied fruits.

Dobos Torte

YIELD:
2 lb, 10 oz (1 kg, 218 g)

	U.S.	Metric
Eggs, separated	1 lb 5 oz	600 g
Heavy cream	½ pt	225 g
Granulated sugar	8 oz	225 g
Bread flour	6 oz	168 g

1. Beat the egg yolks until light, and add the cream.
2. In a separate bowl, beat the egg whites, but not too stiff.
3. Add egg whites to egg yolk mixture.
4. Fold flour into egg mixture.
5. Grease baking pans, and dust with flour.
6. Spread batter on pans in very thin, round shapes.
7. Bake at 400°F (205°C).
8. When cold, assemble eight layers together with chocolate buttercream, trim the sides, and frost the top with caramel sugar.

■ Fédora Cake (Chocolate Sponge)

Bake a Vienna chocolate sponge cake in rings. When cold, cut each into four layers, and fill with aganasse cream. Mask the top and sides with the same cream, and then cover the sides with chocolate cake crumbs. Decorate the top with rosettes of aganasse cream, and sprinkle a pinch of chopped pistachio nuts on each rosette.

■ Hungarian Cake (Coffee Sponge)

Cut up a Vienna coffee sponge cake into very small square pieces, mix together with coffee buttercream, place between two thin, round layers of the same sponge cake. The cake should be about 2 inches (5 cm) thick. Chill in the refrigerator. When stiff, frost all over with chocolate fondant, and sprinkle a few chopped pistachio nuts and candied violets on top.

▪ Jamia Cake (Chocolate Sponge)

Bake a Vienna chocolate sponge cake in rings, and when cold, cut each cake into four layers. Fill with rum-flavored buttercream. Frost all over with pink fondant, and decorate the top with the same buttercream.

Linzer Torte

YIELD:
4 lb, 6¹/₄ oz (1 kg, 990 g)

	U.S.	Metric
Salted butter	1 lb	450 g
Granulated sugar	1 lb	450 g
Almond flour, unroasted	¹/₂ lb	225 g
Egg yolks	10 oz	280 g
Eggs	3¹/₂ oz	100 g
Bread flour	1 lb	450 g
Cinnamon	¹/₄ oz	7 g
Baking powder	1 oz	28 g
Rind of lemons, grated	2	2

1. Cream the butter, sugar, and almond flour.
2. Gradually add the egg yolks.
3. Add the whole eggs.
4. Fold the flour, cinnamon, baking powder, and grated lemon rinds into the mixture.
5. Fill a cake ring about one-fourth full.
6. Cut a wafer paper a little smaller than the ring. Spread a ¹/₄ inch (6 mm) layer of raspberry jam on the paper, and place on top of the mixture in the ring.
7. Add another layer of batter.
8. Dress bars across the top and a border around the edge from the same batter using a small tube.
9. Wash all over with egg yolks, and sprinkle the top with sliced almonds.
10. Bake at 325°F (165°C).

■ Marguerite Cake (Walnut Sponge)

Bake a Vienna walnut sponge cake in rings. When cold, cut each into four layers and fill with coffee buttercream. Cover all over with the same buttercream, dip the sides into finely chopped roasted almonds, and decorate the top with the same buttercream pressed through a star tube.

■ Mocha Cake (Coffee Sponge)

Bake a Vienna coffee sponge cake in rings. When cold, cut each cake into four layers, fill with coffee buttercream, and frost all over with a coffee fondant. Decorate the top with the same buttercream pressed through a star tube.

■ Pisinger Cake (Walnut Sponge)

Bake a Vienna walnut sponge cake in rings. When cold, cut each into four layers, and fill with praline buttercream. Cover all over with sweet chocolate coating, and sprinkle the top with pistachio nuts and candied violets before the coating is dry.

■ Rimgo-Janji Cake (Bohemian Cake)

Make the same as Bohemian Cake. Assemble four layers with chocolate buttercream, mask all over with the same buttercream, cover the top and sides with chocolate powder, and dust lightly with 6× sugar.

■ Sacher Torte (Crème d'Or Cake)

Make the same as Crème d'Or Cake, but fill with apricot jam instead of aganasse cream.

■ Suzanne Cake (Walnut Sponge)

Bake a Vienna walnut sponge cake in rings. When cold, cut each into four layers, and fill with pistachio buttercream. Frost all over with chocolate icing, and decorate the top with the same buttercream pressed through a star tube.

■ Trilby Cake (Chocolate Sponge)

Bake a Vienna chocolate sponge cake in rings. When cold, cut each into four layers and fill with pistachio buttercream. Cover the top with pistachio almond paste, mask the sides with the same buttercream, place granulated chocolate or chocolate shot all around, and decorate the top with chocolate buttercream pressed through a star tube.

🐝 Buttercreams

Buttercreams, or *crème au beurre,* as they are known and loved in France, are very fine and delicious creams that are made of sweet butter, eggs, sugar, and other ingredients and are made in various flavors. They are used in France, Belgium, and Hungary in most pastries, cakes, and *petits fours* either as a filler, for topping, or to decorate.

Plain Buttercream, French Style

YIELD:
5 lb, 10 oz (2 kg, 562 g)

	U.S.	Metric
Water	1 pt	450 g
Granulated sugar	2 lb	900 g
Glucose (or corn syrup)	4 oz	112 g
Egg yolks	7 oz	200 g
Sweet butter	2 lb	900 g

1. Boil water, sugar, and glucose to 240°F (115°C) and then remove from the heat.
2. Beat the egg yolks.
3. Stir sugar into egg yolks. Whisk mixture until it is cold and resembles a thick cream.
4. Place butter in a warm basin, and work it until creamy.
5. Gradually add the egg mixture to the butter.

NOTE: Any flavor may be used in this cream.

Coffee Buttercream, French Style

YIELD:
20 lb, 8 oz (9 kg, 270 g)

	U.S.	Metric
Water	2 qt	1 liter, 8 dl
Coffee	1 lb	450 g
Granulated sugar	6 lb	2 kg, 700 g
Glucose	1 lb	450 g
Egg yolks	1 lb 10 oz	730 g
Sweet butter	7 lb	3 kg, 150 g

1. Prepare coffee from the water and coffee.
2. Boil the coffee with the sugar and glucose to 240°F (115°C).
3. Beat the egg yolks, adding sugar slowly, and whisk until cold.
4. Place the sweet butter in a warm basin, and work it until creamy. Gradually add the egg mixture.

Buttercream 1, Hungarian Style

YIELD:
15 lb (6 kg, 750 g)

	U.S.	Metric
Granulated sugar	4 lb	6 kg, 750 g
Egg whites	2 lb	1 kg, 800 g
Water	3 pt	1 kg, 350 g
Sweet butter	6 lb	2 kg, 700 g

1. Boil the sugar with the water to 240°F (115°C).
2. Pour the syrup very slowly into the egg whites beaten very stiff, and then whisk until cold.
3. Put the butter in a warm basin, and work it until creamy.
4. Gradually add the meringue to the butter.

NOTE: Any flavor may be used with this cream.

Buttercream 2, Hungarian Style

YIELD:
8 lb (3 kg, 600 g)

	U.S.	Metric
Sweet butter	4 lb	1 kg, 800 g
Fondant	4 lb	1 kg, 800 g

1. Place the butter into a warm basin, and work it until very creamy.
2. Gradually add the fondant.

NOTE: Any flavor may be used with this cream.

Crème Aganasse, Hungarian Style

YIELD:
9 lb, 8 oz (4 kg, 275 g)

	U.S.	Metric
Heavy cream	2 qt	1 kg, 800 g
Granulated sugar	2 lb	900 g
Sweet chocolate	2 lb	900 g
Bitter chocolate	1½ lb	675 g

1. Bring half the cream and the sugar to a boil.
2. Add the sweet and bitter chocolate.
3. Stir well with an egg whip until the cream is very smooth; then add the rest of the cream.
4. Set aside to cool.

NOTE: In cold weather, 1 lb of bitter chocolate is sufficient.

Buttercream, Belgian Style

YIELD:
3 lb, 8 oz (1 kg, 566 g)

	U.S.	Metric
Make 1 qt of boiled custard with:		
Egg yolks	6 oz	160 g
Granulated sugar	1 lb	450 g
Milk	1 qt	900 g
Bread flour	2 oz	56 g

When cold, add 2 lb of very fine and creamy sweet butter, a little at a time. Any flavor may be used with this cream.

■ Chocolate Buttercream

Add melted bitter chocolate to any of the buttercreams, and mix well. Smooth until a fine chocolate flavor has been obtained.

🍎 Frangipane

Frangipane is an almond cream that is used as a basis for French pastry and also as a filling.

Frangipane 1

YIELD:
4 lb, 12 oz (2 kg, 212 g)

	U.S.	Metric
Sweet butter	1 lb	450 g
Almond paste	1 lb	450 g
Granulated sugar	1 lb	450 g
Eggs	1 lb, 10 oz	730 g
Bread flour	4 oz	112 g

1. Cream butter, sugar, and half the almond paste together well.
2. Add the eggs, a little at a time.
3. Gradually add the remaining almond paste.
4. Fold in the flour.
5. Set aside until needed.

NOTE: Any spirit flavor may be added, if desired.

Frangipane 2

YIELD:
4 lb, 4 oz (1 kg, 962 g)

	U.S.	Metric
Sweet butter	1 lb	450 g
Almond paste	1 lb	450 g
Confectioner's sugar	1 lb	450 g
Eggs	1 lb, 2 oz	500 g
Bread flour	4 oz	112 g

1. Cream the butter and almond paste until very smooth.
2. Add the sugar.
3. Gradually add the eggs.
4. Fold in the flour.

🍒 Meringue

When making meringue, see that all your utensils are very clean and that your sugar is entirely free from flour. The least particle of flour in the sugar will make the meringue heavy and give it an oily appearance. Your egg whites must be very clean and entirely free from any yolk; they also must be very cold before you begin to beat them.

There are three different methods of making meringue: One is known as *French meringue* or *common meringue,* another is known as *Italian meringue* and is made by boiling the sugar, and the third is known as *Swiss meringue* and is beaten in a *bain-marie,* or double boiler.

French Meringue

YIELD:
6 lb (2 kg, 700 g)

	U.S.	Metric
Egg whites	2 lb	900 g
Granulated sugar	4 lb	1 kg, 800 g

1. Beat the egg whites in a kettle; allow the machine to run at medium speed for 2 minutes and then advance the machine to high speed.
2. When the whites are light and fluffy, gradually add half the sugar while the mixer is running.
3. When the mixture is firm and smooth, remove the kettle from the machine and mix in the rest of the sugar with a skimmer or spatula. The meringue is then ready for pies and general work. When used for meringue shells, however, it is necessary to add another pound of sugar.

NOTE: Meringue shells, kisses, and fancy meringue should be baked at 225°F (105°C) so that it will not color. Meringue for pies or topping meringue should be baked at 400°F (205°C); it will then brown nicely.

Italian Meringue

YIELD:
9 lb, 8 oz (4 kg, 275 g)

	U.S.	Metric
Granulated sugar	5 lb	2 kg, 250 g
Water	1 qt	900 g
Egg whites	2 lb	900 g
4× sugar	1/2 lb	225 g

1. Boil the granulated sugar and water to 244°F (115°C).
2. When the sugar is at about 230°F (110°C), put the egg whites in a mixer and let the machine run at medium speed for 1 minute.
3. Advance the machine to high speed, and add the 4× sugar slowly.
4. When the boiled sugar is ready, remove from the heat and pour it slowly, in a thin running stream, over the egg whites while the mixer is running at medium speed.
5. Beat until cold.

NOTE: When properly made, this meringue is firm and very smooth and is used mostly for creams, fancy meringue, pastries, and cakes.

Swiss Meringue

YIELD:
3 lb (1 kg, 350 g)

	U.S.	Metric
Egg whites	1 lb	450 g
Granulated sugar	2 lb	900 g

1. Beat the egg whites and sugar in a copper kettle over a pan of boiling water.
2. Beat until very warm.
3. Remove from heat, and place in mixer.
4. Beat until cold.

NOTE: All these meringues may be beaten by hand instead of by machine. Any desired flavoring or coloring may be added; they should be mixed in very lightly when the meringue is ready.

❦ Pastry Cream (Crème Pâtissière)

Pastry cream, or custard cream, plays an important part in the making of pastry, and for this reason, should be well made. Smoothness and flavor are especially important, and therefore, great care should be taken during the mixing and boiling processes. Milk should be boiled with half the sugar and the vanilla when vanilla beans are used; the eggs or egg yolks should be well beaten with the rest of the sugar, and then the flour should be well mixed with the eggs and sugar. When the milk boils, a part of the milk should be mixed with the eggs, and then all should be mixed together and boiled over high heat for 1 minute or more, stirring continually with a whip to prevent the cream from burning and at the same time ensure a thorough mixing and obtain a smooth cream. When butter is added, do so when the cream is removed from the range, and if vanilla extract is used, add it when the cream is cold. Never allow the sugar and eggs to stand without mixing, because the sugar will curdle the eggs, small, hard lumps will form, and the mixture will have to be strained before using. In this way, you will lose about one-fourth the value of your eggs, and the cream will be grainy instead of smooth; therefore, it is very important that the sugar and eggs should be mixed immediately upon being combined.

Vanilla Pastry Cream

YIELD:
3 lb, 3 oz (1 kg, 424 g)

	U.S.	Metric
Milk	1 qt	900 g
Vanilla beans	2	56 g
Granulated sugar	8 oz	224 g
Egg yolks	6 oz	160 g
Bread flour	3 oz	84 g

1. Boil the milk, vanilla beans, and half the sugar.
2. Mix the egg yolks, the remaining sugar, and the flour well.
3. Add a part of the boiling milk to the egg mixture; then combine the mixture with the remaining milk and mix for 1 minute.
4. Pour into a clean, dry, flat pan, and remove the vanilla beans.

Vanilla Pastry Cream (Large Quantity)

YIELD:
12 lb, 6 oz (5 kg, 567 g)

	U.S.	Metric
Milk	1 gal	3 kg, 600 g
Vanilla beans	2	56 g
Granulated sugar	2½ lb	1 kg, 125 g
Egg yolks	1 lb	450 g
Bread flour	12 oz	336 g

1. Treat the same as Pastry Cream 1.
2. If vanilla extract is used, add it when the cream is cold.

Almond Pastry Cream

YIELD:
3 lb (1 kg, 376 g)

	U.S.	Metric
Almond paste	4 oz	112 g
Granulated sugar	4 oz	112 g
Egg yolks	6 oz	168 g
Bread flour	3 oz	84 g
Milk	As needed	
Milk	1 qt	900 g

1. Rub the almond paste, granulated sugar, egg yolks, and bread flour with a little milk in a bowl.
2. Bring the quart of milk to a boil, add to the almond mixture, and return to a boil.
3. Remove from heat, remove from kettle, and set aside to cool.

■ Chocolate Pastry Cream

For chocolate pastry cream, use the same formulas as for the vanilla pastry creams and add 3 oz (84 g) of bitter chocolate for every quart (900 g) as soon as the mixture is removed from the heat. Double the amount of vanilla.

■ Coffee Pastry Cream

Coffee pastry cream may be made by using the same formulas as for the vanilla pastry creams, only using one-half cream and one-half black coffee or one-half milk and one-half coffee or by using coffee extract and not using the vanilla.

■ Fruit Pastry Cream

As soon as the vanilla pastry cream is removed from the heat, add $\frac{1}{2}$ lb (225 g) of assorted chopped candied fruits and 4 oz (112 g) of kirsch for every quart (900 g) of cream; or add kirsch flavoring as soon as the cream is cold.

■ Praline Pastry Cream

As soon as the vanilla pastry cream is removed from the heat, add 6 oz (168 g) of praline and a little coffee extract for every quart (900 g) of pastry cream.

🍎 French Fruit Tarts

Fruit tarts, or *tourtes au fruits,* as they are known in France, resemble somewhat our popular dish called pie. However, even though practically the same ingredients are used for both, the difference in appearance, as well as in flavor, is considerable. The most popular, and indeed the most dainty, French fruit tarts are the open round tarts with a raised border. Almost any kind of fruit may be used for a French fruit tart. Pastry rings are placed on greased baking sheets, and these are lined with rolled-out paste (short crust); the raised border is nogged, and the bottom of the paste is docked to prevent blistering. The difference between a fruit tart and a tartlet is often misunderstood. The tartlet is made in individual plain or fancy round molds. All French fruit tarts should be baked at 375°F (190°C).

Short Crust

YIELD:
63 lb (28 kg, 400 g)

	U.S.	Metric
Bread flour	30 lb	13 kg, 500 g
Salted butter, kneaded	20 lb	9 kg
Salt	½ lb	225 g
Granulated sugar	1½ lb	675 g
Eggs	1 lb, 2 oz	500 g
Water	5 qt	4 kg, 500 g

1. Make a well in the center of the flour.
2. Place the kneaded butter, salt, sugar, eggs, and water in the well.
3. Work gradually into a paste.

NOTE: It is important that the mixing of the ingredients not be done too rapidly. When the paste is thoroughly kneaded, allow it to rest in a cool place for at least 12 hours before using.

Almond Tart (Petit Viellée)

Puff paste, on six turns   *Scraps*
Frangipane cream

1. Roll out a piece of scrap puff paste about ¼ inch (6 mm) thick, and cut round with the point of a knife.
2. Place on a wet pan, wash the borders with water, and spread with ½ inch (1 cm) of frangipane cream, leaving about 1 inch of the border uncovered all around. Wash the border with egg wash.
3. Roll out a round piece of puff paste on six turns, rolling it out a little larger than the first (bottom) piece.
4. Place this on top of the filled bottom, pressing the sides down well and then cutting the surplus off with the point of a sharp knife.
5. Cut a pattern on top with the point of a sharp knife, wash with egg wash, and bake at 375°F (190°C).

Apple Tart

Short crust
Applesauce
Cooking apples
Granulated sugar
Hot apricot jelly

1. Place a lightly greased pastry ring on a baking sheet.
2. Roll short crust out about ¼ inch (6 mm) thick, and line the ring with dough. Special care must be taken to fold the paste edges of the rings carefully, the raised border being nogged.
3. Dock the bottom of the paste, and fill halfway with applesauce.
4. Peel, core, and slice cooking apples very thin.
5. Place sliced apples on top of the applesauce so that each slice overlaps another slice, arranging the apples from the outer circle and working toward the center, placing them so that each circle of fruit overlaps another circle.
6. Dredge the surface with granulated sugar.
7. Bake at 375°F (190°C).
8. When done, remove the ring. When cold, cover the top with hot apricot jelly.

■ Apricot Tart

Place a lightly greased pastry ring on a baking sheet. Then roll short crust out about ¼ inch (6 mm) thick, and line the ring as for Apple Tart. Sprinkle some cake crumbs in the bottom, and then fill with halved apricots and arrange so that each apricot overlaps another, working from the outer circle toward the center and placing them so that each circle of fruit overlaps another circle. Dredge the surface with granulated sugar, and bake at 375°F (190°C). When done, remove the ring. When cold, cover the top with hot apricot jelly.

■ Apricot Tart à la Crème

Bake a tart shell until brown; then fill the shell about three-fourths full with boiled custard, well flavored with vanilla. Arrange some halved, stewed, and well-drained apricots on top of the custard. Cover with a well-reduced hot apricot jelly, and sprinkle a few chopped pistachio nuts on top.

■ Blackberry Tart

Prepare a pastry ring as for Apricot Tart, and sprinkle in the bottom 4× sugar mixed with 1 oz (28 g) of cornstarch to every pound (450 g) of sugar used. Fill the tart three-fourths full with blackberries, and sprinkle some of the same sugar on top. Bake at 375°F (190°C). When done, remove from the ring. When cold, cover the top with a hot red currant jelly.

NOTE: Blueberry, huckleberry, and raspberry tarts, etc., are made the same way.

■ Cherry Tart

Prepare a ring the same as for Apricot Tart, and sprinkle some cake crumbs in the bottom. Fill with red pitted cherries, and dredge the surface with granulated sugar. Bake at 375°F (190°C). When done, remove the ring. When cold, cover the top with hot currant jelly.

■ Gooseberry Tart

Make the same as Cherry Tart, but use gooseberries instead, and cover the top with hot apricot jelly.

■ Peach Tart

Prepare a ring the same as for Apricot Tart, place a layer of boiled custard in the bottom, and finish with halved peaches the same as for Apricot Tart (or sliced peaches arranged as for Apple Tart). Bake at 375°F (190°C). When baked and cold, cover with hot apricot jelly. This also may be made the same as Apricot Tart à la Crème by using stewed peaches.

■ Pear Tart

Prepare a ring the same as for Apple Tart. Place a layer of custard in the bottom, and finish with sliced pears, the same as for Apple Tart. Bake at 375°F (190°C). When baked and cold, cover the fruit with hot apricot jelly.

■ Pineapple Tart

Prepare a ring the same as for Apple Tart, and place a layer of boiled custard in the bottom. Arrange slices of pineapple over the custard so that each slice overlaps another. Bake at 375°F (190°C). When baked and cold, cover the fruit with a hot apricot jelly.

🍎 French Sweet Dough Products

These sweet dough products are rich and tasty yeast breads that can be served at any time of day. Plain, they are a welcome addition to a breakfast buffet, or with the appropriate garnishes they are a substantial dessert item.

Parisian Brioche

YIELD:
3 lb, 4 oz (1 kg, 410 g)

	U.S.	Metric
Bread flour	1 lb	450 g
Milk	4 oz	112 g
Yeast, compressed	1 oz	28 g
Eggs	14 oz	400 g
Salt	1/2 oz	14 g
Granulated sugar	1 1/2 oz	42 g
Salted butter	13 oz	364 g

1. Make a sponge with one-fourth of the flour, milk, and the yeast, and let it rise.
2. Mix well the eggs, salt, and sugar with the rest of the flour, and add to the sponge.
3. Beat well until smooth; then add the butter, and beat again until it is light and does not stick to your hands.
4. Let proof, and when ready, knock down and place in the refrigerator overnight.
5. When ready, divide into small pieces as for rolls, round them, and place in greased tins with ribbed edges. Make a hole in the center of each with your finger.
6. Roll out another very small piece the shape of a pear. Place this on the top, and push the point in the hollow with your finger.
7. Let proof.
8. When half ready, wash well with egg. Make three small incisions in the bottom with a pair of scissors.
9. Finish proofing.
10. Bake at 425°F (220°C).

NOTE: These are delicious for breakfast or afternoon tea.

Brioche Flamande

YIELD:
4 lb, 6 oz (1 kg, 970 g)

	U.S.	Metric
Bread flour	2 lb	900 g
Yeast	2 oz	56 g
Milk	10 oz	280 g
Salt	1/2 oz	14 g
Granulated sugar	3 oz	84 g
Eggs	11 oz	300 g
Salted butter	12 oz	336 g

1. Make a sponge with one-fourth of the flour, yeast, and milk.
2. Mix the same as for Parisian Brioche, and beat well.
3. Let rise, and when ready, knock it down.
4. Cut and roll up as for Parisian Brioche, but place on baking pans instead of in tins.
5. Finish same as Parisian Brioche.

Savarin Cake

YIELD:
4 lb, 4 oz (2 kg, 354 g)

	U.S.	Metric
Eggs	1 lb, 2 oz	500 g
Bread flour	2 lb	900 g
Yeast	1 1/2 oz	42 g
Milk	12 oz	336 g
Granulated sugar	4 oz	112 g
Salt	1/2 oz	14 g
Salted butter	1 lb	450 g

1. Treat the same as for Brioche Flamande.
2. When ready, fill in savarin molds or ring molds, and set to proof.
3. When proofed, bake at 375°F (190°C).
4. When baked, turn out and fill the molds one-fourth full of hot syrup (20° on the sugar scale) flavored with kirsch.
5. Replace the savarin, and let stand for 15 minutes; then turn out on a wire rack.
6. Cover all over with a well-reduced apricot sauce flavored with kirsch.

NOTE: This is very often served on a silver platter with whipped cream or ice cream in the center.

■ Breton

Bake a savarin mixture in small barquette tins. Unmold and saturate with hot rum syrup. Cut each crossways and fill with whipped cream. Place a little well-reduced apricot jelly on top, and top with a few chopped pistachio nuts.

■ Baba Rum

The same dough is used as for Savarin Cake. Mix in a few sultana raisins, and bake in baba or pop-over molds. When baked, dip in a hot syrup flavored with rum, and serve in a dish surrounded with a little rum-flavored syrup.

Gugelhupf

YIELD:
3 lb, 14¹/₂ oz (1 kg, 596 g)

	U.S.	Metric
Bread flour	¹/₂ lb	225 g
Yeast	1 oz	28 g
Milk, lukewarm	6 oz	225 g
Salted butter	¹/₂ lb	225 g
Granulated sugar	6 oz	168 g
Eggs	9 oz	250 g
Lemons, juice and rind	2	2
Salt	¹/₂ oz	14 g
Bread flour	1 lb	450 g
Milk	6 oz	168 g

1. Make a sponge with the ¹/₂ lb (225 g) of flour, yeast, and lukewarm milk.
2. Cream the butter, sugar, eggs, lemon juice and rind, and salt well.
3. When the sponge is ready, mix well with the creamed mixture.
4. Add 1 lb of bread flour and milk to make a medium soft dough.
5. Fill in well-greased molds sprinkled with almonds.
6. Set to proof.
7. When ready, bake at 400°F (205°C).

3

Petits Fours and Fancy Cakes

Petits fours may be divided into two different classes: *petits fours glacés* and *petits fours secs*. *Petits fours glacés* are very small, fancy cakes made from different sponges and cake mixtures and filled with creams, fruit jams and jellies, etc. They are made in various forms and combinations and are iced or glazed with colored fondants or jams and jellies. When properly made, not only are they delicious in flavor, but they are also very attractive and dainty in appearance.

Petits fours secs are small, fancy cakes made from cookie doughs, egg whites, almond paste, almond dust or flour, jams, jellies, and many other ingredients. When properly and carefully made according to formulas, they are also very delicious and attractive and are good sellers. Special attention and care also should be given to the baking of *petits fours secs*, since they should always be well done and of the proper color.

The names *friandise* and *mignardise* are often found on the menus of some hotels and restaurants, and these are simply fancy names given to *petits fours glacés* and *petits fours secs* when served mixed for parties.

Petits fours glacés are usually made from plain sponge cake or frangipane pound cake, covered with buttercream, and then placed in the refrigerator to harden. They are then cut into fancy forms, glazed with fondants of various colors and flavors, and decorated with fondant pressed through a cornet or with royal icing.

It is a good idea to bake one pan of sponges somewhat thinner than usual, about ¾ inch (2 cm) thick; this will be found very handy for *petits fours glacés* and also will save much time and labor.

SPONGES FOR PETITS FOURS GLACÉS

Biscuit Arlequins

YIELD:
4 lb, 8 oz (2 kg, 100 g)

	U.S.	Metric
Egg yolks	11 oz	300 g
Granulated sugar	1 lb	450 g
Bitter chocolate	1/2 lb	225 g
Salted butter	1/2 lb	225 g
Egg whites	1 lb	450 g
Bread flour	1/2 lb	225 g
Almond powder, made from roasted almonds	1/2 lb	225 g

1. Beat the egg yolks with 1/2 lb (225 g) of sugar.
2. Melt the butter with the bitter chocolate.
3. In a separate bowl, beat the egg whites until very stiff, and add the other 1/2 lb of sugar.
4. Mix the egg whites into the egg yolk mixture.
5. Add the flour and almond powder.
6. Add the butter and chocolate.
7. Bake at 325°F (165°C) in square baking pans.

Biscuit Caprice

YIELD:
5 lb, 9 oz (2 kg, 495 g)

	U.S.	Metric
Egg yolks	11 oz	320 g
Granulated sugar	1 1/2 lb	675 g
Egg whites	1 lb, 5 oz	600 g
Bread flour	1/2 lb	225 g
Almond powder, made from roasted almonds	1 lb	450 g
Salted butter, melted	1/2 lb	225 g

1. Beat the egg yolks with half the sugar.
2. In a separate bowl, beat the egg whites with the remaining sugar until very firm.
3. Fold the egg whites into the egg yolks.
4. Sift the flour and almond powder together, and fold into the egg mixture.
5. Fold in the melted butter.

6. Pour batter into prepared baking pans. The cake should not be over ¾ inch thick.
7. Bake at 350°F (175°C).

Biscuit Manqué

YIELD:
5 lb, 4 oz (2 kg, 345 g)

	U.S.	Metric
Egg yolks	11 oz	320 g
Egg whites	1 lb	450 g
Granulated sugar	1 lb	450 g
Bread flour	1 lb	450 g
Walnut powder, made from roasted walnuts	1 lb	450 g
Salted butter, melted	½ lb	225 g

1. Beat the egg yolks with half the sugar.
2. In a separate bowl, beat the egg whites with the remaining sugar until very stiff.
3. Fold the egg whites into the egg yolks.
4. Fold in the flour, walnut powder, and then the melted butter.
5. Bake in square baking pans, or drop onto paper in shapes about the size of a quarter.
6. Bake at 325°F (165°C).

Biscuit Progrès

YIELD:
3 lb, 4 oz (1 kg, 462 g)

	U.S.	Metric
Egg whites	1 lb	450 g
Granulated sugar	1 lb	450 g
Almond powder, made from roasted almonds	1 lb	450 g
Bread flour	4 oz	112 g

1. Beat the egg whites until very firm, and then fold in the sugar.
2. Sift together the almond powder and flour, and fold into the egg mixture.
3. Dress through a plain tube to form small balls about the size of a quarter or any other desired shape onto greased pans dusted with flour.
4. Bake at 325°F (165°C).

Pâte à Biscuit

YIELD:
4 lb, 2 oz (1 kg, 825 g)

	U.S.	Metric
Eggs	1 lb, 2 oz	500 g
Egg yolks	7 oz	200 g
Granulated sugar	1 lb	200 g
Bread flour	1 lb	450 g
Salted butter, melted	½ lb	225 g

1. Beat the eggs, egg yolks, and sugar in a pan over low heat until warm.
2. Remove from heat and continue to beat until cold.
3. Add the flour.
4. Add the melted butter.
5. Bake in square cake pans lined with paper at 325°F (165°C).

Pâte à Biscuit with Almonds

YIELD:
4 lb, 1 oz (1 kg, 836 g)

	U.S.	Metric
Egg yolks	1 lb, 2 oz	200 g
Eggs	14 oz	400 g
Granulated sugar	1 lb	450 g
Bread flour	½ lb	225 g
Almond powder, made from roasted almonds	12 oz	336 g
Salted butter, melted	½ lb	225 g

1. Beat the egg yolks, eggs, and sugar in a pan over low heat until warm.
2. Remove from heat, and continue to beat until cold.
3. Add the flour, almond powder, and then the melted butter.
4. Bake at 325°F (165°C) in square, flat, paper-lined baking sheets.

Pâte à Caraques

YIELD:
4 lb, 4 oz (1 kg, 961 g)

	U.S.	Metric
Salted butter	1 lb	450 g
Granulated sugar	1 lb	450 g
Eggs	1 lb, 2 oz	500 g
Almond powder, made from roasted almonds	½ lb	225 g
Bread flour	12 oz	336 g

1. Cream the butter and sugar.
2. Gradually add the eggs and almond powder.
3. Mix in the flour.
4. Bake at 325°F (165°C) in square, flat baking sheets.

Fruit Pudding Cake

YIELD:
5 lb, 8 oz (2 kg, 467 g)

	U.S.	Metric
Salted butter	1 lb	450 g
Granulated sugar	1 lb	450 g
Eggs	1 lb, 2 oz	500 g
Bread flour	14 oz	392 g
Sultana raisins	½ lb	225 g
Candied cherries	½ lb	225 g
Candied fruits, assorted	½ lb	225 g

1. Cream butter and sugar until very light.
2. Gradually add the eggs.
3. Mix in the flour.
4. Cut the fruit in small pieces, and add to batter.
5. Bake at 325°F (165°C) in square, flat baking sheets.

PETITS FOURS GLACÉ

■ Adul

Cut out some round shapes from the biscuit manqué, top with some well-reduced apricot marmalade, and cover all over with a thin, warm, rum-flavored fondant.

Africaine

Cut a biscuit caprice crossways, and fill with a cream made from the following:

YIELD:
1 lb, 4 oz (563 g)

	U.S.	Metric
4× sugar	¹/₂ lb	225 g
Almond paste	¹/₂ lb	225 g
Sweet butter	4 oz	112 g
Rum syrup	To taste	

1. Chill in the refrigerator.
2. When set, cut out with an oval cutter, and cover all over with chocolate fondant.
3. Place a half pistachio nut on top.

■ Algériennes

Press some chestnuts through a sieve, and mix with butter and a little kirsch flavoring to make a cream. Press a small drop of the cream onto a piece of round manqué cake the size of a quarter. Place another cake on top. Cover all over with chocolate fondant, and sprinkle the top with chopped pistachio nuts.

■ Alice

Cut some small squares from fruit pudding cake. Dress on top with chopped candied fruits flavored with kirsch. Cover all over with a thin, warm fondant, and place a piece of candied fruit on top.

■ Americus

Cut a pâte à biscuit crossways and fill with chestnut buttercream. Chill in the refrigerator until set. Cut in domino shapes, cover all over with pistachio fondant, and sprinkle chopped pistachio nuts on top.

■ Anita

Cut an almond pâte à biscuit crossways, and fill with chopped preserved pineapple mixed with apricot jam. Cut into squares, cover all over with rum-flavored fondant, and decorate.

■ Arlequins

Cut round cakes from biscuit arlequins. Dress raspberry buttercream to a long point on the cakes. Chill in the refrigerator. When set, cover all over with pistachio fondant. When the fondant has dried, cut the top open with a knife dipped in hot water.

■ Avello

Cut some oval shapes from biscuit caprice. Dress praline buttercream on top. Sprinkle some chopped brown candied nougat on top, and chill. When set, cover all over with vanilla fondant.

■ Bar le Duc Tart

Line some small tart molds with any of the cookie doughs and bake. When cold, fill with red or white currant jam, and sprinkle a pinch of chopped pistachio nuts on top.

■ Belloca

Cut some round cakes from biscuit arlequins, and dress on top a round ball of chocolate buttercream. Chill. When set, cover all over with coffee fondant mixed with chopped walnuts.

■ Bombes Fruits with Pistachio

Put two drops of biscuit manqué together with plenty of hazelnut buttercream. When set, dip them into coffee fondant, and roll in finely chopped hazelnuts.

■ Boules au Chocolate

Cut out small, round cakes from biscuit arlequins. Dress on top a round ball of chocolate buttercream, sprinkle granulated chocolate all over, and chill to harden.

■ Boules with Pistachio Nuts

Cut out small, round cakes from pâte à caraques. Dress on top a small ball of pistachio buttercream, and sprinkle chopped pistachio nuts all over.

■ Buffalo

Line very small tartlet molds with pure almond paste, and bake at 410°F (210°C). When cold, unmold and fill them with apricot marmalade flavored with rum. Glaze with pistachio fondant.

■ Caprice

Cut a pâte à biscuit crossways and fill with praline buttercream. When set, cut in rectangular shapes and glaze all over with pistachio fondant mixed with chopped pistachio nuts. Sprinkle a few chopped pistachio nuts on top.

■ Cendrillon

Cut an almond pâte à biscuit crossways. Fill with coffee buttercream and reassemble. Chill. When the buttercream has set, cut out with an oval fancy cutter. Dress on top a little mocha cream, place a quarter of a walnut on top, and cover all over with coffee fondant.

■ Chocolate Manqué

Prepare a chocolate syrup of 18° on the Baumé sugar scale. Cut round shapes with a cutter from biscuit manqué, and dip into the syrup. When cold, cover all over with chocolate fondant, and decorate with aganasse cream.

■ Clairettes

Cut a pâte à caraque crossways, and fill with pistachio buttercream. Cut in small triangles, dip into chocolate fondant, and place a half pistachio nut on top.

■ Danswan

Cut round cakes from biscuit progrès. Dress on top a rum-flavored buttercream mixed with currants. Chill. When set, cover all over with rum-flavored, yellow-tinted fondant, and place a currant on top.

■ Manqué with Rum

Prepare a rum syrup of 22° on the Baumé sugar scale. Cut round shapes with a cutter from biscuit manqué, dip into the rum syrup, and cover with a yellow, rum-flavored fondant.

■ Marquise

Cut a thin layer from biscuit arlequins. Top with a layer of pistachio buttercream and then a thin layer of biscuit caprice. Top this with a layer of mocha cream and then another layer of biscuit arlequins. Chill. When set, cover all over with sweet chocolate coating, and cut into small squares.

■ Parisians

Thinly line small, oval-shaped tins with pure almond paste. Bake in a hot oven. When cold, remove from the tins, fill, and decorate the top with vanilla buttercream pressed through a very small fancy tube.

■ Petits Choux

Petits choux are small cream puffs filled with vanilla-flavored whipped cream and dusted with sugar or covered with fondant.

■ Pudding Bordelaise

Prepare a rum syrup of 18° on the Baumé sugar scale. Cut a fruit pudding cake into square shapes, and dip into the syrup. When cold, dip into red currant jelly, cover all over with chopped walnuts, and dust very lightly with 4× sugar.

■ Pudding au Kirsch

Prepare a kirsch syrup of 18° on the Baumé sugar scale. Cut a fruit pudding cake into round shapes, and dip into the syrup. When cold, cover all over with kirsch fondant and decorate.

■ Pudding with Rum

Prepare a rum syrup of 18° on the Baumé sugar scale. Cut a fruit pudding cake into squares, and dip into the syrup. When cold, cover all over with a light green fondant flavored with rum, and place a half pistachio nut on top.

■ Russie

Cut some oval shapes from biscuit manqué. Dress on top a kirsch-flavored buttercream. Cover all over with finely chopped, roasted almonds, and chill. When set, powder with 4× sugar.

■ Shanzy

Cut out some round shapes of fruit pudding cake. Place on top a large preserved strawberry, cover all over with orange fondant, and decorate with pink fondant.

■ Snow Balls

Cut out small, round cakes from biscuit manqué. Dress on top a ball of buttercream, and then press another piece of cake on top. When set, dip them into vanilla fondant, and roll in freshly grated coconut.

■ Suprême

Cut some round shapes from pâte à caraques. Dress on top, to a point, a cream made from praline, heavy cream, and sweet chocolate. When set, cover all over with pistachio fondant, and decorate with chocolate fondant pressed through a cornet.

■ Turinos

Cut some round shapes from pâte à caraques. Dress on top a chestnut buttercream, and chill. When set, glaze all over with vanilla fondant, and sprinkle chocolate shot on top.

❦ Fancy Cakes

Fancy cakes are usually made from plain pound cake covered with buttercream of different flavors, cut in various shapes, and then iced with fondant of different flavors and colors. When the icing is dry, they are decorated on top with royal icing in the form of fruit, flowers, birds, and many other designs.

Bake a pound cake mixture in pans about ½ inch (1 cm) thick. When cold, spread a buttercream on top about ⅛ inch (3 mm) thick, and mark with a knife for cutting. Press buttercream through a plain tube in the form of a ball or any other desired form on each section, and chill overnight. Next morning, cut where marked, place the cakes on a wire rack, and ice all over with various colored and flavored fondants. When dry, decorate as desired.

Take another sheet of pound cake, spread buttercream on top a little thicker than before, and chill. When hard, cut out with fancy cutters and place on a wire rack. Ice all over with fondant of different colors and flavors. When dry, decorate with a royal icing in the form of birds, flowers, etc.

Another sheet of pound cake can be cut in rectangular shapes, iced white, and then decorated with chocolate fondant to represent dominos. Others may be cut square or any shape desired, iced with different flavored and colored fondants, and then decorated with chocolate fondant pressed through a cornet, candied fruits, jellies, etc.

Spread the top of another sheet of pound cake with finely chopped, candied cherries mixed with a little apricot jam. Cut into squares, and ice with a thin pink fondant. When dry, place a dot of chocolate fondant on top, and dip the dot in finely chopped pistachio nuts. This also may be made with pineapple and iced lightly with a yellow, pineapple-flavored fondant. When dry, place a piece of candied pineapple on top.

A layer cake mixture may be substituted for pound cake by using only half the baking powder called for in the recipe.

There are no standard rules or recipes for the making of fancy cakes. The preceding are simply a few suggestions that should aid materially in making cakes that are very rich in flavor as well as in appearance and are at the same time very little trouble and expense.

PETITS FOURS SECS

Almond Bars

YIELD:
3 lb, 8 oz (1 kg, 575 g)

	U.S.	Metric
Line a baking pan with cookie dough, and then fill with the following mixture:		
Granulated sugar	1 lb	450 g
Almonds, chopped	1 lb	450 g
Bitter chocolate	1 oz	450 g
Egg whites	8 oz	225 g

1. Combine all ingredients, and cook over high heat until the mixture has nearly reached the boiling point.
2. Spread out evenly over the cookie dough, and bake at 325°F (165°C).
3. When baked and cold, cut into small bars.

■ Alumettes

Roll out a piece of puff paste quite thin, cover all over with royal icing (not too stiff), and cut into bars 2 × ½ inch (5 × 1 cm). Let stand for 30 minutes. Bake at 325°F (165°C).

Biarritz

YIELD:
1 lb, 7 oz (769 g)

	U.S.	Metric
Egg whites	11 oz	320 g
Granulated sugar	½ lb	225 g
Almond powder, made from roasted almonds	4 oz	112 g
Bread flour	4 oz	112 g

1. Beat the egg whites (not too stiff).
2. Add the sugar, almond powder, and flour.
3. Dress with a bag in round, flat wafers onto greased pans.
4. Bake at 325°F (165°C).
5. When cold, spread sweet chocolate on the flat side with a small palette knife.

Beignets with Cherries

YIELD:
2 lb, 10 oz (1 kg, 276 g)

	U.S.	Metric
Almond paste	1 lb	450 g
Granulated sugar	1/2 lb	225 g
Egg whites	11 oz	320 g
Candied cherries, finely chopped	1/2 lb	225 g
Bread flour	2 oz	56 g
Red food coloring	As needed	

1. Combine the almond paste, sugar, and half the egg whites, and mix well until very smooth.
2. Add the cherries, flour, and food coloring.
3. In a separate bowl, beat the remaining egg whites until very firm.
4. Fold the egg whites into the dough.
5. Fill small paper soufflé cups three-quarters full, place a half cherry on top, and dust with 4× sugar.
6. Bake at 325°F (165°C).

NOTE: These also may be made with orange or pineapple.

Langues de Chats (Cats' Tongues)

YIELD:
6 lb, 4 oz (2 kg, 811 g)

	U.S.	Metric
Sweet butter	1 lb	450 g
Confectioner's sugar	2 lb	900 g
Vanilla extract	To taste	
Egg whites	1 1/2 lb	675 g
Bread flour	1 lb, 12 oz	786 g

1. Cream the butter and sugar well.
2. Add vanilla and then the egg whites, a little at a time.
3. Fold in the flour.
4. Dress in long shapes, about 3 inches (8 cm) long, through a small, plain tube onto lightly greased pans.
5. Bake at 350°F (175°C).

Chocolate Logs

YIELD:
12 lb (5 kg, 400 g)

	U.S.	Metric
Almond paste	5 lb	2 kg, 250 g
4× sugar	5 lb	2 kg, 250 g
Egg whites	1½ lb	675 g
Bitter chocolate, melted	8 oz	225 g

1. Combine the almond paste, sugar, and half the egg whites, and work until very smooth.
2. Add the chocolate and the remaining egg whites.
3. Press through a very large star tube in long strips onto greased pans dusted with flour. Set aside to dry overnight.
4. Bake at 450°F (230°C). When cold, cut into small logs.
5. Dip the ends in well-reduced apricot syrup and then in chopped pistachio nuts, or if desired, the ends may be dipped into sweet chocolate coating and placed on paper to dry.

Chocolate Tips

YIELD:
5 lb, 8 oz (2 kg, 475 g)

	U.S.	Metric
Almond paste	1 lb	450 g
Granulated sugar	2 lb	900 g
Egg whites	2 lb	900 g
Bread flour	8 oz	225 g

1. Combine the almond paste, ½ lb of the sugar, and half the egg whites. Rub well together until very smooth.
2. Beat the remaining egg whites and the remaining sugar to make a firm meringue.
3. Mix the meringue into the almond paste.
4. Fold in the flour.
5. Dress through a small, plain tube in the shape of small lady fingers onto greased pans dusted with flour.
6. Sprinkle all over with sliced nuts or coconut.
7. Bake at 300°F (150°C).
8. When cold, place two cakes together with apricot jam between, dip the ends into sweet chocolate coating, and place on paper to dry.

Cigarettes

YIELD:
3 lb, 5 oz (1 kg, 480 g)

	U.S.	Metric
Sweet butter	10 oz	280 g
Confectioner's sugar	1 lb	450 g
Heavy cream	½ pt	225 g
Egg whites	11 oz	300 g
Bread flour	8 oz	225 g

1. Cream the butter, sugar, and heavy cream together well.
2. In a separate bowl, beat the egg whites until stiff.
3. Fold the egg whites into the creamed mixture.
4. Fold in the flour.
5. Dress in flat balls, the size of a quarter, through a plain tube onto lightly greased pans.
6. Bake at 350°F (175°C).
7. When baked, remove from the oven and roll up on a ½ inch (1 cm) dowel to form a cigarette shape.
8. When cold, fill with aganasse cream or buttercreams of different flavors.

Cyrano

YIELD:
3 lb, 14 oz (1 kg, 744 g)

	U.S.	Metric
Almond paste	1 lb	450 g
Sweet butter	½ lb	225 g
Eggs, separated	1 lb, 2 oz	500 g
Granulated sugar	1 lb	450 g
Bread flour	4 oz	112 g

1. Cream the almond paste and butter.
2. Add the egg yolks two at a time.
3. In a separate bowl, beat the egg whites with the sugar to make a firm meringue.
4. Fold meringue into the almond paste mixture.
5. Fold in the flour.
6. Bake at 325°F (165°C) in a paper-lined pan.
7. When cold, glaze the top with a well-reduced apricot jelly.
8. Sprinkle chopped pistachio nuts on top and cut into small bars or squares.

Duchesses

YIELD:
3 lb, 12 oz (1 kg, 687 g)

	U.S.	Metric
Hazelnut powder, made from roasted hazelnuts	1 lb	450 g
Heavy cream	½ pt	225 g
Bread flour	4 oz	112 g
Egg whites	1 lb	450 g
Confectioner's sugar	1 lb	450 g

1. Mix well together the hazelnut powder, cream, and flour.
2. Beat the egg whites with the sugar to a soft meringue.
3. Fold the meringue into the hazelnut powder mixture.
4. Press through a small, plain tube in round, flat balls onto greased pans.
5. Bake at 325°F (165°C).
6. When baked, place two cakes together with aganasse cream. Dust all over with 4× sugar.

Favorites

YIELD:
4 lb, 15 oz (2 kg, 164 g)

	U.S.	Metric
Sweet butter	1 lb	450 g
Powdered sugar	1 lb, 10 oz	730g
Egg whites	1 lb	450 g
Bread flour	1 lb, 3 oz	534 g
Lemon rind, grated	1	1

1. Cream well together the butter, sugar, and grated lemon rind.
2. Add the egg whites a little at a time.
3. Fold in the flour.
4. Dress onto greased pans through a plain tube in shapes the size of a quarter.
5. Bake at 350°F (175°C).

Jan Hagel

YIELD:
10 lb, 10 oz (4 kg, 506 g)

	U.S.	Metric
Sweet butter	2 lb	900g
Brown sugar, no. 10	2½ lb	1 kg, 125 g
Eggs	14 oz	400 g
Milk	½ pt	225 g
Bread flour	4 lb	1 kg, 800 g
Cinnamon, ground	1 oz	28 g
Baking powder	1 oz	28 g

1. Cream the butter, sugar, and eggs.
2. Add the milk.
3. Sift the flour, cinnamon, and baking powder together. Add to the creamed mixture to form a smooth dough.
4. Chill overnight.
5. Roll out the dough very thin, and place on lightly greased baking pans.
6. Wash all over with egg wash, and sprinkle on top with sliced nuts and granulated sugar.
7. Bake at 350°F (175°C).
8. When baked and while hot, cut into bars 3 × 1 inch (8 × 3 cm) and dust lightly with 4× sugar.

Fancy Kisses

YIELD:
8 lb (3 kg, 600 g)

	U.S.	Metric
Granulated sugar	4 lb	1 kg, 800 g
Water	1 qt	900 g
Egg whites	2 lb	900 g

1. Boil the sugar and water to 242°F (116°C).
2. In a separate bowl, beat the egg whites until very stiff.
3. Add the boiled sugar slowly to the egg whites while continuing to beat at medium speed until cold.
4. Dress through a star tube in fancy shapes onto greased and flour-dusted pans.
5. Bake at 250°F (120°C).

Lady Fingers 1

YIELD:
4 lb, 2¹/₂ oz (1 kg, 867 g)

	U.S.	Metric
Eggs, separated	1 lb, 8 oz	675 g
Granulated sugar	1 lb, 7¹/₂ oz	660 g
Vanilla extract	1 oz	28 g
Cake flour, sifted	13 oz	364 g
Confectioner's sugar	5 oz	140 g

1. Combine the egg yolks, half the sugar, and the vanilla extract, and beat until light and fluffy. Add the flour.
2. In a separate bowl, beat the egg whites until stiff, adding the remaining sugar gradually while beating.
3. Gently fold the egg whites into the egg yolk mixture.
4. Using a pastry bag fitted with a plain round tube, press the batter onto greased and floured baking sheets in portions approximately 3 inches (8 cm) long. Let stand for about 5 minutes.
5. Bake at 350°F (180°C) for about 8 minutes or until golden brown. Store in a tightly sealed jar.

NOTE: In pastry shops, lady fingers are baked on a piece of heavy cardboard used only for this purpose. They are removed with a flexible spatula while hot. The reason for this is simply that the lady finger mixture, being rather light, is very sensitive to bottom heat. This method is recommended if a clean piece of cardboard at least ¹/₄ inch (6 mm) thick is available.

Lady Fingers 2

YIELD:
10 lb, 9¹/₂ oz (4 kg, 545 g)

	U.S.	Metric
Egg yolks	1 lb, 8 oz	720 g
Granulated sugar	3 lb	1 kg, 350 g
Lemon extract	To taste	
Egg whites	3 lb	1 kg, 350 g
Bread flour	2¹/₂ lb	1 kg, 125 g

1. Beat the egg yolks with half the sugar and the lemon extract.
2. In a separate bowl, beat the egg whites until very stiff, and add the remaining sugar slowly to make a firm meringue.
3. Add the meringue to the egg yolk mixture and mix well.

4. Fold in flour.
5. Dress in finger shapes through a plain tube onto paper.
6. Dust with powdered sugar.
7. Bake at 350°F (175°C).

Lady Fingers 3

YIELD:
3 lb (1 kg, 350 g)

	U.S.	Metric
Eggs	1 lb	450 g
Granulated sugar	1 lb	450 g
Bread flour, sifted	1 lb	450 g

1. Combine the eggs and sugar, and beat over low heat until warm.
2. Remove from heat and continue beating until cold.
3. Mix in the sifted flour.
4. Dress in finger shapes through a plain tube onto paper.
5. Dust with powdered sugar.
6. Bake at 350°F (175°C).

Macaroons 1

YIELD:
11 lb, 8 oz (5 kg, 175 g)

	U.S.	Metric
Almond paste	5 lb	2 kg, 250 g
Granulated sugar	5 lb	2 kg, 250 g
Egg whites	1½ lb	675 g

1. Rub the almond paste, sugar, and some of the egg whites together until very smooth.
2. Gradually add the remaining egg whites.
3. Dress onto paper through a plain tube.
4. Bake at 325°F (165°C) on double pans.
5. Do not allow macaroons to become dry on top—the sooner they are put in the oven the better. Wet the macaroons with a slightly damp towel before putting them in the oven.

Macaroons 2

YIELD:
6 lb, 12 oz (3 kg, 36 g)

	U.S.	Metric
Almond paste	2½ lb	1 kg, 125 g
Granulated sugar	3 lb	1 kg, 350 g
Egg whites	1 lb	450 g
Rice flour	4 oz	112 g

Treat the same as Macaroons 1.

Chocolate Macaroons

YIELD:
13 lb, 10 oz (6 kg, 130 g)

	U.S.	Metric
Almond paste	5 lb	2 kg, 250 g
Granulated sugar	6 lb	2 kg, 700 g
Egg whites	2 lb	900 g
Bitter chocolate	10 oz	280 g

1. Combine the almond paste, sugar, and half the egg whites, and work well together until very smooth.
2. Slowly add the remaining egg whites and the chocolate.
3. Dress onto paper through a plain tube, and wet the same as the other macaroons.
4. Bake at 350°F (175°C).

Coconut Macaroons

YIELD:
6 lb, 4 oz (2 kg, 712 g)

	U.S.	Metric
Coconut, shredded	2 lb	900 g
Granulated sugar	3 lb	1 kg, 250 g
Rice flour	4 oz	112 g
Egg whites	1 lb	450 g

1. Mix the coconut, sugar, and egg whites well.
2. Add the flour.
3. Place in a pan over low heat, and warm to a medium heat.
4. Dress onto paper through a plain tube.
5. Bake at 350°F (175°C).

Fancy Macaroons

YIELD:
11 lb, 8 oz (5 kg, 175 g)

	U.S.	Metric
Almond paste	*5 lb*	*2 kg, 250 g*
4× sugar	*5 lb*	*2 kg, 250 g*
Egg whites	*1½ lb*	*675 g*

1. Rub the almond paste, sugar, and some of the egg whites together well. Add the remaining egg whites a little at a time to make a smooth paste.
2. Dress through a large star tube in different fancy shapes onto lightly greased pans dusted with flour.
3. Decorate the tops with candied fruits, raisins, almonds, or angelica.
4. Let stand overnight to dry.
5. Bake at 450°F (220°C).
6. As soon as they become a nice, light brown color, remove from the oven.
7. Wash well with plain hot syrup or a glacé mixture made by boiling 1 qt of water with ½ oz of starch.

■ Fancy Macaroons (with Fondant, Jams, and Jellies)

Prepare the same as for fancy macaroons. Dress through a large star tube in round, oval, or any other desired shapes onto greased pans dusted with flour. Make an impression in the center of each with a stick or with your finger (first dipped into cold water to prevent sticking), and let stand overnight to dry. Bake at 450°F (220°C). When cold, fill the indentations with jams, jellies, or fondants of different flavors and colors.

■ Lemon Macaroons

Treat the same as orange macaroons, but use lemons instead of oranges. Color slightly yellow, and place a piece of candied lemon peel on top.

Orange Macaroons

YIELD:
11 lb, 14 oz (5 kg, 346 g)

	U.S.	Metric
Almond paste	5 lb	2 kg, 250g
Orange rinds, grated	5	56 g
Granulated sugar	5 lb	2 kg, 250 g
Egg whites	1 lb, 12 oz	790 g
Orange coloring	As needed	

1. Combine the almond paste, grated orange rinds, sugar, and some of the egg whites, and work well until very smooth.
2. Add the remaining egg whites and the coloring.
3. Dress onto paper through a plain tube.
4. Place a piece of candied orange peel on top.
5. Wet slightly with a damp towel.
6. Bake at 325°F (165°C) on double pans.

Parisian Macaroons

YIELD:
14 lb (6 kg, 300 g)

	U.S.	Metric
Almond paste	5 lb	2 kg, 250 g
Confectioner's sugar	7 lb	3 kg, 150 g
Egg whites	2 lb	900 g

1. Combine almond paste, sugar, and half the egg whites.
2. Slowly add the remaining egg whites.
3. Place in a pan over moderate heat, stirring constantly until hot.
4. Remove from heat, and dress quickly through a small, plain tube onto greased pans dusted with flour.

5. Let stand overnight to dry.
6. Bake at 350°F (175°C).

NOTE: These macaroons will run a little flat and, when baked, will have a shiny finish.

■ Parisian Split Macaroons

Prepare and treat the same as Parisian macaroons. Dress the mixture onto paper in oval shapes, and let stand overnight to dry. Cut a deep incision down the center three-fourths of its length with a sharp knife. Bake at 350°F (175°C).

Mokke Anversoise

YIELD:
7 lb, 1 oz (3 kg, 184 g)

	U.S.	Metric
Sweet butter	2 lb	900 g
Granulated sugar	1 lb, 12 oz	786 g
Lemon rinds, grated	2	28 g
Egg yolks	4 oz	120
Cake flour	3 lb	1 kg, 350 g

1. Cream the butter, sugar, and grated lemon rinds.
2. Add the egg yolks.
3. Mix in the flour to make a dough.
4. Chill until firm.
5. Divide dough into 1-lb pieces, and roll into long bars.
6. Roll the bars in coarse granulated sugar.
7. Flatten each bar slightly, and chill overnight.
8. Cut into ¼-inch (6-mm) slices, and place flat side down on clean pans. Draw a stripe across each bar with pastry cream.
9. Bake at 325°F (165°C).

Mokke Hollandaise

YIELD:
4 lb (1 kg, 800 g)

	U.S.	Metric
Sweet butter	1 lb	450 g
Granulated sugar	2 lb	900 g
Vanilla extract	To taste	
Bread flour	1 lb	450 g

1. Cream the butter, sugar, and vanilla together.
2. Work in the flour, and chill.
3. Roll into 12-oz (336-g) bars, and then roll in coarse granulated sugar.
4. Chill overnight.
5. Cut into $\frac{1}{4}$-inch (6-mm) slices, place flat side down on clean pans, and put a dot of red currant jelly in the center of each.
6. Bake at 325°F (165°C).

Mousseline Poudrés

YIELD:
3 lb, 12 oz (1 kg, 737 g)

	U.S.	Metric
Almond paste	1 lb	450 g
Sweet butter	$\frac{1}{2}$ lb	225 g
Confectioner's sugar	1 lb	450 g
Eggs, separated	1 lb, 2 oz	500 g
Bread flour	4 oz	112 g

1. Cream the almond paste, butter, and half the sugar together well.
2. Add the egg yolks a little at a time.
3. In a separate bowl, beat the egg whites with the remaining sugar to make a meringue.
4. Fold the meringue into the egg yolk mixture.
5. Fold in the flour.
6. Fill a paper-lined, greased, 1-inch-deep (25-mm deep) pan about three-quarters full with the batter.
7. Bake at 325°F (165°C).
8. When cold, dust all over with 4× sugar and cut into 1-inch (25-mm) squares.

Pains d'Amande

YIELD:
8 lb, ¹/₂ oz (3 kg, 614 g)

	U.S.	Metric
Sweet butter	1 lb	450 g
Brown sugar, no. 10	2¹/₂ lb	1 kg, 125 g
Water	¹/₂ pt	225 g
Cinnamon, ground	¹/₄ oz	7 g
Blanched almonds, chopped	1 lb	450 g
Bread flour	3 lb	1 kg, 350 g
Baking soda	¹/₄ oz	7 g

1. Melt the butter with the sugar and water.
2. Add the cinnamon and almonds.
3. Remove from heat and cool.
4. When cold, mix in the flour and baking soda.
5. Press into a 1¹/₂-inch-deep (4-cm deep) paper-lined pan. Chill overnight.
6. Cut into bars of equal width and thickness. Then cut the bars into thin slices, and place on greased pans (not too close together).
7. Bake at 350°F (175°C).

Palets de Dames

YIELD:
4 lb (1 kg, 800 g)

	U.S.	Metric
Sweet butter	1 lb	450 g
Granulated sugar	1 lb	450 g
Vanilla extract	To taste	
Eggs	1 lb	450 g
Cake flour	1 lb	450 g

1. Cream the butter, sugar, and vanilla together well.
2. Add the eggs a little at a time.
3. Mix in the flour.
4. Dress through a plain tube in round shapes onto greased pans dusted with flour.
5. Bake at 350°F (175°C).

■ Palets de Dames Glacés

Prepare the same as palets de dames. When cold, cover the flat side with a sweet chocolate coating.

■ Palets Fourrées

Prepare the same as palets de dames. When baked, put two together with mocha buttercream or apricot jam, and dust with 4× sugar.

Parisienne

YIELD:
4 lb, 8 oz (2 kg, 25 g)

	U.S.	Metric
Bread flour	2 lb	900 g
Salted butter	1½ lb	675 g
Milk	1 pt	450 g
Salt	To taste	

1. Work all ingredients together the same as for puff paste.
2. Let rest for 2 hours in the refrigerator.
3. Give two turns, the same as for puff paste, by rolling in sugar (as for palmyre leaves).
4. Roll out about ⅛ inch (3 mm) thick, and cut out with a round cutter.
5. Roll out on a *plaque quadrillée* in very thin oval shapes so as to form the open-work pattern.
6. Place on parchment-lined pans.
7. Bake at 400°F (205°C).

Rocher Meringue

YIELD:
5 lb (2 kg, 250 g)

	U.S.	Metric
Water	1 pt	450 g
Granulated sugar	2 lb	900 g
Egg whites	1 lb	450 g
Nuts, sliced	1 lb	450 g

1. Boil water and sugar to 242°F (116°C).
2. In a separate bowl, beat the egg whites.
3. Slowly add the boiled sugar to the egg whites to make a meringue Italienne.
4. Continue beating until nearly cold, and then fold in the sliced nuts.
5. Dress with a teaspoon onto greased pans dusted with flour or lined with parchment paper.
6. Bake at 250°F (120°C).

NOTE: Use whatever nuts you have available; almonds are a good choice, or use shredded coconut for an interesting variation.

Almond Soufflés

YIELD:
2 lb, 8 oz (1 kg, 147 g)

	U.S.	Metric
Almond paste	1 lb	450 g
Granulated sugar	1/2 lb	225 g
Egg whites	13 oz	360 g
Bread flour	4 oz	112 g

1. Work almond paste, sugar, and half the egg whites well until smooth.
2. In a separate bowl, beat the remaining egg whites until stiff.
3. Fold the egg whites into the almond paste mixture.
4. Fold in the flour.
5. Dress through a plain tube into small paper soufflé cups.
6. Sprinkle a pinch of chopped almonds on top, and dust all over with 4× sugar.
7. Bake at 325°F (165°C).

Walnut Soufflés

YIELD:
2 lb, 8 oz (1 kg, 147 g)

	U.S.	Metric
Almond paste	½ lb	225 g
Walnut powder	½ lb	225 g
Granulated sugar	½ lb	225 g
Egg whites	13 oz	360 g
Bread flour	4 oz	112 g

Treat the same as almond soufflés, sprinkle chopped walnut meats on top, and bake at 325°F (165°C).

Tartes Brésiliennes

YIELD:
3 lb, ½ oz (1 kg, 364 g)

	U.S.	Metric
Sweet butter	1 lb	450 g
Granulated sugar	½ lb	225 g
Almond powder, made from roasted almonds	½ lb	225 g
Bread flour	1 lb	450 g
Baking powder	½ oz	14 g

1. Cream the butter, sugar, and almond powder together well.
2. Sift the flour and baking powder together, and then work into the creamed mixture.
3. Chill overnight.
4. When ready, roll out about ⅛ inch (3 mm) thick, cut with a round fancy cutter, and place on clean pans.
5. Bake at 325°F (165°C).
6. When baked, place two together with raspberry jam, and dust the top with 6× sugar.

French Tuiles

YIELD:
2 lb, 14 oz (1 kg, 312 g)

	U.S.	Metric
Granulated sugar	1 lb	450g
Eggs	11 oz	300 g
Almonds, sliced	1 lb	450 g
Bread flour	4 oz	112 g

1. Mix the sugar, eggs, and nuts together well.
2. Add the flour.
3. Dress with a teaspoon onto greased pans or parchment-lined pans, not too close together.
4. Flatten them with a fork, and bake at 325°F (165°C).
5. When baked, and as soon as removed from the oven, place them on broomsticks and bend.

Belgian Tuiles

YIELD:
5 lb, 15¼ oz (2 kg, 676 g)

	U.S.	Metric
Sweet butter	1 lb	450 g
Brown sugar, no. 10	2½ lb	1 kg, 125 g
Cinnamon, ground	¼ oz	7 g
Water	¼ pt	112 g
Almonds, chopped	1 lb	450 g
Bread flour	19 oz	532 g

1. Cream the butter, sugar, and cinnamon.
2. Add the water and almonds.
3. Mix in the flour to make a dough.
4. Chill overnight.
5. When ready, roll up into long bars and cut into small pieces.
6. Place them on well-greased pans or on parchment-lined pans, not too close together.
7. Bake at 325°F (165°C).

NOTE: These tuiles spread out a great deal during the baking process and, when baked, are very thin and really resemble a candy more than a cake.

Vienna Wafers

YIELD:
5 lb, 5¹/₂ oz (2 kg, 384 g)

	U.S.	Metric
Sweet butter	1¹/₂ lb	675 g
Confectioner's sugar	1 lb	450 g
Almond powder, made from roasted almonds	1 lb	450 g
Egg whites	4 oz	120 g
Lemon rinds, grated	2	2
Bread flour	1¹/₂ lb	675 g
Baking powder	¹/₂ oz	14 g

1. Cream butter, sugar, and almond powder.
2. Add the egg whites and the grated lemon rinds.
3. Work in the flour and baking powder.
4. Chill overnight.
5. Roll out in two sheets about ¹/₄ inch (6 mm) thick, and place on separate pans.
6. Bake at 325°F (165°C).
7. When baked and before cold, cut one of the sheets into 1-inch (25-mm) squares, and decorate with royal icing by drawing straight lines crossways. Replace in the oven and bake the royal icing, and cut again while hot (to cut the royal icing).
8. Spread apricot jam on top of the undecorated sheet, place the squares on top, and then cut through the bottom sheet.

COOKIES

Almond Bread Cookies

YIELD:
7 lb, 3 oz (3 kg, 236 g)

	U.S.	Metric
Butter, room temperature	1 lb, 4 oz	562 g
Dark brown sugar, well packed	1 lb, 11½ oz	772 g
Honey	7½ oz	210 g
Eggs, beaten with fork	8 oz	225 g
Cake flour, sifted	2 lb, 10 oz	1 kg, 180 g
Baking soda	¼ oz	7 g
Blanched almonds, whole	10 oz	280 g

1. Cream the butter, brown sugar, and honey together thoroughly.
2. Add the beaten eggs, and blend well.
3. Sift the flour and soda together twice, and then stir it into the butter mixture and mix thoroughly.
4. Stir in the almonds.
5. Chill the dough in the refrigerator until firm, and then shape it into long rolls approximately 1½ inches (4 cm) in diameter.
6. Wrap the rolls in waxed paper, and chill in the freezer or refrigerator until hard.
7. Cut into slices ⅛ inch (3 mm) thick.
8. Arrange the cookies approximately 1 inch (2.5 cm) apart on lightly greased cookie sheets.
9. Bake at 350°F (180°C) for about 12 minutes or until golden brown.

Almond Kisses

YIELD:
9 lb, 12¹/₂ oz (4 kg, 391 g)

	U.S.	Metric
Egg whites	12 oz	336 g
Salt	To taste	
Granulated sugar	6 lb, 14 oz	3 kg, 92 g
Vanilla extract	¹/₂ oz	7 g
Almonds, sliced	8 ¹/₃ cups	956 g

1. Beat the egg whites, salt, sugar, and vanilla extract over hot water until lukewarm or until the sugar is dissolved. Remove from heat and whip until thick and fluffy.
2. Stir in the sliced almonds, and using a tablespoon, drop the batter onto greased and floured baking sheets.
3. Bake at 325°F (165°C) for approximately 25 minutes.
4. Remove the cookies immediately from the sheet, and store in a dry place.

NOTE: The almond cookies can be dipped into melted sweet chocolate for an especially festive appearance. The sliced almonds also can be replaced by chopped pecans or shredded coconut.

Almond Lace Cookies

YIELD:
7 lb, 5 oz (3 kg, 288 g)

	U.S.	Metric
Light corn syrup	1 lb, 14 oz	842 g
Butter	1 lb, 4 oz	562 g
Brown sugar	1 lb, 4 oz	562 g
All purpose flour, sifted	1 lb, 4 oz	562 g
Blanched almonds, finely chopped	1 lb, 11 oz	758 g

1. Place the corn syrup, butter, and brown sugar in a deep saucepan over medium heat, and bring to a slow boil. Remove from heat.
2. Blend the flour and nuts together and gradually add to the warm ingredients. Stir well.

3. Drop the batter in 1-inch (3-cm) portions onto well-greased baking sheets, leaving enough space between each cookie for spreading.
4. Bake at 325°F for 8 minutes or until golden brown. Remove from oven and cool before lifting the cookies from the sheet with a thin, flexible spatula.
5. Place on waxed paper to complete cooling.

NOTE: You can coat the bottoms of these cookies with melted sweet chocolate or roll them around a thick pencil while still warm into a cigarette shape. If the cookies become too hard to roll, return them briefly to the oven to soften.

American Pecan Drops

YIELD:
5 lb, 3 oz (2 kg, 328 g)

	U.S.	Metric
Eggs, beaten	1 lb	450 g
Brown sugar	14 oz	392 g
Granulated sugar	1 lb	450 g
Cake flour	12½ oz	350 g
Salt	¼ oz	7 g
Baking powder	¼ oz	7 g
Pecans, finely chopped	15 oz	420 g
Apricot jam	9 oz	420 g
Confectioner's sugar	As needed	

1. Beat the eggs and sugars together until light and fluffy.
2. Sift the flour, salt, and baking powder together, and fold into the egg batter alternately with the nuts.
3. Using a teaspoon or pastry bag fitted with a round, plain tube, drop the cookies onto greased baking sheets, spacing them about 2 inches (5 cm) apart.
4. Bake at 400°F for about 6 minutes or until the edges start to brown. Remove from the sheets while still warm, and sandwich together in pairs with apricot jam in the center. Dust with confectioner's sugar.

Americana Cookies

YIELD:
6 lb, 3¹/₄ oz (2 kg, 786 g)

	U.S.	Metric
Butter, room temperature	1 lb, 4 oz	562 g
Brown sugar	13¹/₂ oz	378 g
Granulated sugar	1 lb	450 g
Eggs, beaten with fork	8 oz	225 g
All purpose flour, sifted	1 lb, 14 oz	842 g
Baking soda	³/₄ oz	21 g
Cinnamon, ground	¹/₂ oz	14 g
Salt	¹/₄ oz	7 g
Lemon rind, grated	¹/₄ oz	7 g
Walnuts, finely chopped	10 oz	280 g

1. Cream the butter and sugars together well.
2. Add the beaten eggs, and continue beating until light and fluffy.
3. Sift the flour, baking soda, cinnamon, and salt together. Stir into the egg batter alternately with the lemon rind and nuts.
4. Work the mixture into a smooth dough.
5. Place the dough in the refrigerator for approximately 15 minutes or until firm.
6. Form the dough into long rolls about 1¹/₂ inches (4 cm) in diameter.
7. Wrap the rolls in waxed paper, and chill in the freezer for approximately 1 hour.
8. Cut into slices about ¹/₄ inch (6 mm) thick.
9. Arrange the slices on greased baking sheets, 2 inches (5 cm) apart, and bake at 375°F (190°C) for about 8 minutes or until golden brown.

Anise Cookies

YIELD:
8 lb, 10 ³/₄ oz (3 kg, 901 g)

	U.S.	Metric
Eggs	2 lb	900 g
Granulated sugar	2 lb, 12 oz	1 kg, 238 g
All purpose flour	3 lb, 12 oz	1 kg, 686 g
Double-acting baking powder	¹/₄ oz	7 g
Anise seeds	2¹/₂ oz	70 g

1. Cream the eggs and sugar until the mixture becomes thick (about the consistency of whipped cream).
2. Sift the flour with the baking powder. Gently fold the sifted ingredients and the anise seeds into the egg mixture.
3. Using a teaspoon or a pastry bag fitted with a plain tube, drop 1-inch (3-cm) portions of the cookie dough approximately 1 inch (3 cm) apart onto greased and floured baking sheets. Let stand at room temperature overnight.
4. Bake at 350°F (180°C) for approximately 10 to 12 minutes.

Anise Sponge Cookies

YIELD:
3 lb, 12¼ oz (1 kg, 692 g)

	U.S.	Metric
Eggs	1 lb, 8 oz	675 g
Granulated sugar	7½ oz	210 g
All purpose flour, sifted	1 lb, 11½ oz	772 g
Anise seeds	1¼ oz	35 g

1. Beat the eggs and sugar vigorously over hot water until warm [approximately 110°F (43°C)]. Remove from heat and continue beating until cold and thick (consistency should be that of whipped cream).
2. Combine the sifted flour with the anise seeds, and fold into the egg mixture.
3. Using a pastry bag fitted with a ½-inch (1-cm) plain round tube, squeeze 1-inch (3-cm) cookies onto greased and floured baking sheets, spacing them about 2 inches (5 cm) apart. Allow the cookies to dry for 6 hours at room temperature.
4. Bake at 325°F (170°C) for 10 to 12 minutes or until golden brown.

Brandy Snaps

YIELD:
11 lb, 5¹/₂ oz (5 kg, 103 g)

	U.S.	Metric
All purpose flour, sifted	2 lb, 8 oz	1 kg, 125 g
Granulated sugar	2 lb	900 g
Ginger, ground	1¹/₄ oz	35 g
Molasses	2 lb, 8 oz	1 kg, 125 g
Butter, melted	2 lb, 8 oz	1 kg, 125 g
Heavy cream, whipped	1 lb, 4 oz	562 g
Brandy	1¹/₄ oz	35 g
Sweet chocolate, grated	7 oz	196 g

1. Sift the flour, sugar, and ginger together twice.
2. Boil the molasses in a deep saucepan. Remove from heat, and stir in the melted butter. While stirring constantly, add the sifted ingredients, and mix to a smooth batter.
3. Using a pastry bag fitted with a round tube or a tablespoon, drop the cookies at least 3 inches (8 cm) apart onto greased baking sheets.
4. Bake at 275°F (135°C) for approximately 15 minutes or until the edges start to brown.
5. Immediately remove from the sheet, and roll each cookie around a broomstick, a small rolling pin, or the handle of a wooden spoon until it is the shape of a cigarette. Cool.
6. Combine the whipped cream, brandy, and grated chocolate, and fill the cooled cookies.
7. Store in a tightly closed container in the refrigerator or freezer until needed. Remove from the freezer approximately 10 minutes before serving.

Cats' Tongues (Langues de Chats)

YIELD:
4 lb, 2 oz (1 kg, 854 g)

	U.S.	Metric
Butter	1¹/₄ lb	562 g
Fine granulated sugar	1 lb	450 g
Egg whites	1 lb	450 g
Cake flour, sifted	14 oz	392 g

1. Cream the butter and sugar together until light.
2. Add the egg whites, a little at a time, beating well after each addition. Scrape the sides and bottom of the bowl from time to time to avoid lumps.

3. Stir in the sifted flour, and blend all ingredients well to obtain a smooth batter.
4. Place the batter in a pastry bag fitted with a 1/6-inch (4-mm) round pastry tube, and squeeze in portions about 3 inches (8 cm) long onto lightly greased and floured baking sheets.
5. Bake at 425°F (220°C) for 8 minutes or until the edges start to brown.

NOTE: The mixture should be of a rather soft consistency; depending on the size of the eggs used, a little more or less flour may be necessary. In order to test the consistency, drop a tablespoonful onto a greased pie plate, and place it in the oven. If the mixture expands and becomes too thin during baking, add a little more flour to the batter. If the mixture does not expand, add a little more egg white or heavy cream to soften the batter to the proper consistency.

Chocolate Chip Cookies

YIELD:
7 lb, 12¼ oz (3 kg, 430 g)

	U.S.	Metric
Butter, softened	1 lb, 4 oz	562 g
Brown sugar	13 oz	364 g
Granulated sugar	1 lb	450 g
Eggs, beaten	8 oz	225 g
Milk, cold	5 oz	140 g
Cake flour, sifted	1 lb, 11 oz	758 g
Baking soda	3/4 oz	21 g
Semisweet chocolate chips	1 lb, 4 oz	562 g
Pecans, finely chopped	14½ oz	408 g

1. Cream the butter and sugars together until light. Add the beaten eggs and cold milk, and blend well.
2. Sift the flour and baking soda together, and stir into the egg mixture.
3. Fold in the chocolate chips and nuts.
4. Using a teaspoon or a pastry bag fitted with a plain, round tube, drop the cookies 1½ inches (4 cm) apart onto prepared baking sheets.
5. Bake at 400°F (205°C) for approximately 15 minutes or until golden brown.

Chocolate Chocolate Chip Cookies

YIELD:
7 lb, 12 oz (3 kg, 481 g)

	U.S.	Metric
Butter, softened	1 lb, 4 oz	562 g
Granulated sugar	1 lb	450 g
Brown sugar	13 oz	364 g
Eggs, beaten	8 oz	225 g
Red food coloring	15 drops	
Unsweetened chocolate, melted over hot water	10 oz	280 g
All purpose flour, sifted	1 lb, 12 oz	786 g
Baking powder	½ oz	14 g
Almond extract	½ oz	14 g
Walnuts or pecans, finely chopped	10 oz	280 g
Semisweet chocolate chips	1 lb, 2 oz	506 g

1. Cream the butter and sugars together until light. Add the beaten eggs, and continue creaming.
2. Stir in the red food coloring and melted chocolate.
3. Sift together the flour and baking powder, and fold into the egg batter alternately with the almond extract, nuts, and chocolate chips.
4. Using a teaspoon or pastry bag fitted with a round tube, drop the dough onto greased baking sheets.
5. Bake at 375°F (180°C) for about 10 minutes or until firm.

■ Chocolate Ice Box Cookies

Follow the recipe for Americana cookies. Add 5 oz (140 g) of unsweetened chocolate, melted over hot water, simultaneously with the sifted ingredients.

Chocolate Pinwheels (Half-and-Half's)

YIELD:
6 lb, 2³/₄ oz (2 kg, 774 g)

	U.S.	Metric
Butter	1 lb, 4 oz	562 g
Granulated sugar	1 lb, 6¹/₂ oz	632 g
Vanilla extract	1 oz	28 g
Lemon rind, grated	¹/₄ oz	7 g
Eggs	8 oz	225 g
All purpose flour, sifted	2 lb, 4 oz	1 kg, 12 g
Baking powder	¹/₂ oz	14 g
Walnuts or pecans, finely ground	5 oz	140 g
Salt	¹/₂ oz	14 g
Unsweetened chocolate, melted	5 oz	140 g
Milk	As needed	

1. Cream the butter, sugar, vanilla extract, and lemon rind together.
2. Stir in the eggs.
3. Sift together the flour, baking powder, ground nuts, and salt. Add this to the butter mixture.
4. Blend all ingredients well, but do not overmix.
5. Divide the dough into two equal parts, and mix the chocolate into one part.
6. Wrap each half of the dough in waxed paper, and chill in the refrigerator for at least 1 hour or until firm enough to roll.
7. Roll out each half of the chilled dough on waxed paper to form a rectangle approximately 12 × 10 inches (30 × 25 cm).
8. To form pinwheels, brush half the dough with milk, and place the other half on top of it. Press gently with your hands to secure the two pieces, and cut away any uneven parts.
9. Roll the dough as you would a jelly roll, and place in the freezer or refrigerator until firm.
10. Slice cookies approximately ¹/₆ inch (4 mm) thick, and bake at 375°F (190°C) for 8 to 10 minutes.

NOTE: To form half-and-half's, form each half of the dough into a sausage-shaped roll approximately 2 inches (5 cm) in diameter; do not roll out. Wrap each half in waxed paper, and chill in the freezer or refrigerator until firm. Then cut each roll in half lengthwise with a sharp knife. Brush each cut surface with milk, and press the vanilla and chocolate halves together. Chill again until firm. Slice cookies approximately ¹/₆ inch (4 mm) thick, and bake at 375°F (190°C) for 8 to 10 minutes.

Cigarettes

YIELD:
6 lb, 7 oz (2 kg, 893 g)

	U.S.	Metric
Butter, softened	10 oz	280 g
Superfine granulated sugar	1 lb	450g
Light cream	10 oz	280 g
All purpose flour	1 lb, 4 oz	562 g
Almonds, finely grated	7 oz	196 g
Clear apricot jam	2 lb, 8 oz	1 kg, 125 g

1. Cream the butter and sugar until light and fluffy. Gradually stir in the cream.
2. Add the flour, and blend to a smooth dough.
3. Spread dough in a thin [$\frac{1}{10}$-inch (2-mm)], even sheet on the baking sheet.
4. Sprinkle with almonds.
5. Bake at 350°F (180°C) for approximately 5 minutes.
6. Cut into squares immediately, and roll each square around a stick to form cigarette shape. If the dough becomes too hard to roll, return it to the oven to soften. When cool, fill the cookies with apricot jam.

Coconut Delight

YIELD:
5 lb, 12 oz (2 kg, 583 g)

	U.S.	Metric
Butter, softened	1 lb, 4 oz	562 g
Superfine granulated sugar	1 lb	450 g
Eggs, separated	8 oz	225 g
Lemon rinds, grated	2 oz	56 g
Salt	To taste	
All purpose flour, sifted	1 lb, 4 oz	562 g
Candied cherries, chopped	13 oz	364 g
Coconut, shredded	13 oz	364 g
Confectioner's sugar	As needed	

1. Cream the butter and sugar together until light. Add the egg yolks, lemon rind, salt, and sifted flour.
2. Mix gently into a smooth dough, and then blend in the finely chopped cherries. Chill the dough in the refrigerator for approximately 1 hour.
3. Shape the chilled dough into 1-inch (3-cm) balls, and place them side by side on waxed paper until all the dough has been used.
4. Beat the egg whites until foamy. Dip each ball into the egg whites, and immediately roll it in the coconut.
5. Place the cookies on prepared baking sheets, and bake at 350°F (180°C) for about 20 to 25 minutes or until golden brown.
6. Remove from the oven, dust with confectioner's sugar, and cool.

▪ Coconut Ice Box Cookies

Use $7\frac{1}{2}$ oz (190 g) of slightly toasted, shredded coconut instead of the walnuts in the recipe for Americana cookies.

Curled Wafers

YIELD:
3 lb, 2 oz (1 kg, 403 g)

	U.S.	Metric
Granulated sugar	1 lb, $8\frac{1}{2}$ oz	689 g
Cake flour	10 oz	280g
Egg whites	12 oz	336 g
Almonds, finely chopped	3 oz	84 g
Lemon rind, grated	$\frac{1}{2}$ oz	14 g

1. Mix all ingredients together to form a smooth dough.
2. Using a pastry bag fitted with a plain tube, drop onto greased baking sheets. Leave enough space for the cookies to spread.
3. Bake at 350°F (180°C) for 10 to 12 minutes or until the edges begin to brown.
4. Remove from oven, and while still warm, curl the wafers around a pencil into a cigarette shape. If the cookies are too hard, return them briefly to the oven to soften. Cool.

▪ Date Ice Box Cookies

Add 12 oz (336 g) of finely chopped dates to the recipe for Americana cookies.

Florentine Cookies

YIELD:
8 lb, 15 oz (4 kg, 17 g)

	U.S.	Metric
Heavy cream	2 lb, 8 oz	1 liter, 1.25 dl
Granulated sugar	2 lb	900 g
Blanched almonds, finely chopped	1 lb, 4 oz	562 g
Candied fruit, finely chopped	1 lb, 14 oz	842 g
All purpose flour	7 oz	196 g
Sweet chocolate, melted	14 oz	392 g

1. Blend the cream, sugar, almonds, fruit, and flour together to form a smooth batter. *Do not overmix.*
2. With a tablespoon, drop the cookie mixture onto greased baking sheets, spacing them at least 2 inches (5 cm) apart.
3. Flatten the cookies with a fork dipped in cold water.
4. Bake at 300°F (150°C) for approximately 10 minutes or until the edges begin to color.
5. Remove from the pan and place on waxed paper to cool.
6. Melt the chocolate over hot water, stirring rapidly. Cool to lukewarm, and spread the bottom of each cooled cookie with some of the chocolate.
7. Let stand in a cool place until the chocolate hardens. Store in a tightly covered jar.

Fruit Kisses

YIELD:
4 lb, 11¹/₂ oz (2 kg, 120 g)

	U.S.	Metric
Glazed mixed fruits, finely diced	13¹/₂ oz	378 g
Brandy, good quality	14 oz	392 g
Egg whites	1 lb	450 g
Granulated sugar	2 lb	900 g

1. Soak the fruits in brandy overnight, and then drain thoroughly and dry with a towel.
2. Beat the egg whites until stiff, adding the sugar gradually while beating.
3. Fold in the drained diced fruit.
4. Using a tablespoon, drop the cookies onto greased and floured baking sheets approximately 2 inches (5 cm) apart.
5. Bake at 250°F (120°C) for about 40 to 50 minutes or until dry.
6. Remove immediately from the sheet, and store in a dry place.

Hermits

YIELD:
12 lb, 12¹/₂ oz (5 kg, 736 g)

	U.S.	Metric
All purpose flour, sifted	2 lb, 14 oz	1 kg, 292 g
Double-acting baking powder	1¹/₂ oz	35 g
Cinnamon, ground	¹/₄ oz	7 g
Mace, ground	¹/₄ oz	7 g
Butter, softened	1 lb, 14 oz	842 g
Dark brown sugar	2 lb, 11 oz	1 kg, 208 g
Eggs	1 lb	450 g
Egg yolks	4¹/₂ oz	126 g
Walnuts or pecans, chopped	10 oz	280 g
Seedless raisins	2 lb, 8 oz	1 kg, 125 g
Red glazed cherries, small dice	13 oz	364 g
Confectioner's sugar	As needed	

1. Sift together the flour, baking powder, and spices.
2. Cream the butter and sugar together thoroughly.
3. Add the eggs and egg yolks a little at a time, beating well after each addition, and scraping the sides and bottom of the bowl frequently to ensure a smooth batter.
4. Stir in the sifted dry ingredients, nuts, raisins, and cherries.
5. Drop the batter 2 inches (5 cm) apart onto greased and floured baking sheets.
6. Bake at 375°F (190°C) for approximately 15 minutes or until golden brown. When cool, dust heavily with confectioner's sugar.

Leckerli

YIELD:
10 lb, 13 oz (4 kg, 858 g)

	U.S.	Metric
Granulated sugar	1 lb	450 g
Honey	1 lb, 14 oz	842 g
Candied orange and lemon peel, diced	1 lb, 11 oz	758 g
Blanched almonds, sliced	15 oz	420 g
Cake flour, sifted	3 lb, 2 oz	1 kg, 406 g
Nutmeg, ground	1/4 oz	7 g
Cinnamon, ground	1/2 oz	14 g
Baking soda	3/4 oz	21 g
Salt	1/2 oz	14 g
Lemon rind, grated	1/2 oz	14 g
Confectioners' sugar	12 1/2 oz	350 g
Water	1 lb, 4 oz	562 g

1. Bring the sugar and honey just to a boil. Remove from heat and add the candied citrus peels and almonds. Cool to lukewarm.
2. Sift the flour, nutmeg, cinnamon, baking soda, and salt together.
3. Sprinkle grated lemon rind over the flour, and gradually stir the sifted ingredients into the syrup.
4. Knead the mixture to form a dough of rolling consistency.
5. Place the dough in a bowl and cover with aluminum foil. Let stand at room temperature for at least 1 day.
6. Roll out the dough to approximately 1/3 inch (8 mm) thick on a floured board, and cut into round or square shapes.

7. Bake at 350°F (180°C) for approximately 10 to 12 minutes or until golden brown.
8. Meanwhile, boil the confectioner's sugar and water together until the syrup reaches 235°F (112°C) on a candy thermometer.
9. Brush syrup over the hot cookies immediately upon removal from the oven.

Madeleines

YIELD:
4 lb, 13 oz (2 kg, 162 g)

	U.S.	Metric
Eggs	1 lb	450 g
Egg yolks	13 oz	364 g
Granulated sugar	1 lb	450 g
All purpose flour, sifted	1 lb, 4 oz	562 g
Lemon rind, grated	2 oz	56 g
Clarified butter, melted	10 oz	280 g

1. Place the eggs, egg yolks, and sugar in a bowl, and beat at moderate speed for about 12 minutes or until the batter is thick and pale in color. Remove from mixer and stir in the sifted flour and grated lemon rind.
2. Gently fold in the butter; avoid pouring in the sediment and residue.
3. Using a tablespoon or a pastry bag fitted with a plain tube, drop the batter onto greased and floured Madeleine molds.
4. Bake at 350°F (180°C) for approximately 15 minutes or until golden brown.
5. Unmold immediately and cool.

Old Fashioned Cookies

YIELD:
13 lb, 7¼ oz (6 kg, 51 g)

	U.S.	Metric
Shortening	1 lb	450 g
Butter	1 lb, 4 oz	562 g
Light brown sugar	2 lb, 8 oz	1 kg, 125 g
Granulated sugar	12 oz	336 g
Eggs	1 lb	450 g
All purpose flour, sifted	4 lb, 6 oz	1 kg, 968 g
Salt	To taste	
Baking soda	¾ oz	21 g
Cream of tartar	½ oz	14 g
Candied fruits, finely chopped	2 lb, 8 oz	1 kg, 125 g

1. Combine the shortening and butter, and cream the mixture with the sugars.
2. Add the eggs.
3. Stir in the remaining ingredients, and knead to a smooth dough of rolling consistency.
4. Shape the dough into long rolls.
5. Wrap the rolls in waxed paper, and place them in the refrigerator for approximately 2 hours to harden.
6. Cut into slices ¼ inch (6 mm) thick.
7. Place the cookies on greased baking sheets, and bake at 375°F (190°C) for 8 minutes or until golden brown.

Palais des Dames

YIELD:
5 lb, 12 oz (2 kg, 585 g)

	U.S.	Metric
Butter	1 lb, 4 oz	562 g
Granulated sugar	1 lb	450 g
Eggs	1 lb, 8 oz	675 g
Egg yolks	4 oz	112 g
Lemon rind, grated	½ oz	14 g
All purpose flour, sifted	1 lb, 4 oz	562 g
Currants	7½ oz	210 g

1. Cream the butter and sugar together until light.
2. Add the eggs and egg yolks, a little at a time, beating well after each addition.
3. Stir in the grated lemon rind.
4. Fold in the flour and currants.
5. Using a tablespoon or a pastry bag fitted with a plain round tube, drop the cookies onto greased and floured baking sheets. Each cookie should be about 1 inch (3 cm) in diameter.
6. Bake at 400°F (205°C) for approximately 12 minutes or until the edges start to brown.

Peanut Butter Spritz Cookies

YIELD:
6 lb, 1¹/₂ oz (2 kg, 737 g)

	U.S.	Metric
Shortening	*l lb, 1 oz*	*478 g*
Butter	*15 oz*	*420 g*
Peanut butter	*8 oz*	*225 g*
Confectioners' sugar	*12¹/₂ oz*	*350 g*
Egg yolks	*4 oz*	*112 g*
Lemon rind, grated	*2 oz*	*56 g*
Cake flour, sifted	*2 lb, 7 oz*	*1 kg, 96 g*
Salt	*Pinch*	*Pinch*

1. Cream shortening, butter, peanut butter, and sugar together until light and smooth.
2. Add the egg yolks and grated lemon rind, and blend well.
3. Sift the cake flour and salt together. Add to the egg mixture, and work to a smooth batter.
4. Force through a cookie press or pastry bag fitted with a star tube onto greased and floured baking sheets.
5. Bake at 375°F (190°C) for approximately 10 minutes or until golden brown.

Pecan Cherry Kisses

YIELD:
4 lb, 4 oz (1 kg, 909 g)

	U.S.	Metric
Red glazed cherries	1 lb, 3 oz	534 g
Pecans, chopped	10 oz	280 g
Cake flour	2½ oz	70 g
Egg whites	12 oz	336 g
Granulated sugar	1 lb, 8½ oz	689 g

1. Blend the cherries, pecans, and cake flour together well.
2. Beat the egg whites until stiff, adding the sugar gradually while beating.
3. Gently fold the egg white mixture into the dry ingredients.
4. Using a tablespoon, drop the batter onto baking sheets lined with parchment paper.
5. Bake at 250°F (120°C) for approximately 40 minutes. Cool and store in a dry place.

Raisin Drops

YIELD:
10 lb, 4¾ oz (4 kg, 628 g)

	U.S.	Metric
Shortening	8 oz	225 g
Butter	10 oz	280 g
Brown sugar	12½ oz	350 g
Granulated sugar	1 lb	450 g
Eggs	1 lb	450 g
Molasses	1 lb, 14 oz	842 g
Cake flour, sifted	2 lb, 10 oz	1 kg, 180 g
Double-acting baking powder	2 oz	56 g
Salt	¼ oz	7 g
Cinnamon, ground	¼ oz	7 g
Nutmeg, ground	¼ oz	7 g
Seedless raisins	1 lb, 11½ oz	772 g

1. Combine the shortening and butter, and cream together with the sugars.
2. Add the eggs and blend thoroughly.
3. Stir in the molasses.
4. Add the remaining ingredients, leaving the raisins for last, and mix well.
5. Drop the cookies onto greased and floured baking sheets approximately $1\frac{1}{2}$ inches (4 cm) apart using a pastry bag fitted with a large plain tube.
6. Bake at 375°F (190°C) for about 12 minutes or until done.

Refrigerator Cookies

YIELD:
8 lb, $10^{1}/_{4}$ oz (3 kg, 890 g)

	U.S.	Metric
Shortening	1 lb	450 g
Butter	1 lb, 4 oz	562 g
Granulated sugar	1 lb	450 g
Light brown sugar	$12\frac{1}{2}$ oz	350 g
Eggs	8 oz	225 g
Milk	8 oz	225 g
Vanilla extract	$1\frac{1}{4}$ oz	42 g
All purpose flour	2 lb, 13 oz	1 kg, 264 g
Baking soda	$\frac{1}{2}$ oz	14 g
Salt	$\frac{1}{2}$ oz	14 g
Nutmeg, ground	$\frac{1}{4}$ oz	7 g
Cinnamon, ground	$\frac{1}{4}$ oz	7 g
Almonds, finely ground	10 oz	280 g

1. Cream the shortening and butter with the sugars, and then mix in the eggs, milk, and vanilla extract.
2. Sift all the remaining ingredients together, and add them to the butter mixture. Blend well, but do not overmix.
3. Form the dough into sausage-shaped rolls approximately 2 inches (5 cm) in diameter.
4. Wrap the rolls in waxed paper, and chill until firm (in the freezer for approximately 1 hour or the refrigerator for about 2 hours).
5. Slice the chilled dough into cookies approximately $\frac{1}{4}$ inch (6 mm) thick, and bake on greased and floured cookie sheets at 375°F (190°C) for approximately 6 minutes or until golden brown.

Southern Lace Cookies

YIELD:
8 lb, 5³/₄ oz (3 kg, 757 g)

	U.S.	Metric
Butter	10 oz	280g
Brown sugar	1 lb, 9 oz	702g
Granulated sugar	2 lb	900 g
Eggs	1 lb	450 g
All purpose flour	1 lb, 4 oz	562 g
Baking powder	³/₄ oz	21 g
Pecans, finely chopped	1 lb, 4 oz	562 g
Almonds, finely chopped	10 oz	280 g

1. Cream butter and sugars together. Add the eggs and continue beating for approximately 3 or 4 minutes.
2. Sift the flour and baking powder together, and add to the egg mixture alternately with the nuts. Blend all ingredients thoroughly.
3. Chill in the refrigerator for about 1 hour.
4. Drop the cookies 2 inches (5 cm) apart onto greased and floured baking sheets.
5. Bake at 375°F (190°C) for approximately 6 to 8 minutes or until golden brown.
6. Remove from the sheet while still warm, and place on waxed paper or aluminum foil to cool.

Spritz Cookies

YIELD:
3 lb, 10¹/₄ oz (1 kg, 636 g)

	U.S.	Metric
Butter	1¹/₄ lb	562 g
Superfine granulated sugar	12 oz	336 g
Egg yolks	1 lb	450 g
Cake flour, sifted	1 lb, 2 oz	506 g
Salt	To taste	
Lemon rind, grated	¹/₄ oz	7 g
Blanched almonds	As needed	

1. Cream the butter and sugar together until very light and fluffy.
2. Add the egg yolks a little at a time, scraping the sides and bottom of the bowl after each addition.
3. Add the sifted flour, salt, and grated lemon rind. Do not overmix, but blend all ingredients well.
4. This batter should be forced through a cookie press onto greased and floured baking sheets. If a press is not available, squeeze the mixture through a pastry bag fitted with a no. 3 star tube.
5. Garnish the center of each cookie with an almond or candied cherry.
6. Bake at 375°F (190°C) for about 8 to 10 minutes or until the edges start to brown.

NOTE: If the batter is too soft, add a little more sifted flour; if it is too stiff to be pressed through a pastry bag or cookie press, add a tablespoon of milk.

Tea Drops

YIELD:
6 lb, 15¼ oz (3 kg, 127 g)

	U.S.	Metric
Butter	1 lb, 4 oz	562 g
Granulated sugar	1 lb	450 g
Eggs	1 lb, 8 oz	675 g
Orange rind, grated	1¼ oz	35 g
All purpose flour, sifted	2 lb, 8 oz	1 kg, 125 g
Currants	10 oz	280 g

1. Cream the butter, and then gradually add the sugar and eggs. Beat until light and fluffy.
2. Add the grated orange rind.
3. Fold in the flour, alternately with the currants.
4. Blend all ingredients thoroughly.
5. Using a teaspoon or a pastry bag fitted with a round tube, drop the dough in 1-inch (3-cm) portions onto greased baking sheets.
6. Bake at 360°F (180°C) for approximately 10 to 12 minutes.

Whipped Cream Ginger Snaps

YIELD:
6 lb, 5¼ oz (2 kg, 845 g)

	U.S.	Metric
All purpose flour	1 lb, 4 oz	562 g
Granulated sugar	1 lb, 6 oz	618 g
Ginger, ground	1¼ oz	35 g
Dark molasses	1 lb, 2 oz	506 g
Butter, melted	1 lb, 4 oz	562 g
Heavy cream, whipped	1 lb, 4 oz	562 g

1. Sift the flour, sugar, and ginger together twice.
2. Boil the molasses in a deep saucepan. Remove from heat, and stir in the melted butter. While stirring constantly, add the sifted ingredients, and mix to a smooth batter.
3. Using a pastry bag fitted with a round tube or a tablespoon, drop the cookies at least 3 inches (8 cm) apart onto greased baking sheets.
4. Bake at 275°F (135°C) for approximately 15 minutes or until the edges start to brown.
5. Immediately remove from the sheet, and roll each cookie around a broomstick, small rolling pin, or the handle of a wooden spoon until it is the shape of a cigarette.
6. Cool and fill with whipped cream. Store in a tight container in the refrigerator.

❦ Brownies

Brownies, generally considered a type of cookie, stand alone as one of America's favorite dessert items. They are quick to prepare, easy to store, travel well, and are guaranteed to please, and so are ideal for large gatherings, buffets, and picnic lunches.

Americana Brownies

YIELD:
9 lb, 1¹/₂ oz (4 kg, 86 g)

	U.S.	Metric
Shortening	8 oz	225 g
Butter	10 oz	280 g
Granulated sugar	3 lb	1 kg, 350 g
Eggs	1 lb, 8 oz	675 g
Unsweetened chocolate	15 oz	420 g
All purpose flour, sifted	1 lb, 4 oz	562 g
Double-acting baking powder	¹/₂ oz	14 g
Salt	To taste	
Cinnamon, ground (optional)	To taste	
Pecans, chopped	10 oz	280 g
Walnuts, chopped	10 oz	280 g

1. Combine the shortening and butter, and cream with the sugar and eggs until light.
2. Melt the chocolate over hot water, and add to the egg mixture. Blend well.
3. Sift the flour, baking powder, salt, and cinnamon together, and stir into the chocolate mixture.
4. Add the nuts.
5. Pour into greased pans, and bake at 350°F (180°C) for approximately 40 minutes.
6. Ice with quick brownie icing, and cut into squares.

Black and White Squares

YIELD:
5 lb, 13 oz (2 kg, 609 g)

	U.S.	Metric
Shortening	7 oz	196 g
Butter	7 oz	196 g
Granulated sugar	2 lb	900 g
Eggs	8 oz	225 g
Egg yolks	7 oz	196 g
Cake flour, sifted	9 oz	252 g
Double-acting baking powder	¹/₂ oz	14 g
Salt	To taste	
Pecans or walnuts, chopped	15 oz	420 g
Unsweetened chocolate, melted	7¹/₂ oz	210 g

1. Cream the shortening and butter with the sugar until light.
2. Add the eggs and egg yolks. Blend well to obtain a smooth batter.
3. Stir in flour, baking powder, salt, and chopped nuts, and mix thoroughly.
4. Divide dough into two equal parts.
5. Add the melted chocolate to one part, and spread immediately on the bottom of prepared pan. Refrigerate for approximately 30 minutes, until firm.
6. Spread the white mixture over the chocolate.
7. Bake at 350°F (180°C) for approximately 25 minutes.
8. Cool, then ice with chocolate icing or dust with confectioner's sugar.

Brownies

YIELD:
6 lb, 13¹/₂ oz (3 kg, 74 g)

	U.S.	Metric
Unsweetened chocolate	10 oz	280 g
Butter, softened	1 lb, 4 oz	562 g
Red food coloring	15 drops	15 drops
Cake flour, sifted	14 oz	392 g
Baking powder	¹/₂ oz	14 g
Salt	1 oz	28 g
Eggs	1 lb	450 g
Granulated sugar	2 lb	900 g
Vanilla extract	1 oz	28 g
Walnuts, broken	15 oz	420 g

1. Melt the chocolate over hot water, and cool to lukewarm.
2. Add the butter and food coloring, and mix well.
3. Sift the flour, baking powder, and salt together twice.
4. Beat the eggs and sugar with a fork. Add the vanilla, and blend into the chocolate mixture.
5. Stir in the sifted ingredients and walnuts, and work to a smooth batter.
6. Pour into greased and floured pans, and bake at 350°F (180°C) for approximately 30 to 40 minutes.
7. Remove from the oven and cool. Ice with quick brownie icing.

Pecan Fudge Brownies

YIELD:
6 lb, 2³/₄ oz (2 kg, 773 g)

	U.S.	Metric
Butter	*1 lb, 4 oz*	*562 g*
Light brown sugar	*1 lb, 8 ³/₄ oz*	*696 g*
Eggs, lightly beaten	*1 lb*	*450 g*
Unsweetened chocolate	*10 oz*	*280 g*
Cake flour, sifted	*9 oz*	*252 g*
Vanilla extract	*1 oz*	*28 g*
Seedless raisins	*8 oz*	*225 g*
Pecans, chopped	*10 oz*	*280 g*

1. Cream the butter and sugar together well. Gradually add the beaten eggs, and blend to a smooth mixture.
2. Melt the chocolate over hot water, and add to the creamed mixture.
3. Stir in the sifted flour, vanilla, raisins, and pecans. Scrape the sides and bottom of the bowl to ensure a perfect blending.
4. Spread the mixture into a pan lined with greased paper, and bake at 350°F (177°C) for approximately 35 to 40 minutes. Cool and ice with chocolate icing for pecan fudge brownies.

Raisin and Date Brownies

YIELD:
7 lb, 1³⁄₄ oz (3 kg, 192 g)

	U.S.	Metric
Butter	1 lb, 4 oz	562 g
Light brown sugar	6¹⁄₄ oz	175 g
Granulated sugar	8 oz	225 g
Cocoa powder	4 oz	112 g
Milk, heated	10 oz	280 g
Eggs	1 lb	450 g
Cake flour, sifted	1 lb, 3¹⁄₂ oz	548 g
Milk	10 oz	280 g
Seedless raisins	10 oz	280 g
Dates, chopped	10 oz	280 g

1. Combine the butter and sugars together, and beat until light and fluffy.
2. Mix the cocoa powder with the hot milk until smooth, and then add the butter and sugar mixture.
3. Add the eggs a little at a time, beating well after each addition. Scrape the sides and bottom of the bowl to ensure a smooth batter.
4. Add the sifted flour alternately with the milk.
5. Stir in the raisins and dates.
6. Pour into greased and floured pans, and bake at 350°F (180°C) for approximately 35 to 40 minutes or until golden brown.

BROWNIE ICING

Chocolate Icing for Pecan Fudge Brownies

YIELD:
4 lb, 7 oz (1 kg, 992 g)

	U.S.	Metric
Granulated sugar	2 lb	900 g
Light brown sugar	12$\frac{1}{2}$ oz	350 g
Corn syrup	6 oz	168 g
Milk	1 lb, 4 oz	562 g
Unsweetened chocolate	10 oz	280 g
Butter	5 oz	140 g
Vanilla extract	1 oz	28 g
Red food coloring	$\frac{1}{2}$ oz	14 g

1. Boil the sugars, corn syrup, and milk in a deep saucepan over moderate heat until all ingredients are dissolved.
2. Add the chocolate and continue cooking until the temperature reaches 325°F (165°C) and the mixture forms a soft ball; stir from time to time.
3. Remove from the heat, and cool to lukewarm.
4. Place in a mixing bowl, and add the butter, vanilla extract, and food coloring.
5. Beat until smooth, and spread icing over cooled brownies.

Quick Brownie Icing

YIELD:
2 lb, 3$\frac{1}{2}$ oz (996 g)

	U.S.	Metric
Butter	10 oz	280 g
Unsweetened chocolate, grated	7$\frac{1}{2}$ oz	210 g
Confectioners' sugar, sifted	1 lb, 2 oz	506 g

1. Melt the butter with the grated chocolate in a deep saucepan. Stir constantly, and remove from heat as soon as bubbles appear.
2. Add the sugar, and work until smooth, beating vigorously until spreading consistency is reached.
3. Spread the icing over cooled brownies.

NOTE: If the icing is too stiff, stir in 5 tablespoons or so of warm milk while beating rapidly. If it is too soft, stir in additional confectioner's sugar.

CHAPTER 4

Puddings, Sweets, and Sauces

❦ Puddings

Puddings are among the most popular desserts served and are generally the most economical and profitable as well. They should be made, however, according to the formulas given and not by guesswork. A well-prepared pudding is always a good seller. During the summer months, chilled puddings are delightful, whereas in cold weather, hot puddings are usually preferred.

There are six varieties of puddings: steamed, boiled, baked, soufflé, chilled, and frozen. Generally speaking, the most popular puddings are the baked, chilled, and soufflé varieties, in that order.

For *à la carte* service, the soufflé pudding is especially attractive and appropriate. These puddings should be made only at serving time, and they should be kept in a *bain marie,* or double boiler, to keep them light and fluffy. For this reason, soufflé puddings are not practical dishes to be served in American-plan hotels or in cafeterias because their preparation entails too much labor and attention. They are often served when they have fallen and are then tough and heavy. Soufflé puddings are best, and very light, when made and served in individual portions. Chilled puddings are also attractive when made in small individual cups and then removed from the cup and served very cold in a deep dish with a very cold sauce.

Steamed puddings are somewhat heavy and should be served only in cold weather. Frozen puddings are different ice cream combinations and really belong with the ice cream desserts.

BAKED PUDDINGS

Apple Rice Pudding 1

YIELD:
12 lb, 7¼ oz (5 kg, 527 g)

	U.S.	Metric
Milk	5 qt	4 kg, 500 g
Rice	1 lb	450 g
Egg yolks	4 oz	120 g
Granulated sugar	1 lb	450 g
Vanilla extract	¼ oz	7 g
Apples, stewed, sliced	As needed	

1. Bring the milk to a boil in a double boiler or steam kettle.
2. Add the rice, and stir well with an egg whip to obtain a perfect mixture and also to prevent the rice from sticking together.
3. Let boil slowly until the rice is tender, stirring occasionally to keep the rice from sticking to the kettle and forming lumps. Simmer from 1½ to 2 hours or until the rice is tender.
4. Mix the egg yolks, sugar, and vanilla together in a separate bowl. Make a liaison, adding a small amount of hot milk to the egg mixture.
5. Mix the egg mixture with the rice, and remove from the heat.
6. Place a layer of apples in a pudding pan or dish, and then fill the dish three-quarters full with the rice mixture.
7. Place the pan or dish in a *bain marie* or water bath.
8. Bake at 380°F (195°C) until light brown in color.
9. When ready, serve with cream.

NOTE: If a softer pudding is desired, some milk may be added to the mixture.

Apple Rice Pudding 2

YIELD:
12 lb, 8¼ oz (5 kg, 647 g)

	U.S.	Metric
Milk	4 qt	3 kg, 600 g
Rice	1 lb	450 g
Egg yolks	8½ oz	240 g
Granulated sugar	1 lb	450 g
Vanilla extract	¼ oz	7 g
Heavy cream	1 qt	900 g
Apples, stewed, sliced	As needed	

Prepare the same as Apple Rice Pudding 1.

Apple Tapioca Pudding 1

YIELD:
10 lb, 8¼ oz (4 kg, 747 g)

	U.S.	Metric
Milk	4 qt	3 kg, 600 g
Pearl tapioca	1 lb	450 g
Egg yolks	8½ oz	240 g
Granulated sugar	1 lb	450 g
Vanilla extract	¼ oz	7 g
Apples, stewed, sliced	As needed	

Prepare and serve the same as Apple Rice Pudding 1.

■ Apple Tapioca Pudding 2

Prepare the same as for Apple Tapioca Pudding 1, but add 11½ oz of egg yolks instead of 8½ oz, and mix 1 qt of heavy cream with the eggs and sugar.

Bread and Butter Pudding

YIELD:
28 lb, 10 oz (12 kg, 881 g)

	U.S.	Metric
Sandwich bread	6 lb	2 kg, 700 g
Sweet butter	1½ lb	675 g
Seeded muscat raisins	1 lb	450 g
Eggs	3 lb	1 kg, 350 g
Granulated sugar	3 lb	1 kg, 350 g
Vanilla extract	2 oz	56 g
Milk	7 qt	6 kg, 300 g

1. Slice bread very thin, and remove the crust.
2. Cut each slice in half, and dip in melted butter.
3. Place bread in a pudding dish, overlapping each slice. When individual dishes are used, serve three slices to a pudding.
4. Sprinkle a few raisins on top. If any butter is left, mix in with the custard.
5. Prepare a cold custard from the eggs, sugar, vanilla, and milk. Strain.
6. Pour the custard over the bread.
7. Place the dishes or pan in a *bain marie* or water bath.
8. Bake at 380°F (195°C).
9. When custard is done and the bread is a light brown color, remove from the oven.
10. Serve hot with cream or fruit sauce on the side.

Cabinet Pudding

YIELD:
3 lb, 11 oz (1 kg, 677 g)

	U.S.	Metric
Milk	1 qt	900 g
Granulated sugar	6 oz	168 g
Eggs	11 oz	300 g
Vanilla extract	To taste	
Plain sponge cake	½ lb	225 g
Sultana raisins	3 oz	84 g

1. Prepare a custard with the milk, sugar, eggs, and vanilla. Strain.
2. Cut the sponge cake into $\frac{1}{2}$-inch (1-cm) cubes.
3. Grease and dredge with sugar 10 pudding molds or cups.
4. Place the sponge in the cups, and sprinkle the raisins on top.
5. Pour the custard over the raisins.
6. Place the cups in a *bain marie*.
7. Bake at 400°F (205°C) until the custard is done.
8. When baked, turn out on a hot dish, and serve surrounded by hot vanilla custard sauce.

Canadian Pudding

YIELD:
7 lb, 9 oz (3 kg, 389 g)

	U.S.	Metric
Tapioca	1 lb	450 g
Eggs	2 lb	900 g
Lemon rinds, grated	2	2
Apple sauce	1 qt	900 g
Preserved ginger, shredded	$\frac{1}{2}$ lb	225 g
Heavy cream	1 qt	900 g
Nutmeg, ground	$\frac{1}{4}$ oz	7 g
Cinnamon, ground	$\frac{1}{4}$ oz	7 g

1. Cook 1 lb of tapioca as for apple tapioca pudding.
2. Beat the eggs, lemon rinds, and apple sauce together.
3. Add the ginger, cream, nutmeg, and cinnamon.
4. Pour into a pudding pan or pudding dishes.
5. Place in a *bain marie*.
6. Bake at 380°F (195°C) until light brown in color.
7. Serve hot with cream.

■ Diplomat Pudding

Prepare and bake the same as Cabinet Pudding, only instead of raisins, use 6 oz of assorted candied fruits, and serve with melba sauce.

Farina Pudding

YIELD:
16 lb, 5 oz (7 kg, 320 g)

	U.S.	Metric
Milk	6 qt	5 kg, 400 g
Farina	1 lb	450 g
Egg yolks	4 oz	120 g
Granulated sugar	1 lb	450 g
Heavy cream	1 qt	900 g

1. Bring the milk to a boil in a double boiler or steam kettle.
2. Add the farina, and cook slowly, stirring constantly until it becomes a mush.
3. Remove from heat.
4. Mix the egg yolks well with the sugar and cream. Make a liaison by adding a small amount of hot milk, and then add the mixture to the farina.
5. Pour into pudding dishes, and place in a *bain marie*.
6. Bake at 380°F (195°C) until light brown in color.
7. Serve hot with cream.

Indian Pudding

YIELD:
11 lb, 13 oz (5 kg, 325 g)

	U.S.	Metric
Milk	4 qt	3 kg, 600 g
Yellow corn meal	1 lb	450 g
Molasses	1/2 pt	225 g
Granulated sugar	1 lb	450 g
Lemon rind, grated	1	1
Eggs	1 lb, 5 oz	600 g

1. Bring the milk to a boil in a double boiler or steam kettle.
2. Add the corn meal, cook slowly until it becomes a mush, and then remove from heat.
3. Beat the molasses, sugar, lemon rind, and eggs together well, and add to the corn meal.
4. Pour mixture into pudding dishes or pans, and place in a *bain marie.*
5. Bake at 380°F (195°C) until light brown in color.
6. Serve hot with whipped cream on the side.

Mercédes Pudding

YIELD:
17 lb (7 kg, 650 g)

	U.S.	Metric
Milk	4 qt	3 kg, 600 g
Almond paste	2 lb	900 g
Eggs	2 lb	900 g
Granulated sugar	2 lb	900 g
Plain sponge cake (or lady fingers)	1½ lb	675 g
Candied cherries	½ lb	225 g
Macaroons	1 lb	450 g

1. Grease and dredge with flour 40 pudding molds or cups.
2. Prepare a custard by first boiling the milk and then adding the almond paste. Boil together a few seconds and remove from heat. Mix the eggs and sugar together, and add to the milk. Mix thoroughly with a whip and strain.
3. Cut the cake, cherries, and macaroons in small pieces. Mix them together and fill the molds about three-quarters full.
4. Pour the custard over the mixture in the cups.
5. Place the molds in a *bain marie.*
6. Bake at 375°F (190°C).
7. When baked, remove from the molds and serve on a hot dish with a kirsch-flavored custard sauce.

■ Minute Tapioca Pudding

Prepare the same as Sago Pudding, using minute tapioca instead of sago.

Rice Pudding

YIELD:
12 lb, 7¹/₂ oz (5 kg, 614 g)

	U.S.	Metric
Milk	4 qt	3 kg, 600 g
Rice	1 lb	450 g
Egg yolks	7 oz	200 g
Granulated sugar	1 lb	450 g
Vanilla extract (or two vanilla beans)	¹/₂ oz	14 g
Heavy cream	1 qt	900 g

1. Boil the milk in a double boiler or steam kettle.
2. When boiling, add the rice and cook very slowly, stirring occasionally to prevent burning.
3. When rice is tender, remove from heat.
4. Mix the eggs, sugar, vanilla, and cream well. Add to the rice.
5. Pour into pudding dishes, and place in a *bain marie.*
6. Bake at 380°F (195°C) until light brown in color.
7. Serve hot with cream.

NOTE: When vanilla beans are used, they should be split and cooked with the milk and rice and removed before the eggs are added.

Sago Pudding

YIELD:
14 lb, 2¼ oz (6 kg, 357 g)

	U.S.	Metric
Milk	5 qt	4 kg, 500 g
Sago	1 lb	450 g
Heavy cream	1 pt	450 g
Granulated sugar	1 lb	450 g
Vanilla extract		
(or one vanilla bean)	¼ oz	7 g
Eggs, separated	1 lb, 2 oz	500 g

1. Boil the milk in a double boiler or steam kettle. If vanilla bean is used, split and boil with the milk.
2. Add the sago, and cook slowly. Stir constantly until it becomes a mush, and then remove from heat. Remove the vanilla bean, if used.
3. Add the cream, sugar, vanilla, and egg yolks, making a liaison.
4. In a separate bowl, beat the egg whites until very stiff, and mix into the sago.
5. Pour the mixture into pudding dishes or pans, and place in a *bain marie*.
6. Bake at 380°F (195°C) until light brown in color.
7. Serve hot with cream.

CHILLED PUDDINGS

Banana Bavarian Pudding

YIELD:
17 lb, 6 oz (7 kg, 813 g)

	U.S.	Metric
Gelatin	6 oz	168 g
Milk	4 qt	3 kg, 600 g
Confectioner's sugar	2½ lb	1 kg, 125 g
Heavy cream	1 qt	900 g
Egg whites	2 lb	900 g
Bananas, medium sized, sliced very thin	12	1 kg, 120 g

1. Dissolve the gelatin in 1 qt (900 g) of milk.
2. Boil the remaining milk with half the sugar.
3. Remove from heat, add the gelatin, and strain. Place in a bowl over ice to cool.
4. Whip the cream until stiff.
5. Make a meringue from the egg whites and the remaining sugar.
6. When the pudding is cool and just before it begins to set, add the whipped cream.
7. Fold in the meringue and the bananas.
8. Fill small ramekins or pudding cups, and place in the refrigerator to set.
9. When set, unmold and serve in a cold dish with a cold vanilla mousseline sauce around it.

Chocolate Bavarian Pudding

YIELD:
16 lb, 7 oz (7 kg, 396 g)

	U.S.	Metric
Milk	4 qt	3 kg, 600 g
Bitter chocolate	1 lb	450 g
Gelatin	6 oz	168 g
Heavy cream	1 qt	900 g
Egg whites	2 lb	900 g
Powdered sugar	3 lb	1 kg, 350 g
Vanilla extract	1 oz	28 g

1. Dissolve the gelatin in 1 qt (900 g) of the milk.
2. Boil the remaining milk with half the sugar and the chocolate, stirring continually with a whip until well mixed.
3. Remove from heat, add the gelatin, and strain.
4. Prepare the same as Banana Bavarian Pudding, and serve with a kirsch-flavored mousseline sauce around it.

Coffee Bavarian Pudding

YIELD:
14 lb, 6 oz (6 kg, 468 g)

	U.S.	Metric
Gelatin	6 oz	168 g
Milk	2 qt	1 kg, 800 g
Strong black coffee	2 qt	1 kg, 800 g
Confectioner's sugar	2 lb	900 g
Heavy cream	1 qt	900 g
Egg whites	2 lb	900 g
Caramel, for coloring	As needed	

1. Dissolve the gelatin in 1 qt (900 g) of the milk.
2. Boil the coffee and remaining milk with half the sugar.
3. Remove from heat, add the gelatin, and strain.
4. When cold, add the caramel, and treat the same as Banana Bavarian Pudding. Serve surrounded by cold coffee mousseline.

■ Melba Bavarian Pudding

Melba Bavarian Pudding is made the same as Vanilla Bavarian Pudding but is served with melba sauce.

■ Praline Bavarian Pudding

Prepare the same as Vanilla Bavarian Pudding, adding 1 1/2 lb (675 g) of praline to the milk while boiling. Serve with a chocolate mousseline sauce.

Strawberry Bavarian Pudding

YIELD:
16 lb, 6 oz (7 kg, 368 g)

	U.S.	Metric
Gelatin	6 oz	168 g
Milk	3 qt	2 kg, 700 g
Confectioner's sugar	2 lb	900 g
Strawberry juice	2 qt	1 kg, 800 g
Strawberry extract	As needed	
Red food coloring	As needed	
Heavy cream	1 qt	900 g
Egg whites	2 lb	900 g

1. Dissolve the gelatin in 1 qt (900 g) of the milk.
2. Boil the remaining milk with half the sugar.
3. Remove from heat, add the gelatin, and strain.
4. Add the strawberry juice, extract, and coloring. Allow the mixture to cool.
5. Meanwhile, whip the cream until stiff.
6. Make a stiff meringue of the egg whites and the remaining sugar.
7. When the pudding has cooled, add the whipped cream and fold in the egg whites.
8. Fill pudding cups or ramekins with the pudding and refrigerate.
9. When set, unmold on a cold dish, and serve with a cold strawberry sauce.

NOTE: During the fresh fruit season, add 1 qt of finely chopped fresh strawberries to the mixture, or replace the strawberries with other fresh fruit (pear, peach, raspberry, etc.) and serve with a sauce the same flavor as the fruit used.

Vanilla Bavarian Pudding

YIELD:
14 lb, 8 oz (6 kg, 528 g)

	U.S.	Metric
Confectioner's sugar	2 lb	900 g
Milk	4 qt	3 kg, 600 g
Gelatin	6 oz	168 g
Heavy cream	1 qt	900 g
Vanilla extract (or four vanilla beans)	2 oz	56 g
Egg whites	2 lb	900 g

1. Dissolve the gelatin in 1 qt (900 g) of the milk.
2. Boil the remaining milk and half the sugar. If vanilla beans are being used, split them and boil with the milk.
3. Remove from heat, add the gelatin, strain, and cool.
4. Meanwhile, whip the cream until stiff.
5. Make a meringue of the egg whites and the remaining sugar.
6. When the pudding is cold, add the vanilla extract and whipped cream. If vanilla beans are being used, remove them before adding the cream. Fold in the meringue.
7. Fill pudding cups or ramekins with the pudding and refrigerate.
8. When set, unmold on a cold dish and serve with a vanilla mousseline sauce.

▬ Walnut Bavarian Pudding

Walnut Bavarian Pudding is made the same as the Vanilla Bavarian Pudding by adding 3 lb (1 kg, 350 g) of finely chopped walnut meats to the mixture. It is served with a coffee mousseline sauce.

NOTE: Almond, Date, Fig, Filbert, Pistachio, and Raisin Bavarian Puddings are made the same way as the Walnut Bavarian Pudding. Almond Bavarian Pudding is served with a vanilla mousseline sauce; Date Bavarian Pudding is served with an apricot sauce flavored with kirsch; Fig Bavarian Pudding is served with an apricot sauce; Filbert Bavarian Pudding is served with a praline sauce; Pistachio Bavarian Pudding is served with a kirsch-flavored mousseline sauce; and Raisin Bavarian Pudding is served with a rum-flavored mousseline sauce. Any of these puddings may be made in large molds to serve four or more. When firmly set, unmold on a folded napkin, and serve the sauce in a separate bowl.

▬ Charlotte Puddings

Charlotte Puddings may be made in the same flavors as Bavarian puddings. Line the molds or ramekins with lady fingers, fill the centers with Bavarian pudding, and refrigerate. When set, unmold on a cold dish, and decorate with whipped cream before serving.

SOUFFLÉ PUDDINGS

Apricot Soufflé Pudding

YIELD:
13 lb (5 kg, 875 g)

	U.S.	Metric
Milk	2 qt	1 kg, 800 g
Granulated sugar	1½ lb	675 g
Salted butter	1 lb	450 g
Bread flour	1 lb	450 g
Eggs, separated	3 lb, 9 oz	1 kg, 600 g
Candied apricots, cut into small pieces	1 lb	450 g
Apricot jam	1 lb	450 g

1. Boil the milk with half the sugar.
2. Work the butter and flour into a paste, and add to the boiling milk.
3. Cook, stirring to a smooth paste, and then remove from heat.
4. Add the egg yolks a little at a time, and then add the apricots and apricot jam.
5. Make a meringue with the egg whites and remaining sugar.
6. Fold the meringue into the mixture.
7. Fill pudding molds or greased tins dredged with sugar three-quarters full, and place in a *bain marie.*
8. Bake at 375°F (190°C).
9. When baked, remove from the oven and place pan over low heat. Keep the water in the *bain marie* boiling constantly to prevent the pudding from falling.
10. When ready to serve, remove from the molds and place in deep dishes. Serve with hot apricot sauce.

Chocolate Soufflé Pudding

YIELD:
3 lb, 8 oz (1 kg, 568 g)

	U.S.	Metric
Eggs, separated	1 lb, 2 oz	500 g
Granulated sugar	1 lb	450 g
Salted butter	½ lb	225 g
Bitter chocolate	½ lb	225 g
Rice flour	6 oz	168 g

1. Beat the egg yolks well with half the sugar.
2. Melt the butter and chocolate together and let cool.
3. Beat the egg whites with the remaining sugar to make a meringue.
4. Fold the meringue into the egg yolks. Fold in the rice flour and then the butter and chocolate.
5. Fill greased pudding molds, dredged in sugar, three-quarters full, and place in a *bain marie.*
6. Bake at 375°F (190°C).
7. Serve with hot vanilla custard sauce.

Date Soufflé Pudding

YIELD:
7 lb, 6 oz (3 kg, 331 g)

Prepare the same as for Vanilla Soufflé Pudding, adding to the mixture 2 lb (900 g) of dates, finely chopped. Serve with melba sauce mixed with chopped dates.

Fig Soufflé Pudding

YIELD:
7 lb, 6 oz (3 kg, 331 g)

Prepare the same as for Vanilla Soufflé Pudding, adding 2 lb (900 g) of finely chopped figs to the mixture. Serve with a small preserved fig on top and apricot sauce all around it.

Montmorency Soufflé Pudding

YIELD:
7 lb, 6 oz (3 kg, 331 g)

Prepare the same as for Vanilla Soufflé Pudding, adding to the mixture 2 lb (900 g) of finely chopped preserved cherries and a little red food coloring. Serve with hot kirsch-flavored apricot sauce.

Orange Soufflé Pudding

YIELD:
5 lb, 4 oz (2 kg, 375 g)

	U.S.	Metric
Milk	1 qt	900 g
Granulated sugar	½ lb	225 g
Bread flour	½ lb	225 g
Salted butter	½ lb	225 g
Oranges, zest only	4	4
Lemon, zest only	1	1
Eggs, separated	1 lb, 13 oz	800 g
Orange food coloring	As needed	

1. Boil the milk with half the sugar.
2. Combine the flour, butter, and the orange and lemon zest to form a paste, and add to the boiling milk.
3. Continue to cook until smooth, and then remove from the heat.
4. Add the egg yolks a little at a time, and then add the food coloring.
5. Beat the egg whites with the remaining sugar to make a meringue, and then fold into the egg yolk mixture.
6. Fill pudding cups, and bake the same as for Apricot Soufflé Pudding.
7. Serve with hot orange custard sauce.

■ Pudding Soufflé Saxon

Prepare the same as for Orange Soufflé Pudding, using six lemons instead of the oranges and yellow food coloring instead of orange. Serve with hot lemon custard sauce.

Strawberry Soufflé Pudding

YIELD:
7 lb, 6 oz (3 kg, 331 g)

Prepare the same as for Vanilla Soufflé Pudding, adding 1 qt (900 g) of fresh strawberries cut in half and a little red food coloring. Serve with hot strawberry sauce.

Vanilla Soufflé Pudding

YIELD:
5 lb, 6 oz (2 kg, 431 g)

	U.S.	Metric
Milk	1 qt	900 g
Granulated sugar	1/2 lb	225 g
Salted butter	1/2 lb	225 g
Bread flour	1/2 lb	225 g
Eggs, separated	1 lb, 13 oz	800 g
Vanilla extract	2 oz	56 g

1. Boil the milk with half the sugar.
2. Work the butter and flour together to form a paste, and add to the boiling milk.
3. Continue to cook, stirring constantly, until smooth. Remove from heat.
4. Add the egg yolks a little at a time, and then add the vanilla.
5. Make a meringue by beating the egg whites with the remaining sugar. Fold into the egg yolk mixture.
6. Fill greased pudding molds, dredged with sugar, three-quarters full, and place in a *bain marie*.
7. Bake at 375°F (190°C).
8. When baked, serve with vanilla custard sauce.

NOTE: For Blueberry Soufflé Pudding, add 1 qt (900 g) of blueberries to the vanilla soufflé pudding mixture, and serve with hot blueberry sauce.

STEAMED PUDDINGS

Blueberry Pudding

YIELD:
7 lb, 8 oz (3 kg, 367 g)

	U.S.	Metric
Salted butter	¾ lb	338 g
Granulated sugar	1½ lb	675 g
Egg whites	15 oz	420 g
Cake flour	1½ lb	675 g
Baking powder	¾ oz	21 g
Milk	12 oz	338 g
Blueberries	1 qt	900 g
Cinnamon, ground	To taste	

1. Cream the butter and sugar together well.
2. Beat the egg whites until stiff, and gradually add to the creamed mixture.
3. Sift the flour and baking powder together. Gradually add to the mixture, alternately with the milk.
4. Fold in the blueberries, and flavor to taste with cinnamon.
5. Fill tins three-quarters full, and cover.
6. Steam for 1½ hours.
7. Serve with hard sauce or lemon custard sauce.

Coconut Pudding

YIELD:
6 lb, 5 oz (2 kg, 839 g)

	U.S.	Metric
Granulated sugar	1½ lb	675 g
Salted butter	12 oz	336 g
Egg whites	1½ lb	675 g
Cake flour	1½ lb	675 g
Coconut, shredded	1 lb	450 g
Baking powder	1 oz	28 g

1. Cream the sugar and butter.
2. Add the egg whites a little at a time, and then fold in the flour, coconut, and baking powder. Mix well.
3. Fill molds three-quarters full, and cover.
4. Steam for 1¼ hours.
5. Serve with hot vanilla custard sauce.

Macaroon Pudding

YIELD:
6 lb, 8 oz (2 kg, 960 g)

	U.S.	Metric
Granulated sugar	¹/₂ lb	225 g
Salted butter	1 lb	450 g
Eggs, separated	1 lb, 5 oz	600 g
Macaroons	2 doz	225 g
Milk, heated	10 oz	280 g
Cake crumbs	2 lb	900 g
Sultana raisins	10 oz	280 g

1. Cream the sugar and butter well.
2. Add the egg yolks a little at a time.
3. Place the macaroons in a bowl with some hot milk. When soaked, press them dry, and add to the sugar mixture.
4. Add the cake crumbs and raisins.
5. Beat the egg whites until stiff, and fold into the mixture.
6. Fill molds three-quarters full, and cover.
7. Steam for 1 hour.
8. Serve with hot apricot sauce.

Normande Pudding

YIELD:
9 lb, 12¹/₂ oz (4 kg, 438 g)

	U.S.	Metric
Apples	15	2 kg, 250 g
Bread crumbs	1 lb	450 g
Granulated sugar	12 oz	336 g
Cinnamon, ground	1 tsp	11 g
Milk	1 qt	900 g
Eggs	1 lb, 2 oz	500 g

1. Peel, core, and chop the apples. Place them in a mixing bowl with the bread crumbs, sugar, and cinnamon, and stir well.
2. Add the milk. Gradually add the eggs, and mix thoroughly.
3. Pour into a well-greased mold and cover.
4. Steam for 2 hours.
5. Serve with hot apricot sauce.

Plum Pudding

YIELD:
10 lb, 15 oz (4 kg, 900 g)

	U.S.	Metric
Salted butter	1 lb	450 g
Granulated sugar	1 lb	450 g
Eggs	1 lb, 2 oz	500 g
Lemons, rind and juice	4	4
Bread flour	1 lb	450 g
Sultana raisins	2 lb	900 g
Currants	2 lb	900 g
Cinnamon	1 oz	28 g
Nutmeg	½ oz	14 g
Cloves	½ oz	14 g
Molasses	½ pt	225 g
Brandy	1 pt	450 g
Citron peel, chopped	1 lb	450 g

1. Cream the butter and sugar together.
2. Add the eggs a little at a time. Add the rind and juice of the lemons, and then add the bread flour.
3. In a separate bowl, mix the raisins, currants, cinnamon, nutmeg, cloves, molasses, and brandy.
4. Grind the citron peel until fine, and add to the raisin mixture.
5. Add the egg mixture to the raisin mixture, and mix well.
6. Fill bowls or pudding molds and cover. Steam for 3 to 3½ hours.
7. Serve with a hot, rum-flavored custard sauce or hard sauce.

❦ Cold Sweets

These cold sweets can be the basis of the most elegant desserts offered to customers. Plate an individual serving with a light, crisp cookie such as a tuile, and complement with a tangy sauce or two to create an edible masterpiece.

Banana Bavarian Cream

YIELD:
7 lb, 8 oz (3 kg, 422 oz)

	U.S.	Metric
Milk	1 qt	900 g
Granulated sugar	1 lb	450 g
Egg yolks	3 oz	80 g
Gelatin	1½ oz	42 g
Bananas, medium size, mashed	6	800 g
Bananas, medium size, sliced	2	250 g
Heavy cream, lightly whipped	1 qt	900 g

1. Bring the milk to a boil with half the sugar.
2. Meanwhile, beat egg yolks well with remaining sugar.
3. When the milk comes to a boil, remove from heat and add the egg mixture.
4. Dissolve the gelatin in a little water, and add to the mixture. Blend thoroughly.
5. Strain through a fine sieve or strainer, and place on ice to cool, stirring occasionally to prevent cream from adhering to the sides of the bowl.
6. When cold and ready to set, strain the mashed bananas and add the strained pulp and the banana slices to the mixture.
7. Fold in the whipped cream and fill Bavarian molds, cups, or desired containers. Refrigerate.
8. When set, unmold on a cold dish and serve surrounded by French vanilla custard sauce.

NOTE: To unmold Bavarian creams, dip the container in warm water for a moment, and then turn the mold over on a cold dish. Hold the mold and dish together, and give a sharp jerk with your hand. The cream will drop out of the form.

All Bavarian creams may be made in large molds or individual forms. Do not fully whip the heavy cream or it will become overwhipped when it is mixed into the Bavarian cream.

Chocolate Bavarian Cream

YIELD:
5 lb, 10 oz (2 kg, 540 g)

	U.S.	Metric
Milk	1 qt	900 g
Granulated sugar	1 lb	450 g
Bitter chocolate	6 oz	168 g
Egg yolks	3 oz	80 g
Gelatin	1 oz	28 g
Vanilla extract	1/2 oz	14 g
Heavy cream, lightly whipped	1 qt	900 g

1. Boil the milk with half the sugar and the chocolate.
2. Meanwhile, beat the egg yolks with the remaining sugar.
3. When the milk is boiling, remove from heat.
4. Add the egg mixture to the milk. Then add the gelatin, dissolved in a little water.
5. Strain the mixture, and cool over ice.
6. When cool, add the vanilla and the whipped cream.
7. Fill molds and refrigerate.
8. When set, unmold on a cold dish and serve surrounded by French vanilla custard sauce.

Coffee Bavarian Cream

YIELD:
5 lb, 11¹/₂ oz (2 kg, 628 g)

	U.S.	Metric
Milk	1 qt	900 g
Ground coffee	6 oz	168 g
Granulated sugar	1 lb	450 g
Egg yolks	6 oz	168 g
Gelatin	1¹/₂ oz	42 g
Heavy cream, lightly whipped	1 qt	900 g

1. Boil the milk and the coffee with half the sugar. Let stand while preparing egg yolks, well covered, and then strain.
2. Beat the egg yolks with the remaining sugar. Dissolve the gelatin in a little water.

3. Add the egg yolks to the milk mixture, and then add the gelatin.
4. Strain again, and set on ice to cool.
5. When ready to set, fold in the whipped cream.
6. Fill the molds and refrigerate.
7. When ready, serve with a cold coffee mousseline sauce.

■ Marquisette Bavarian Cream

Prepare the same as for Vanilla Bavarian Cream. Serve with a cold chocolate sauce or a chocolate mousseline sauce.

■ Melba Bavarian Cream

Prepare a Vanilla Bavarian Cream. Serve with a melba sauce.

Strawberry Bavarian Cream

YIELD:
6 lb, 1¹/₂ oz (2 kg, 742 g)

	U.S.	Metric
Milk	1 pt	450 g
Gelatin	1¹/₂ oz	42 g
Granulated sugar	1 lb	450 g
Strawberry pulp	1 qt	900 g
Heavy cream, lightly whipped	1 qt	900 g

1. Boil the milk with half the sugar, and then remove from heat.
2. Dissolve the gelatin in a little water, add the hot milk and sugar, and strain.
3. Add the strawberry pulp and the remaining sugar to the mixture.
4. Place on ice to cool, stirring from time to time to keep the mixture from adhering to the sides of the bowl.
5. When cold and ready to set, fold in the whipped cream.
6. Fill molds and refrigerate.
7. When ready, unmold on a cold dish and serve with cold strawberry mousseline sauce.

NOTE: Raspberry, Peach, and Apricot Bavarian Creams are made the same way.

Vanilla Bavarian Cream

YIELD:
5 lb, 10 oz (2 kg, 530 g)

	U.S.	*Metric*
Milk	*1 qt*	*900 g*
Granulated sugar	*1 lb*	*450 g*
Gelatin	*1½ oz*	*42 g*
Egg yolks	*8 oz*	*224 g*
Vanilla extract (or one vanilla bean)	*½ oz*	*14 g*
Heavy cream, lightly whipped	*1 qt*	*900 g*

1. Boil the milk with half the sugar, and then remove from heat. If vanilla bean is used, split and boil with the milk.
2. Dissolve the gelatin in a little water, and add to the hot milk and sugar.
3. Beat the egg yolks and the remaining sugar together.
4. Combine the two mixtures, strain, and place on ice to cool.
5. When cold, add the vanilla (when extract is used) and the whipped cream.
6. Fill molds and refrigerate to set.
7. When ready, unmold on a cold dish and serve with a cold French custard sauce.

Walnut Bavarian Cream

YIELD:
7 lb, 10 oz (3 kg, 430 g)

Prepare a Vanilla Bavarian Cream. When ready to set, mix in 2 lb (900 g) of ground walnut meats and a little rum flavoring. Fill the molds and refrigerate to set. When ready, unmold on a cold dish and serve with a cold coffee mousseline sauce.

NOTE: Filbert, Pistachio, and Praline Bavarian Creams are made the same way as Walnut Bavarian Cream. Simply substitute the desired nuts. The Filbert Bavarian Cream is served with a praline sauce, the Pistachio Bavarian Cream with a kirsch sauce, and the Praline Bavarian Cream with a chocolate sauce.

■ Chocolate Charlotte

Line the bottom of a plain charlotte mold with a plain jelly. When set, sprinkle some chocolate shot on top, and then line the sides with lady fingers. Fill the center with Chocolate Bavarian Cream. Refrigerate to set. When ready, unmold on a cold platter and decorate the sides with whipped cream.

NOTE: Charlottes may be made in small individual forms, but they are most attractive when made in large forms.

■ Coffee Charlotte

Line the bottom of a plain charlotte mold with a layer of coffee jelly. Line the sides with lady fingers, and fill the center with Coffee Bavarian Cream. Refrigerate to set. Unmold onto cold dishes and decorate with whipped cream.

■ Charlotte Romaine

Trim lady fingers as needed to line the bottoms and sides of charlotte molds. Mix Walnut Bavarian Cream with 1 lb (450 g) of assorted diced, stewed fruit and refrigerate. When ready, unmold on a cold platter and decorate the sides with whipped cream and walnut halves.

■ Charlotte Russe

Trim lady fingers as needed to line the bottoms and sides of charlotte molds, and then fill with whipped cream and chill. Turn out onto a chilled platter and decorate with whipped cream. Charlotte Russe may be made in individual paper cups using fancy cupcake liners instead of molds. This method eliminates unmolding and speeds serving. Use the russe as the main item of a plated dessert, with appropriate garnishes.

■ Strawberry Charlotte

Line the bottom of a plain charlotte mold with strawberry jelly, and then line the sides with lady fingers. Fill the center with Strawberry Bavarian Cream. Refrigerate to set, and then unmold onto a cold dish. Decorate with whipped cream and strawberries.

NOTE: Raspberry, Peach, and Apricot Charlottes are made the same way as the Strawberry Charlotte.

■ Vanilla Charlotte

Line the bottom of a plain charlotte mold with a layer of sweet jelly. Decorate with sliced almonds and a round piece of dried apricot at the center, arranged to form a daisy. Line the sides with lady fingers, and fill the center with Vanilla Bavarian Cream. Refrigerate to set. Unmold onto a cold dish and decorate with whipped cream.

■ Walnut Charlotte

Line the bottom of a plain charlotte mold with a layer of sweet jelly, and decorate with walnuts. Line the sides with lady fingers, and fill the center with Walnut Bavarian Cream. When set, unmold on a cold dish and decorate with walnuts and whipped cream.

NOTE: Filbert, Pistachio, and Praline Charlottes are made the same as the Walnut Charlotte.

Rice à l'Imperatrice

YIELD:
4 lb, 13¼ oz (2 kg, 185 g)

	U.S.	Metric
Milk	1 qt	900 g
Rice	6 oz	168 g
Granulated sugar	8 oz	225 g
Vanilla extract	¼ oz	14 g
Assorted candied fruit, diced	10 oz	280 g
Gelatin	1 oz	28 g
Egg yolks	4 oz	120 g
Heavy cream, whipped	1 pt	450 g

1. Bring the milk to a boil in a double boiler, and then add the rice. Cook slowly until the rice is tender, stirring occasionally to prevent sticking.
2. When the rice is done, add half the sugar, the vanilla, and the candied fruit.
3. Dissolve the gelatin in a little water, and add to the rice mixture.
4. Beat well together the egg yolks and remaining sugar. Add to the rice mixture and mix well.
5. Place the rice mixture over ice to cool, stirring occasionally.
6. When cold and ready to set, fold in the cream. Pour into a fancy form, and refrigerate to set.
7. When set, unmold on a cold platter and decorate with candied fruit and whipped cream.

Lemon Jelly

YIELD:
1 lb, 4¹/₂ oz (600 g)

	U.S.	Metric
Gelatin	1¹/₂ oz	42 g
Lemons	6	6
Granulated sugar	1 lb	450 g
Egg whites	2 oz	60 g

1. Soak the gelatin in a little cold water.
2. Thinly peel lemons, and set peels aside. Juice lemons, and strain the juice.
3. Place the peels in a pan with the juice, sugar, and 2 egg whites.
4. Drain the soaked gelatin, and add sufficient water to make 1 qt of liquid. Then add the slightly beaten egg whites last.
5. Whisk all together over high heat until mixture boils. Reduce heat, and simmer gently for about 10 minutes.
6. Remove from heat, strain, and mold.

■ Orange Jelly

Prepare the same as for Lemon Jelly, but use the juice and rind of five oranges and one lemon.

■ Jellied Raspberries

Prepare 1 qt of orange jelly, and then select about 1 qt of fine ripe raspberries. Pick raspberries carefully, remove stems, and insert thin strips of angelica in place of the stems. Place a plain jelly mold in ice, mask the inside with half-set jelly, and set the raspberries with alternate layers of jelly, continuing until the mold is filled. Do not attempt to set a fresh layer of fruit until the previous layer is firm or the effect of the mold, when turned out, will be spoiled. When firm, remove from the mold by dipping into lukewarm water for a moment. Decorate with whipped cream and raspberries, and serve on a cold dish.

NOTE: Jellied Strawberries, Blackberries, etc. are prepared the same way.

■ Peach à l'Ambassadrice

Prepare a Vanilla Bavarian Pudding, mix with diced pineapple, pour into flat molds, and place over ice to set. When set, unmold on a round dish, place half a stewed peach on top, and cover all over with vanilla mousseline sauce. For a large service, prepare in a flat savarin mold, then unmold, arrange peaches neatly on top, and glaze with a well-reduced cold apricot sauce. Fill the center with mousseline sauce mixed with sliced peaches, and decorate all around with whipped cream, and serve.

NOTE: Apricots, apples, figs, strawberries, raspberries, pears, etc. are served the same way.

■ Savarin Chantilly

Prepare a savarin the same as for Savarin Kirsch (see Hot Sweets), place on a silver platter, and fill the center with sweetened whipped cream flavored with vanilla. Decorate with whipped cream.

■ Savarin Glacé

Prepare a savarin as for Savarin Kirsch (see Hot Sweets), place on a platter, and fill the center with desired flavor of ice cream. Decorate with whipped cream and serve.

■ Savarin Mont-Blanc

Prepare a Savarin Kirsch (see Hot Sweets), place on a platter, decorate all over with a marron mixture pressed through a small, plain tube to resemble a nest, then fill the center in a dome shape with whipped cream. Serve with a cold kirsch-flavored mousseline sauce.

Marron Mixture

YIELD:
2 lb, 4 oz (1 kg, 112 g)

	U.S.	Metric
Glazed chestnuts	1 lb	450 g
Sweet butter	½ lb	225 g
Confectioner's sugar	½ lb	225 g
Kirsch	½ cup	112 g

1. Press the chestnuts through a sieve.
2. Combine chestnuts with butter and sugar, and work into a paste. Keep the mixture rather firm.
3. Flavor with kirsch.

■ Savarin Nesselrode

Bake a savarin cake, unmold, saturate with hot rum syrup, and place on a round silver dish. Whip some heavy cream and combine with broken chestnuts and apricot marmalade. Fill center of savarin cake with cream mixture, and decorate all over with whipped cream.

Soufflé New Ocean

YIELD:
7 lb, 6 oz (3 kg, 290 g)

	U.S.	Metric
Bananas, sliced	12	1 kg, 800 g
Granulated sugar	½ lb	225 g
Boiled custard cream	1 qt	900 g
Gelatin	1 oz	28 g
Heavy cream, whipped	½ pt	225 g
Powdered macaroons	4 oz	112 g
Sweet chocolate, grated	As needed	

1. Sprinkle sugar over bananas and set aside.
2. Add gelatin to custard cream and chill.
3. When custard cream is cold, add whipped cream and macaroons.
4. Arrange the cream and bananas in soufflé dishes in alternate layers. Cover the top with whipped cream, and sprinkle all over with grated chocolate.

Strawberry Shortcake

YIELD:
5 lb, 12 oz (2 kg, 594 g)

	U.S.	Metric
Butter	1 lb	450 g
Granulated sugar	6 oz	168 g
Salt	To taste	
Egg yolks	4 oz	120 g
Cake flour	3 lb	1 kg, 350 g
Baking powder	2 oz	56 g
Milk	1 pt (approx.)	450 g

1. Rub well together the butter, sugar, and salt, and then add the egg yolks.
2. Mix the flour and baking powder thoroughly between your hands, and then add enough milk to make a smooth dough.
3. Roll out about ³⁄₄ inch (18 mm) thick, and cut with a round cutter.
4. Place on greased pans, and bake at 450°F (230°C).
5. When cool, split crosswise, place half in a deep dish, and fill with fresh crushed ripe strawberries mixed with confectioner's sugar. Then place the other half on top. Cover all over with crushed strawberries, and decorate with a little whipped cream.

🍎 Hot Sweets

Cherries Jubilee and Baked Alaska are two instantly recognized desserts that are guaranteed to impress. Here are these two, and some interesting variations, along with many hot sweets that can form the basis for elegant and satisfying desserts.

Apple Charlotte

YIELD:
2 lb, 2 oz (954 g)

	U.S.	Metric
Cooking apples	1 lb	450 g
Sweet butter	2 oz	56 g
Water	4 oz	112 g
Granulated sugar	4 oz	112 g
Sandwich bread	6 oz	168 g
Clarified butter, warm	2 oz	56 g

1. Peel, core, and slice the apples.
2. Place the apples in a pan with the sweet butter, water, and sugar.
3. Cover and stew gently until the apples are tender.

4. Meanwhile, butter a plain charlotte mold, and line the bottom and sides with thin slices of sandwich bread dipped in clarified butter.

5. When apples are ready, pour them into the mold on top of the bread. Place a round of bread on top.

6. Bake in a *bain marie* at 400°F (205°C) for 30 to 40 minutes.

7. When the bread is quite crisp and golden brown in color, take out of the oven and remove the top crust.

8. Unmold Apple Charlotte onto a hot dish, and pour a kirsch-flavored apricot sauce around the base.

■ Apple Meringue

Cut a sponge cake in rounds and place on dishes. Drain a stewed apple and place on top of the cake. Using a pastry bag with a star tube, fill with plain meringue and press out to cover the apple and cake completely. Dust with granulated sugar and bake at 425°F (220°C). Remove from the oven when the meringue is nicely browned and serve hot.

NOTE: Peach and Pear Meringue are made the same way.

Apricot Condé

	YIELD: *2 lb, 15 oz (1 kg, 316 g)*	
	U.S.	*Metric*
Milk	*1 qt*	*900 g*
Rice	*4 oz*	*112 g*
Granulated sugar	*4 oz*	*112 g*
Egg yolks	*3 oz*	*80 g*
Sultana raisins	*4 oz*	*112 g*

1. Bring the milk to a boil, and add the rice. Cook slowly in a double boiler until the rice is tender. Add the sugar and continue to cook until the mixture is firm.

2. Remove rice mixture from heat, and add egg yolks and raisins.

3. Place in a small charlotte mold and let stand until set.

4. When set, unmold on a round dish, place a half apricot on top, and cover all over with hot apricot sauce.

NOTE: Peach, Pear, Fig, and Apple Condé are prepared and served the same way.

■ Baba Rum

Bake a baba (see French Sweet Dough), and when cold, soak in rum-flavored syrup (18° on the Baumé sugar scale) until the baba swells and is tender. Remove from the syrup and place on a wire rack. Serve in a deep dish with hot rum-flavored syrup around it.

Rum-Flavored Syrup

YIELD:
6 lb, 12 oz (3 kg, 37 g)

	U.S.	Metric
Water	3½ pt	1 kg, 575 g
Granulated sugar	3 lb	1 kg, 350 g
Rum	¼ pt	112 g

1. Combine the water and sugar, and bring to a boil.
2. Remove from heat, and add rum. Use as needed.

■ Chocolate Profiterole

Bake medium-sized cream puffs (see Cream Puff Paste). When cold, fill with vanilla ice cream, place on a dish, and cover all over with hot chocolate sauce.

NOTE: Three cream puffs usually are served to each person in *à la carte* service. For American service, cafeterias, etc., it is more practical to serve one large cream puff per person.

Fig Border à la Condé

YIELD:
3 lb, 3¹/₂ oz (1 kg, 435 g)

	U.S.	Metric
Milk	1 qt	900 g
Rice	4 oz	112 g
Granulated sugar	4 oz	112 g
Egg yolks	3 oz	80 g
Vanilla	¹/₄ oz	7 g
Salted butter	2 oz	56 g
Raisins and candied fruits, mixed	6 oz	168 g

1. Bring the milk to a boil. Add the rice, and cook until tender. Add the sugar, and cook slowly until the mixture is firm.
2. Remove from heat, and add the egg yolks, vanilla, butter, raisins, and candied fruit. Mix well.
3. Place in a buttered border mold (*moule à savarin*).
4. Bake at 400°F (205°C) in a *bain marie*.
5. When the rice is set, remove from oven and unmold onto a hot round dish. Fill the center with stewed figs, and decorate all around with figs and maraschino cherries.
6. Serve hot, with kirsch-flavored apricot sauce.

■ Baked Alaska

Cut a 1-inch-thick (25-mm-thick) oval shape from a sponge cake. Remove some cake from the center, and place the oval on a silver platter. Prepare a soufflé mixture as directed for Omelette Soufflé and set aside. Fill the oval with vanilla ice cream, molding it into a high dome, and cover quickly with the soufflé mixture. Decorate all over with the same mixture forced through a cornet. Dredge with sugar, and bake at 450°F (230°C). Serve immediately.

■ Baked Alaska Jubilee

Cut a 12 × 5 inch (30 × 13 cm) oval of sponge cake 1 inch (25 mm) thick, and then cut from the center a 3 × 4 inch (8 × 10 cm) rectangle. Place the oval on a silver platter. Cut a 3 × 4 inch (8 × 10 cm) piece of stale sandwich bread, and place in the cavity created in the sponge cake. Place a soufflé dish on top of the bread. Mound vanilla ice cream on one side of the soufflé dish and strawberry ice cream on the opposite side. Mold the ice cream toward the center to form a high dome. Prepare Omelette Soufflé as directed. Mask all around with the mixture, covering the sides of the soufflé dish but leaving the top uncovered. Decorate as for Baked Alaska, dredge with sugar, and bake at 450°F (230°C). When baked to a light brown color, remove from the oven and fill the soufflé dish three-quarters full with Cherries Jubilee. Pour kirsch or other spirits over the cherries. Ignite and serve immediately.

■ Baked Alaska Milady

Cut a 2-inch-thick (5-cm-thick) sponge cake into an oval, remove some of the sponge from the center, partly fill with peach jam, and place on a silver platter. Prepare a soufflé mixture as directed for Omelette Soufflé. Mold strawberry ice cream in the cake into a high dome, place a few peach halves on top, and cover quickly with the soufflé mixture. Decorate all over with the same mixture forced through a cornet, dredge with sugar, and bake at 450°F (230°C). When baked, decorate all around with sliced peaches and serve immediately.

NOTE: Baked Alaska Milord is made the same way but using stewed pears rather than peaches and a combination of strawberry and vanilla ice cream.

Cherries Jubilee

YIELD:
2 lb, 4^1/$_2$ oz (1 kg, 25 g)

	U.S.	Metric
Fresh cherries, stewed	*1 lb*	*450 g*
Granulated sugar	*4 oz*	*112 g*
Corn starch or arrowroot	*1/2 oz*	*14 g*
Water	*As needed*	
Red food coloring	*A few drops*	
Kirsch	*1/2 cup*	*112 g*

1. Drain and reserve all the juice from the stewed cherries. Combine 3/4 pt (337 g) of the juice and the sugar, and bring to a boil.
2. Mix the starch with a little water and add to the boiling juice. Return to a boil, stirring constantly.

An arrangement of classic desserts, invitingly placed before a window in Master Chef Karousos' Sea Fare Inn.

Two presentations of napoleons—with pastry cream; with pastry cream and fresh raspberries—served with a dessert wine.

The favorite cheesecake of the Sea Fare Inn—with a fresh strawberry and raspberry sauce.

Chocolate cake and apricot cake.

Raspberry tart and apple tart.

Two presentations of cream puffs: three small puffs with vanilla ice cream and chocolate sauce; one puff with raspberry sauce, garnished with fresh raspberries.

A selection of pastry creams and sauces, including: almond cream, chocolate pastry cream, coffee pastry cream, strawberry cream, chocolate sauce, chocolate raspberry sauce, and vanilla sauce.

Crêpes suzette flambé, depicted with a photograph of Henri Charpentier (1880–1961), who created the dish for the Prince of Wales.

Bavarian creams. Various presentations, both in glass and on plate. Shown are vanilla Bavarian cream and raspberry Bavarian cream with raspberry sauce.

Mixed petits fours.

Presentations of plated desserts.

A display of various breads.

Croquembouche.

Clockwise from lower left: peach melba, pear compote, peach compote, strawberry compote, apricot compote.

Clockwise from front: vanilla custard, caramel custard, orange custard, orange Grand-Marnier, chocolate custard.

Bread and butter pudding in soufflé dish.

3. Add food coloring and cherries, remove from heat, and place in a chafing dish.
4. Pour kirsch over cherries, ignite, and serve.

NOTE: Strawberries Jubilee and Raspberries Jubilee are prepared the same way. Cherries Jubilee also may be served with any plain ice cream.

■ Savarin Kirsch

Bake a savarin (see French Sweet Dough), and remove from the mold. Fill the mold one-quarter full with hot kirsch-flavored syrup (20° on the Baumé sugar scale). Replace the savarin in the mold, and let stand for 15 minutes. Turn out on a wire rack, and glaze all over with a well-reduced kirsch-flavored apricot sauce. Place on a platter and serve hot, with hot kirsch-flavored syrup on the side.

■ Savarin Flambé Montmorency

Prepare a savarin as for Savarin Kirsch, place on a platter, and fill with Cherries Jubilee. Sprinkle some spirits over the savarin, ignite, and serve flaming.

NOTE: Strawberries, raspberries, or any other fruit may be served the same way.

Banana Soufflé

YIELD:
1 lb, 4¼ oz (580 g)

	U.S.	Metric
Bananas, well ripened	2	300 g
Egg yolks	2 oz	40 g
Granulated sugar	4 oz	112 g
Cornstarch	1 tsp	1 tsp
Vanilla extract	¼ oz	7 g
Egg whites	4 oz	120 g

1. Rub the bananas through a sieve. Add the egg yolks, sugar, cornstarch, and vanilla. Beat the mixture well.
2. Beat the egg whites to a stiff peak, and then fold them into the banana mixture.
3. Fill a buttered and sugared soufflé dish with the mixture, place a few slices of banana on top, and bake at 400°F (205°C). Serve immediately.

NOTE: All soufflés should be baked in a *bain marie,* and served as soon as they are baked. If not served immediately, they will fall and be unfit to eat.

Cheese Soufflé

YIELD:
_1 lb, 12 oz (793 g)_

	U.S.	Metric
Cream (20 percent)	¹/₂ pt	225 g
Salted butter	1 oz	28 g
Potato flour	1 oz	28 g
Gruyère cheese, grated	4 oz	112 g
Eggs, separated	14 oz	400 g
Salt and pepper	To taste	

1. Place the cream and the butter in a pan, and bring to a boil.
2. When boiling, add the flour and stir well until completely mixed. Remove from heat, add the cheese, and stir well.
3. Gradually add the egg yolks, then add salt and pepper to taste, and mix well.
4. Beat the egg whites until firm, and fold into the mixture.
5. Butter and flour a soufflé dish, and pour in mixture.
6. Bake at 450°F (230°C) and serve immediately.

Chocolate Soufflé

YIELD:
_11¹/₂ oz (330 g)_

	U.S.	Metric
Egg yolks	2 oz	40 g
Granulated sugar	4 oz	112 g
Vanilla extract	¹/₄ oz	7 g
Cornstarch	1 tsp	1 tsp
Bitter chocolate, melted	1¹/₂ oz	42 g
Egg whites	4 oz	120 g

1. Beat together the egg yolks, sugar, vanilla, cornstarch (or 1 Tbsp of boiled custard), and chocolate.
2. Beat the egg whites until stiff, and fold into the mixture.
3. Butter a soufflé dish, dredge with sugar, and fill with mixture.
4. Bake at 400°F (205°C). Serve immediately.

Coffee Soufflé

YIELD:
9 1/2 oz (275 g)

	U.S.	Metric
Egg yolks	3 oz	80 g
Granulated sugar	2 oz	56 g
Coffee extract	1/2 oz	14 g
Cornstarch	1 tsp	1 tsp
Egg whites	4 oz	120 g

1. Beat together the egg yolks, sugar, coffee extract, and cornstarch.
2. Beat the egg whites until stiff, and fold into the mixture.
3. Butter a soufflé dish, dredge with sugar, and fill with mixture.
4. Bake at 400°F (205°C). Serve immediately.

Lemon Soufflé

YIELD:
11 1/2 oz (300 g)

	U.S.	Metric
Egg yolks	2 oz	60 g
Granulated sugar	4 oz	112 g
Lemon rinds, grated	2	2
Cornstarch	1 tsp	1 tsp
Egg whites	4 oz	120 g

1. Beat together the egg yolks, sugar, grated lemon rinds, and cornstarch.
2. Beat the egg whites until stiff, and fold into the mixture.
3. Butter a soufflé dish, dredge with sugar, and fill with mixture.
4. Bake at 400°F (205°C). Serve immediately.

■ Soufflé Lily

Prepare a Soufflé Normandy mixture (see following recipe). Butter a soufflé dish, and dredge with sugar. Place a layer of the soufflé mixture in the bottom of the dish. Add a thin layer of red currant jelly and then another layer of the soufflé mixture, repeating alternate layers until the mold is filled. Bake at 400°F (205°C), and serve immediately.

Soufflé Normandy

YIELD:
1 lb, 10 oz (738 g)

	U.S.	Metric
Apples	1 lb	450 g
Granulated sugar	6 oz	168 g
Egg whites	4 oz	120 g
Red food coloring	A few drops	

1. Peel, slice, and cook apples until tender.
2. Rub apples through a sieve into a bowl and add sugar.
3. Beat egg whites until stiff and add to apple mixture. Tint with a little red food coloring.
4. Butter a soufflé dish, dredge in sugar, and fill with mixture.
5. Bake at 400°F (205°C). Serve immediately.

Omelette Soufflé

YIELD:
12¹/₂ oz (356 g)

	U.S.	Metric
Egg yolks	3 oz	80 g
Granulated sugar	3 oz	84 g
Cornstarch	1 tsp	1 tsp
Vanilla	¹/₄ oz	7 g
Egg whites	6 oz	180 g

1. Beat the egg yolks with the sugar, cornstarch, and vanilla.
2. Beat the egg whites until stiff and fold into mixture.
3. Butter a silver platter, and dredge with sugar.
4. Mound the mixture on the platter in a high dome.
5. Use a palette knife to create a pattern all around. Decorate the top and sides with soufflé mixture forced through a cornet. Sprinkle with sugar.
6. Bake at 400°F (205°C). Serve immediately.

Orange Soufflé

YIELD:
10 ¼ oz (285 g)

	U.S.	Metric
Egg yolks	1½ oz	40 g
Granulated sugar	4 oz	112 g
Orange rinds, grated	3	3
Cornstarch	1 tsp	1 tsp
Egg whites	4 oz	120 g
Orange food coloring	A few drops	

1. Beat the egg yolks, sugar, grated orange rind, and cornstarch together.
2. Beat the egg whites until stiff, and fold into the mixture. Add coloring.
3. Butter a soufflé dish, dredge with sugar, and fill with mixture. Decorate the top with a few orange slices.
4. Bake at 400°F (205°C). Serve immediately.

■ Soufflé Palmyre

Prepare a Vanilla Soufflé mixture. Butter a soufflé dish and dredge in sugar. Place a layer of the soufflé mixture in the bottom and then a layer of lady fingers and apricot jam. Continue to alternate layers until the mold is filled. Bake at 400°F (205°C), and serve immediately.

■ Soufflé Royale

Prepare a Lemon Soufflé mixture. Butter a soufflé dish, and dredge in sugar. Place a layer of the soufflé mixture in the bottom and then a layer of finely cut candied fruits and soaked macaroons. Continue to alternate layers until the mold is filled. Decorate the top with assorted candied fruits, and bake at 400°F (205°C). Serve immediately.

Strawberry Soufflé

YIELD:
1 lb, $^{1}/_{4}$ oz (464 g)

	U.S.	Metric
Strawberries, crushed	$^{1}/_{2}$ pt	225 g
Granulated sugar	4 oz	112 g
Cornstarch	$^{1}/_{4}$ oz	7 g
Egg whites	4 oz	120 g

1. Mix the crushed strawberries with the sugar and cornstarch.
2. Beat the egg whites until stiff, and fold into the mixture. Fold in a few strawberry halves.
3. Butter a soufflé dish, dredge with sugar, and fill with mixture.
4. Bake at 400°F (205°C). Serve immediately.

Vanilla Soufflé

YIELD:
$10^{1}/_{2}$ oz (304 g)

	U.S.	Metric
Egg yolks	2 oz	60 g
Granulated sugar	4 oz	112 g
Vanilla extract	$^{1}/_{4}$ oz	7 g
Cornstarch	1 tsp	1 tsp
Egg whites	4 oz	120 g

1. Beat the egg yolks, sugar, vanilla, and cornstarch together.
2. Beat the egg whites until stiff, and fold into the mixture.
3. Butter a soufflé dish, dredge with sugar, and then fill with mixture.
4. Bake at 400°F (205°C). Serve immediately.

❦ Fritters and Pancakes

Use these crêpes as the basis of extraordinary dessert presentations, or include some pleasing fruit fritters on your breakfast menu.

Fritter Batter

YIELD:
2 lb, 13¹/₄ oz (1 kg, 246 g)

	U.S.	Metric
Eggs	7 oz	200 g
Granulated sugar	6 oz	168 g
Salt	¹/₄ oz	7 g
Milk	As needed	
Bread flour	1 lb	450 g
Baking powder	1 oz	28 g
Salted butter, melted	6 oz	168 g

1. Mix together the eggs, sugar, salt, and ¹/₂ pt (225 g) of milk.
2. Sift together the flour and baking powder, and add to the egg mixture. Mix well.
3. Add more milk to make a medium-soft batter, then add the melted butter, and strain.

■ Apple Fritters

Pare and core the desired number of apples, and cut into slices. Dip the slices into fritter batter and drop into hot fat. Fry until soft and golden brown. Dust with confectioner's sugar.

NOTE: Pineapple Fritters and Pear Fritters are made the same way as Apple Fritters.

■ Banana Fritters

Cut bananas in half crosswise and then cut in half again lengthwise. Prepare the same as for Apple Fritters, and serve with lemon sauce.

Crêpe Batter

YIELD:
6 lb, ¹/₂ oz (2 kg, 655 g)

	U.S.	Metric
Eggs	14 oz	400 g
Granulated sugar	¹/₂ lb	225 g
Salt	1 tsp	1 tsp
Milk	1 qt	900 g
Bread flour	2 lb	900 g
Salted butter, melted	¹/₂ lb	225 g

1. Beat together the eggs, sugar, and salt.
2. Add half the milk, and then add the flour. Add the remaining milk and the melted butter. Beat until smooth.

How to Fry Crêpes (French Pancakes)

Place a small omelette pan over high heat. Pour a little melted butter into the pan, and when hot, pour in just enough batter to cover the bottom of the pan. Fry, shaking the pan constantly, until the bottom of the *crêpe* is golden brown. Toss the *crêpe,* and fry on the other side. Place the *crêpe* on a clean towel to absorb excess butter. Roll up, or fold over, and serve on a hot dish. *Crêpes* should be made as thin as possible.

■ Crêpes Mirette

Fry the *crêpe* batter as directed, spread with red currant jelly, and roll. Dredge with icing sugar, mark with a propane torch, and place on a hot platter.

■ Crêpes Normande

Fry the *crêpe* batter as directed, spread with hot apple sauce, and roll up. Then dredge with icing sugar, mark them with a propane torch, and place on a hot platter.

■ Crêpes Suzette

Fry the *crêpe* batter as directed. Spread each *crêpe* with hard sauce, fold in four, and place on a platter. If desired, the *crêpe* may be served plain, with the hard sauce in a separate sauce bowl.

Hard Sauce

YIELD:
4¹/₂ oz (120 g)

	U.S.	Metric
4× sugar	2 oz	56 g
Sweet butter	2 oz	56 g
Orange, grated rind and juice	1	1
Curaçao or Porto wine	To taste	

1. Place the sugar and butter in a small bowl, and cream well together.
2. Add the orange rind and juice, and flavor with Curaçao or wine.

❦ Custards

Custards are an ideal dessert offering for a large group of diners. Pay careful attention to the accompaniments—offer a contrast of textures and colors to make an elegant presentation.

Chocolate Cup Custard

YIELD:
5 lb, 14¹/₂ oz (2 kg, 672 g)

	U.S.	Metric
Milk	2 qt	1 kg, 800 g
Bitter chocolate	6 oz	168 g
Granulated sugar	1 lb	450 g
Egg yolks	8¹/₂ oz	240 g
Vanilla extract	¹/₂ oz	14 g

1. Boil together the milk, chocolate, and half the sugar.
2. Beat well together the eggs, the remaining sugar, and the vanilla. Add the boiling chocolate milk, mix well together, and strain.
3. Place 20 custard cups in a *bain marie*, and fill with mixture, removing the scum from the top of each.
4. Cover with a sheet pan to prevent coloring, and bake at 400°F (205°C).

NOTE: Cup custards are always served in the cup in which they were baked. Therefore, they may be baked less than custards which are to be removed from the mold.

Coffee Cup Custard

YIELD:
5 lb, 10 oz (2 kg, 544 g)

	U.S.	Metric
Milk	2 qt	1 kg, 800 g
Coffee, finely ground	6 oz	168 g
Granulated sugar	12 oz	336 g
Egg yolks	8½ oz	240 g

1. Boil the milk with the coffee and half the sugar; then strain.
2. Beat the eggs with the remaining sugar, add the hot coffee milk, and strain once more.
3. Place 20 custard cups in a *bain marie,* and fill with mixture, removing the scum from the top of each.
4. Cover with a sheet pan to prevent coloring, and bake at 400°F (205°C).

Vanilla Cup Custard

YIELD:
5 lb, 6 oz (2 kg, 430 g)

	U.S.	Metric
Egg yolks	10 oz	280 g
Granulated sugar	12 oz	336 g
Vanilla extract		
(or two vanilla beans split)	½ oz	14 g
Milk, boiling	2 qt	1 kg, 800 g

1. Beat together the eggs, sugar, and vanilla. Add the milk, and strain. If vanilla beans are used, split and boil them with the milk.
2. Place 20 custard cups in a *bain marie,* and fill with mixture, removing the scum from the top of each.
3. Cover with a sheet pan to prevent coloring, and bake at 400°F (205°C).

Caramel Custard

YIELD:
13 lb, 2¹/₂ oz (5 kg, 770 g)

	U.S.	Metric
Granulated sugar	3 lb, 2 oz	1 kg, 406 g
Water	1 pt	450 g
Eggs	3 lb	1 kg, 200 g
Milk	3 qt	2 kg, 700 g
Vanilla extract	¹/₂ oz	14 g

1. Boil the water and 2 lb (900 g) of the sugar together to 328°F (165°C) or until it becomes a dark amber color.
2. Pour into dry molds or cups to cover the bottom about ¹/₄ inch (6 mm).
3. To make custard, beat well together the eggs, remaining sugar, milk, and vanilla extract. Strain.
4. Fill the cups, place in a *bain marie,* and bake at 350°F (175°C).
5. When cold, turn out into a deep dish and serve.

NOTE: To make sure that the custard is done, insert the point of a knife in the center. When no liquid comes to the surface, the custard is done.

Orange Custard

YIELD:
6 lb, 8 oz (2 kg, 940 g)

	U.S.	Metric
Granulated sugar	12 oz	336 g
Eggs	1 lb, 12 oz	800 g
Milk	2 qt	1 kg, 800 g
Orange rinds, grated	6	6
Orange food coloring	A few drops	

1. Lightly grease cups or molds.
2. Beat together the sugar and eggs.
3. Warm the milk with the grated orange rind. When very hot, mix with the eggs and sugar. Add the food coloring, and strain.
4. Fill the cups, place in a *bain marie,* and bake at 350°F (175°C).
5. Serve in a deep dish surrounded by orange mousseline sauce.

❦ Sweet Sauces

Sauces have become a most important component of desserts. Make them with care, ensure that the colors and flavors are vivid, and use scant one-ounce portions that enhance rather than mask the entire dessert presentation.

Apricot Sauce (Cold) for Ice Cream

YIELD:
6 lb (2 kg, 700 g)

	U.S.	Metric
Apricots, canned or fresh pulp (without the juice)	2 qt	1 kg, 800 g
4× sugar	2 lb	900 g

1. Rub apricots through a fine sieve.
2. Combine apricots with sugar, mixing well.
3. Place in a jar and refrigerate until needed.

Apricot Sauce (Hot or Cold)

YIELD:
16 lb, 3 oz (7 kg, 260 g)

	U.S.	Metric
Apricots, canned or fresh pulp (with juice)	1 gal	3 kg, 600 g
Water	2 qt	1 kg, 800 g
Granulated sugar	4 lb	1 kg, 800 g
Lemons, juice of	2	2
Cornstarch or arrowroot (dissolved in a small amount of water)	2 oz	56 g

1. Press apricots through a fine sieve.
2. Add water, sugar, and lemon juice to apricots with juice, and bring to a boil.
3. Stir starch into apricot mixture and return to a boil, stirring constantly. Cook at a boil for 1 minute, strain, and set aside until needed. When served hot, keep the sauce in a double boiler until ready to serve.

Apricot Mousseline Sauce

YIELD:
4 lb, 8 oz (2 kg, 25 g)

	U.S.	Metric
Heavy cream, lightly whipped	¹/₂ pt	225 g
Cold apricot sauce	2 qt	1 kg, 800 g
Apricot brandy	To taste	

Mix well all ingredients and refrigerate until needed.

Delna Sauce

YIELD:
3 lb (1 kg, 350 g)

	U.S.	Metric
Melba sauce	1 pt	450 g
Apricot sauce	1 pt	450 g
Pineapple juice	¹/₂ pt	225 g
Heavy cream, lightly whipped	¹/₂ pt	225 g
Pink food coloring	As needed	
Peach brandy	To taste	

1. Chill all ingredients until very cold.
2. Mix well together and set aside until needed.

Hot Chocolate Sauce (Fudge Sauce)

YIELD:
15 lb (6 kg, 750 g)

	U.S.	Metric
Glucose or corn syrup	2 lb	900 g
Granulated sugar	6 lb	2 kg, 700 g
Water	2 qt	1 kg, 800 g
Bitter chocolate	3 lb	1 kg, 350 g

1. Boil together the glucose, sugar, and water. Add the chocolate and whisk.
2. Return to a boil. Remove from heat as soon as sauce is boiling, and strain.

NOTE: For Cold Chocolate Sauce, add only 2½ lb (1 kg, 125 g) of bitter chocolate. For Chocolate Mousseline Sauce, add 1 pt (450 g) of lightly whipped heavy cream to cold chocolate sauce.

Gourmet Sauce

YIELD:
3 lb, 8 oz (1 kg, 575 g)

	U.S.	Metric
Melba sauce	1 qt	900 g
Pâte à bombe	1 pt	450 g
Heavy cream, lightly whipped	½ pt	225 g
Red food coloring	As needed	
Rum flavoring	To taste	

Mix well all ingredients and set aside until needed.

Hard Sauce

YIELD:
3 lb, 12 oz (1 kg, 687 g)

	U.S.	Metric
Sweet butter	2 lb	900 g
4× sugar	1 lb	450 g
Egg whites	½ lb	225 g
Granulated sugar	4 oz	112 g
Food coloring	As needed	
Flavoring	To taste	

1. Lightly cream butter and 4× sugar.
2. Beat egg whites and granulated sugar to a meringue.
3. Add meringue to butter and sugar.
4. Stir in any flavor and color desired.

Lemon Custard Sauce (Hot)

YIELD:
11 lb, 7 oz (5 kg, 300 g)

	U.S.	Metric
Milk	4 qt	3 kg, 600 g
Granulated sugar	1½ lb	675 g
Egg yolks	1 lb	450 g
Bread flour	4 oz	112 g
Egg whites	11 oz	320 g
Lemons, grated rind and juice	6	6
Yellow food coloring	A few drops	

1. Boil the milk with half the sugar.
2. Cream together the remaining sugar and the egg yolks. Add the flour.
3. Slowly mix in the milk.
4. Return to a boil for a few seconds, and then remove from heat.
5. Beat the egg whites until stiff, and add to the mixture along with the rind and juice of the lemons. Tint with yellow food coloring.
6. Mix together well and strain.

NOTE: Orange Custard Sauce is made the same as Lemon Custard Sauce, by using five oranges, two lemons, and orange food coloring.

Melba Sauce

YIELD:
4 lb, ¹/₂ oz (1 kg, 814 g)

	U.S.	Metric
Raspberry juice, fresh	1 qt	900 g
Red currant jelly	1 pt	450 g
Granulated sugar	1 lb	450 g
Cornstarch or arrowroot	¹/₂ oz	14 g
Water	As needed	

1. Combine raspberry juice, jelly, and sugar. Bring to a boil.
2. Add the starch diluted in a little water, and return to a boil.
3. As soon as the sauce reaches a boil, remove from heat and strain.

Hot Mousseline Sauce 1

YIELD:
3 lb, 12 oz (1 kg, 710 g)

	U.S.	Metric
Egg yolks	6 oz	160 g
Eggs	7 oz	200 g
Granulated sugar	1 lb	450 g
Heavy cream	1 qt	900 g

1. Place all ingredients in a pan and whisk until light and creamy.
2. Place the pan in hot water and whisk until hot.
3. Add any flavor desired.

▪ Hot Mousseline Sauce 2

Any hot sauce may be made into mousseline sauce by adding a meringue made from 4 egg whites and 8 oz (225 g) of granulated sugar to every quart (900 g) of hot sauce and mixing well together.

■ Cold Mousseline Sauce

Any cold sauce may be made into mousseline sauce by adding $\frac{1}{2}$ pt (225 g) of whipped cream to every quart (900 g) of the cold sauce.

Peach Sauce

YIELD:
15 lb, 3 oz (7 kg, 284 g)

Peach Sauce is made by the same formula as Apricot Sauce, only using peaches instead of apricots and adding a little pink food coloring and peach brandy. When fresh peaches are used, add 3 lb (1 kg, 350 g) of granulated sugar and 2 oz of arrowroot to every 6 lb (2 kg, 700 g) of peaches. If you wish to use water in order to reduce the cost, add $\frac{1}{2}$ lb (225 g) of sugar and a $\frac{1}{2}$ oz (14 g) of arrowroot to every quart (900 g) of water used.

Raspberry Sauce (Hot or Cold)

YIELD:
8 lb, 3$\frac{1}{2}$ oz (3 kg, 650 g)

	U.S.	Metric
Water	1 qt	900 g
Granulated sugar	2 lb	900 g
Raspberry juice, fresh	2 qt	1 kg, 800 g
Lemons, juice of	2	2
Cornstarch or arrowroot	1 oz	28 g

1. Bring the water and sugar to a boil. Add the raspberry juice and the juice of the lemons. Then add the starch dissolved in a little water.
2. Return to a boil, remove from heat immediately, and strain.

NOTE: Strawberry Sauce (Hot or Cold) is made the same as Raspberry Sauce by using strawberry juice instead of raspberry juice and adding a little red food coloring.

Vanilla Custard Sauce (Hot)

YIELD:
5 lb, 10 oz (2 kg, 546 g)

	U.S.	Metric
Milk	2 qt	1 kg, 800 g
Granulated sugar	1 lb	450 g
Egg yolks	8½ oz	240 g
Bread flour	1½ oz	42 g
Vanilla extract	½ oz	14 g

1. Bring to a boil the milk and half the sugar.
2. Beat well together the egg yolks and the remaining sugar, and then mix in the flour. Add the boiling milk slowly, and return to a boil, stirring constantly to prevent burning.
3. As soon as the mixture reaches a boil, remove from heat, strain, and add the vanilla. When vanilla beans are used, use one split bean to every 2 qt (900 g) of sauce, and boil with the milk.

NOTE: Coffee Custard Sauce is made the same way by using half milk and half black coffee (or coffee extract).

French Vanilla Custard Sauce

YIELD:
11 lb, 1 oz (4 kg, 950 g)

	U.S.	Metric
Milk	4 qt	3 kg, 600 g
Granulated sugar	2 lb	900 g
Vanilla beans, split	2	2
Egg yolks	1 lb	450

1. Combine the milk, half the sugar, and the vanilla beans in a pan and bring to a boil.
2. Cream well the egg yolks and the remaining sugar.
3. Add the milk slowly to the egg yolks, and heat to 185°F (85°C). Remove from the heat, place on ice, and cool as quickly as possible. Do not allow this sauce to boil, which will cause curdling.

NOTE: This sauce makes an excellent foundation for Mousseline Sauce.

Sabayon

YIELD:
3 lb, 1¹/₂ oz (1 kg, 395 g)

	U.S.	Metric
White wine	1 qt	900 g
Egg yolks	7 oz	200 g
Granulated sugar	¹/₂ lb	225 g
Rum	2¹/₂ oz	70 g

1. Place the wine, egg yolks, and sugar in a double boiler over moderate heat, and beat with a whip until light and creamy. Do not allow the mixture to boil.
2. Remove from heat and add rum.

❦ Fruit Compotes

All compotes should be prepared from fresh fruits when in season. It takes little time to prepare good compotes, and the results using fresh fruits will more than compensate for the trouble involved in their preparation—and not only is their quality better, but they are also less expensive than canned fruits.

Fruits selected for stewing should be of the best quality available and not too ripe. All highly or delicately colored fruits should be cooked in copper or enamel to preserve their natural color. Stewed fruits are often served with a liqueur-flavored syrup.

■ Apple Compote

Select small apples, peel them as thinly as possible, and cut out the core very carefully so as not to break the fruit. Let them simmer in a syrup of 18° (Baumé scale) until tender. The syrup should first be boiled in a flat pan that fits into the oven. Place the apples in the syrup, cover with parchment paper, and cook in the oven until the apples are tender. This method keeps the apples whole and in good shape until served. Serve cold with some of the syrup to which has been added the juice of 1 lemon to every 4 qt (3 kg, 600 g) of syrup.

■ Apricot Compote

Select fresh apricots of high quality that are not too ripe. Make an incision in each near the stem, and remove the stone. Prick the skin, blanch the fruit, and drain carefully. Prepare a syrup of 20° on the Baumé scale, and drop in the apricots. Boil for about 15 minutes or until tender. Serve cold with some of the syrup. If desired, the apricots may be peeled and cut in half.

NOTE: To blanch, bring water to a boil, add the fruit, return to a boil, and remove fruit.

■ Cherry Compote

Wash and stone the cherries. Prepare a syrup of 20° on the Baumé scale, adding the juice of 1 lemon for every quart of syrup, and tint with red food coloring. Drop in the cherries, and boil very gently for about 10 minutes or until tender. Remove from heat and cover. Serve cold with some of the syrup.

■ Peach Compote

Bring some water to a boil, drop in the peaches, and return to a boil. Remove the fruit, and drop into ice water. Remove the skins and drop into a syrup of 22° on the Baumé scale, adding the juice of 1 lemon for every quart of syrup. Boil very gently for about 10 minutes or until tender. Serve cold with some of the syrup.

■ Pear Compote

Select even-sized, ripe cooking pears. Peel them thinly and cook until tender in a syrup of 16° on the Baumé scale, adding the juice of 1 lemon for every quart of syrup. Serve cold with some of the syrup.

■ Plum Compote

Select some large plums, not too ripe, and prick the skin. Prepare a syrup of 18° on the Baumé scale, tint with red food coloring, and drop in the plums. Boil very gently for about 10 minutes or until they are tender. Serve very cold with some of the syrup.

■ Raspberry Compote

Select ripe raspberries, and wash thoroughly. Prepare a syrup of $24°$ on the Baumé scale. Add the juice of 1 lemon to every pound of fruit used, and tint with red food coloring. Bring to a boil, drop in the fruit, and allow to boil for 2 minutes. Serve very cold with some of the syrup.

■ Rhubarb Compote

Peel the skin from young rhubarb and cut into small pieces. Prepare a syrup of $18°$ on the Baumé scale, bring to a boil, and drop in the rhubarb. Cover with parchment paper, and simmer gently until the fruit is tender. Serve very cold with some of the syrup. If desired, rhubarb also may be cooked in the oven following the method used for apples.

■ Strawberry Compote

Select ripe strawberries, and hull and wash them carefully. Prepare a syrup of $22°$ on the Baumé scale. Add the juice of 1 lemon for every pound of berries used, and tint slightly with red food coloring. Bring to a boil, and drop in the fruit. Return to boil, remove from heat, and set aside to cool. Serve very cold with some of the syrup.

CHAPTER 5

Cakes, Pies, Muffins, and Griddle Cakes

❦ Pound Cakes

It is very important to take consistent care with all cakes. All ingredients must be carefully selected and of the best quality, and care should always be taken to have the oven temperature right. Measure carefully. Do not figure on 10 eggs to a pound, since 10 small eggs and 10 large eggs are not the same. Always scale your eggs; this is the only way to obtain uniform results. Many bakers make poor cakes, never obtaining the same result twice, simply because they neglect many slight and seemingly unimportant details such as flour too strong, butter not of the right kind, measuring of eggs by the number, butter and sugar not creamed, and numerous other details of construction and handling. Small causes often spell the difference between the success or failure of the finished product. To obtain proper and uniform results, do not overlook any of these seemingly minor points.

It is also important to be sure that your mixture is not too soft when making fruit cake, because if it is, the fruit will sink to the bottom. If the mixture begins to curdle, add a little flour to bring back the creamy smoothness. Never stir in flour in cake mixtures; always mix in or fold in, since stirring breaks down the air cells formed during the beating process and makes the mixture heavy. The yield will be less, also, and the cake will be heavy when baked.

Plain Pound Cake

YIELD:
16 lb, 2 oz (7 kg, 256 g)

	U.S.	Metric
Salted butter	4 lb	1 kg, 800 g
Confectioner's sugar	4 lb	1 kg, 800 g
Vanilla extract	2 oz	56 g
Eggs	4 lb	1 kg, 800 g
Cake flour, sifted	4 lb	1 kg, 800 g

1. Cream together the butter, sugar, and vanilla until very light and creamy.
2. Add the eggs, a little at a time, and then add the flour, well sifted.
3. Fill paper-lined molds about half full, and bake at 375°F (190°C). If baked in large pans containing approximately 5 lb, the temperature of the oven should not be more than 350°F (175°C).

Maple Pound Cake

YIELD:
8 lb, 9 oz (3 kg, 853 g)

	U.S.	Metric
Salted butter	2 lb	900 g
Maple sugar	1/2 lb	225 g
Brown sugar	1/2 lb	225 g
Confectioner's sugar	1 lb	450 g
Maple extract	1/2 oz	14 g
Eggs	2 lb	900 g
Cake flour	2 1/2 lb	1 kg, 125 g
Baking powder	1/2 oz	14 g

1. Cream well together the butter, sugars, and extract.
2. Add the eggs, a little at a time. Sift the flour with the baking powder, and then mix into the batter.
3. Fill paper-lined molds, and bake at 375°F (190°C).

Oxford Cake

YIELD:
_23 lb, 2 oz (10 kg, 406 g)_

	U.S.	Metric
Salted butter	4 lb	1 kg, 800 g
Confectioner's sugar	5 lb	2 kg, 250 g
Eggs	4 lb	1 kg, 800 g
Cherries, preserved or candied	2 lb	900 g
Pecans	2 lb	900 g
Baking powder	2 oz	56 g
Cake flour	6 lb	2 kg, 700 g

1. Cream well together the butter and sugar.
2. Add the eggs, a little at a time.
3. Add the cherries and pecans.
4. Sift the flour and baking powder together, and mix into batter.
5. Fill paper-lined molds, and bake at 375°F (175°C).

Riche Cake

YIELD:
_17 lb, 2 oz (7 kg, 706 g)_

	U.S.	Metric
Salted butter	3 lb	1 kg, 350 g
Brown sugar, no. 10	3 lb	1 kg, 350 g
Cinnamon, ground	2 oz	56 g
Eggs	3 lb	1 kg, 350 g
Cake flour	3 lb	1 kg, 350 g
Candied fruits, assorted, finely chopped	3 lb	1 kg, 350 g
Sultana raisins	1 lb	450 g
Malaga raisins	1 lb	450 g

1. Cream well together the butter, sugar, and cinnamon until very light.
2. Add the eggs, a little at a time, and then add 2½ lb (1 kg, 125 g) of flour.
3. Combine the candied fruit and raisins, dust with the remaining flour, and mix into the batter. (The fruit is dusted with flour to prevent it from sinking to the bottom of the cake.)
4. Fill paper-lined pans, place some cherry halves on top, and bake at 300 to 325°F (150 to 165°C).

White Mountain Cake

YIELD:
8 lb, 9 oz (3 kg, 853 g)

	U.S.	Metric
Confectioner's sugar	2 lb	900 g
Salted butter	1½ lb	675 g
Egg whites	2 lb	900 g
Banana pulp	1 pt	450 g
Cake flour	2 lb	900 g
Baking powder	1 oz	28 g

1. Cream well together the sugar and butter.
2. Gradually add the egg whites, and then add the banana pulp.
3. Sift together the flour and baking powder, and add to mixture. Mix well.
4. Fill paper-lined pans, sprinkle with granulated sugar, and bake at 350 to 375°F (175 to 190°C).

Wine Cake

YIELD:
18 lb, 3 oz (8 kg, 184 g)

	U.S.	Metric
Salted butter	3 lb	1 kg, 350 g
Confectioner's sugar	4 lb	1 kg, 800 g
Baking soda	1 oz	28 g
Egg yolks	4 lb	1 kg, 800 g
Milk	1 qt	900 g
Cake flour	5 lb	2 kg, 250 g
Cream of tartar	2 oz	56 g

1. Cream well together the butter, sugar, and baking soda.
2. Gradually add the egg yolks and milk.
3. Sift together the flour and cream of tartar, and add to the batter. Mix well.
4. Fill paper-lined pans, and bake at 350°F (175°C).

Light Fruit Cake

YIELD:
14 lb, 1 oz (6 kg, 328 g)

	U.S.	Metric
Currants	2 lb	900 g
Sultana raisins	2 lb	900 g
Candied fruit, chopped	2 lb	900 g
Lemons, grated rind	2	2
Cake flour	2 lb	900 g
Salted butter	2 lb	900 g
Confectioner's sugar	2 lb	900 g
Eggs	2 lb	900 g

1. Mix together the fruits and grated lemon rind, and dust with 4 oz of the flour.
2. Cream well together the butter and sugar.
3. Add the eggs a little at a time.
4. Mix in the remaining flour, and add the fruit.
5. Fill paper-lined pans a little over half full, and bake at 325°F (165°C).

Cherry Cake

YIELD:
10 lb, 1 oz (4 kg, 556 g)

	U.S.	Metric
Cherries, preserved or candied, halved or broken	2 lb	900 g
Wild cherry extract	1 oz	56 g
Salted butter	2 lb	900 g
Confectioner's sugar	2 lb	900 g
Eggs	2 lb	900 g
Cake flour	2 lb	900 g

1. Dust the cherries with a little flour.
2. Cream together the butter, sugar, and extract.
3. Add the eggs a little at a time.
4. Mix in the flour, and then add the cherries.
5. Fill paper-lined pans, sprinkle a few cherry halves on top, and bake at 350°F (175°C).

Dundee Cake

YIELD:
24 lb (10 kg, 800 g)

	U.S.	Metric
Sultana raisins	2 lb	900 g
Citron peel, chopped	2 lb	900 g
Orange peel, chopped	2 lb	900 g
Preserved cherries, chopped	1 lb	450 g
Cake flour	5 lb	2 kg, 250 g
Salted butter	4 lb	1 kg, 800 g
Confectioner's sugar	4 lb	1 kg, 800 g
Eggs	4 lb	1 kg, 800 g

1. Combine the raisins, citron peel, orange peel, and cherries with 1 lb of the flour.
2. Cream well together the butter and sugar.
3. Add the eggs a little at a time. Mix in the remaining flour, and then add the fruit.
4. Fill paper-lined pans three-quarters full, place slices of citron and almond halves on top, and bake at 350°F (175°C).

Fruit Cake

YIELD:
10 lb, 14 oz (4 kg, 892 g)

	U.S.	Metric
Currants	2 lb	900 g
Sultana raisins	1 lb	450 g
Seedless raisins	1 lb	450 g
Citron peel, sliced	4 oz	112 g
Candied fruit, chopped	4 oz	112 g
Brandy	1 pt	450 g
Rum	1 pt	450 g
Salted butter	1 lb	450 g
Confectioner's sugar	1 lb	450 g
Almonds	2 oz	56 g
Nutmeg, ground	$1/2$ oz	14 g
Mace, ground	$1/2$ oz	14 g
Cinnamon, ground	$1/2$ oz	14 g
Allspice, ground	$1/2$ oz	14 g
Eggs	1 lb	450 g
Bread flour, sifted	1 lb	450 g
Walnut meats	2 oz	56 g

1. Soak the fruit for 24 hours in the brandy and rum.
2. Cream together the butter, sugar, and spices.
3. Add the eggs a little at a time.
4. Add the flour, and mix well.
5. Add the soaked fruit and nuts, and mix well.
6. Bake in covered pans at 300°F (150°C).

NOTE: In soaking the fruits for these cakes, the spirits may be replaced by hot syrup and extracts, such as brandy or rum extract. This fruit cake was traditionally prepared as a wedding cake.

Layer Cake Mixture

YIELD:
26 lb, 13 oz (12 kg, 65 g)

	U.S.	Metric
Salted butter	3 lb	1 kg, 350 g
Shortening	1 lb	450 g
Egg coloring	As needed	
Confectioner's sugar	5½ lb	2 kg, 475 g
Eggs	4 lb	1 kg, 800 g
Milk	2 qt	1 kg, 800 g
Cake flour	9 lb	4 kg, 50 g
Baking powder	5 oz	140 g

1. Cream well together butter, shortening, egg coloring, and sugar.
2. Add the eggs gradually, and then add the milk.
3. Sift together the flour and baking powder, and add to the mixture.
4. Pour batter into greased and floured cake pans, and bake at 375°F (190°C).

■ Chocolate Layer Cake

Fill three baked layers with chocolate icing, and frost all over with chocolate icing.

■ Maple Layer Cake

Fill three baked layers with custard cream, and frost all over with maple icing.

■ Marshmallow Layer Cake

Fill three baked layers with marshmallow, cover all over with marshmallow, and sprinkle with chopped walnuts.

■ Vanilla Layer Cake

Fill three baked layers with vanilla custard cream, and frost all over with vanilla icing.

Washington Layer Cake

YIELD:
15 lb, 9 oz (7 kg, 2 g)

	U.S.	Metric
Granulated sugar	4 lb	1 kg, 800 g
Eggs	2 lb	900 g
Egg yolks	2 lb	900 g
Salt	1 oz	28 g
Milk, heated	1 qt	900 g
Vanilla extract	4 oz	112 g
Cake flour	5 lb	2 kg, 250 g
Baking powder	4 oz	112 g

1. Combine the sugar, eggs, egg yolks, and salt in a cake mixer over low heat or over a double boiler with hot water. Beat until light and stiff. Remove from heat.
2. Add hot milk, and beat until cold.
3. Add vanilla.
4. Sift together the flour and baking powder, and add to mixture.
5. Grease and flour layer cake pans, pour in batter, and bake at 375 to 390°F (190 to 200°C).
6. When cooled, fill two layers with raspberry jam, and dust the top with 4× sugar.

Blueberry Cake

YIELD:
43 lb, 10 oz (19 kg, 630 g)

	U.S.	Metric
Salted butter	2 lb	900 g
Shortening	2 lb	900 g
Salt	2 oz	56 g
Confectioner's sugar	7 lb	3 kg, 150 g
Egg coloring	As needed	
Milk	6 qt	5 kg, 400 g
Cake flour	14 lb	6 kg, 300 g
Blueberries	3 qt	2 kg, 700 g
Baking powder	8 oz	225 g

1. Cream together the butter, shortening, salt, sugar, and coloring.
2. Add the milk slowly. Sift the flour with the baking powder, and add to the batter. Mix well until smooth.
3. Add 2 qt of the blueberries, taking care not to break the berries while mixing.
4. Grease and flour pans, and fill with batter.
5. Sprinkle the remaining blueberries on top.
6. Bake at 375°F (190°C).
7. When cool, dust lightly with 4× sugar.

Carlos Cake

YIELD:
15 lb, 4¹/₂ oz (6 kg, 876 g)

	U.S.	Metric
Confectioner's sugar	4 lb	1 kg, 800 g
Salted butter	2 lb	900 g
Almond extract	1 oz	28 g
Vanilla extract	3 oz	84 g
Egg whites	2 lb	900 g
Banana pulp	³/₄ qt	675 g
Cake flour	5 lb	2 kg, 250 g
Cornstarch	¹/₂ lb	225 g
Cream of tartar	¹/₂ oz	14 g

1. Cream together the sugar, butter, and extracts.
2. Whip egg whites until stiff, and gradually add to sugar mixture.
3. Add banana pulp.
4. Sift together the flour, cornstarch, and cream of tartar. Mix thoroughly with banana mixture.
5. Fill deep paper-lined pans, cut the tops with a knife dipped in butter, and bake at 350 to 375°F (175 to 190°C).
6. When cool, frost all over with vanilla icing.

Cupcakes

YIELD:
13 lb, 11 oz (6 kg, 159 g)

	U.S.	Metric
Shortening	2 lb	900 g
Confectioner's sugar	3 lb	1 kg, 350 g
Lemon extract	To taste	
Egg coloring	As needed	
Eggs	2 lb	900 g
Milk	1 qt	900 g
Cake flour	4¹/₂ lb	2 kg, 25 g
Baking powder	3 oz	84 g

1. Cream well together the shortening, sugar, extract, and coloring until very light and creamy.
2. Add eggs gradually, and then add milk.
3. Sift together flour and baking powder, and add to mixture.
4. Grease and flour cups, and fill three-quarters full.
5. Bake at 300°F (200°C).
6. When cool, finish with jams, jellies, marshmallow, buttercreams, etc., and ice with different colored and flavored fondants.

Devil's Food Cake (Boiled Process)

YIELD:
18 lb, 13 oz (8 kg, 450 g)

	U.S.	Metric
Water	1 qt	900 g
Confectioner's sugar	5 lb	2 kg, 250 g
Cocoa powder	1 lb	450 g
Egg yolks	8 oz	225 g
Salted butter, or shortening	2 lb	900 g
Salt	1 oz	28 g
Eggs	2 lb	900 g
Vanilla extract	2 Tbsp	2 Tbsp
Vinegar, distilled white	1 Tbsp	1 Tbsp
Cinnamon, ground	1 oz	28 g
Milk	1 qt	900 g
Baking soda	1½ oz	42 g
Cake flour	4 lb	1 kg, 800 g

1. Bring to a boil the water, 2 lb (900 g) of the sugar, and the cocoa. Remove from heat.
2. Stir in the egg yolks, and then set aside to cool.
3. Cream butter, salt, and the remaining sugar.
4. Add eggs gradually, and then add the cooled chocolate mixture.
5. Add vanilla, vinegar, cinnamon, and the milk, in which the baking soda has been dissolved.
6. Add mixture to flour, and mix.
7. Grease and flour cake pans, and pour in batter.
8. Bake at 375°F (190°C).
9. When cool, fill and top the layers with marshmallow or chocolate icing.

Ginger Cake

YIELD:
8 lb, 15 oz (4 kg, 28 g)

	U.S.	Metric
Baking soda	2 oz	56 g
Water	1 qt	900 g
Shortening	12 oz	336 g
Confectioner's sugar	1/2 lb	225 g
Eggs	7 oz	200 g
Molasses	1 pt	450 g
Ginger, ground	1 oz	28 g
Cinnamon, ground	1/2 oz	14 g
Salt	1/2 oz	14 g
Cake flour	4 lb	1 kg, 800 g

1. Dissolve the baking soda in water.
2. Cream the shortening and sugar.
3. Add the eggs a little at a time. Add molasses, ginger, cinnamon, salt, and water containing the baking soda.
4. Mix in the flour until smooth.
5. Bake in papered pans at 325°F (165°C).
6. When cool, ice the top with chocolate icing, and cut into squares.

❦ Angel Cakes

Angel cakes have always been a light and elegant product, suitable for the basis of lovely dessert presentations. Now more than ever, they are an indispensable menu item. Since they are made without egg yolks or added fat, they have a great appeal for fat- and cholesterol-conscious diners.

Angel Cake 1

YIELD:
5 lb, 4 1/2 oz (2 kg, 375 g)

	U.S.	Metric
Egg whites	2 lb	900 g
Granulated sugar	2 lb	900 g
Bread flour	12 oz	336 g
Cornstarch	8 oz	224 g
Cream of tartar	2 tsp	2 tsp
Lemon extract	To taste	

1. Beat the egg whites until very stiff.
2. Gradually add half the sugar.
3. Sift the flour, cornstarch, and cream of tartar with the remaining sugar. Add to the mixture along with the flavoring, folding in until ingredients are well incorporated.
4. Fill wet pans, and bake at 350°F (175°C).
5. When baked, turn upside down onto paper with the pan to prevent the cake from shrinking.
6. When cold, remove from the pan by pressing down the sides of the cake, and then knocking the pan on the table.
7. Brush off all the crumbs, and ice all over.

Angel Cake 2

YIELD:
5 lb, ¹/₂ oz (2 kg, 262 g)

	U.S.	Metric
Egg whites	2 lb	900 g
Granulated sugar	2 lb	900 g
Bread flour	14 oz	392 g
Cornstarch	2 oz	56 g
Cream of tartar	¹/₂ oz	14 g
Vanilla extract	To taste	

Prepare as for Angel Cake 1.

Chocolate Angel Cake

YIELD:
5 lb, 6¹/₂ oz (2 kg, 430 g)

	U.S.	Metric
Egg whites	2 lb	900 g
Granulated sugar	2 lb	900 g
Bread flour	14 oz	392 g
Cornstarch	4 oz	112 g
Cocoa powder	4 oz	112 g
Cream of tartar	2 tsp	2 tsp

Prepare as for Angel Cake 1, sifting the cocoa with the dry ingredients.

🦃 Cheesecakes

One or more cheesecakes must be featured on every dessert menu, whether you develop a signature cheesecake for your establishment or offer a specialty cheesecake of the day. Their luscious flavor and texture are enormously popular, and they create a perfect main item for satisfying plated desserts.

Americana Cheesecake

YIELD:
29 lb, 7¼ oz (13 kg, 250 g)

	U.S.	Metric
Crust:		
Graham cracker crumbs (approx. 90 single squares, crushed)	1 lb, 7 oz	646 g
Butter, melted	5 oz	140 g
Granulated sugar	5 oz	140 g
Filling:		
Cream cheese, softened	15 lb	6 kg, 750 g
Granulated sugar	5 lb, 8 oz	2 kg, 475 g
Cornstarch	7½ oz	210 g
Salt	1¼ oz	35 g
Eggs	3 lb	1 kg, 350 g
Egg yolks	1 lb, 2 oz	508 g
Light cream	1 lb, 14 oz	842 g
Lemon rind, grated	5 oz	140 g
Vanilla extract	½ oz	14 g

1. Blend the graham cracker crumbs, melted butter, and sugar for the crust.
2. Press firmly into the bottoms of spring-form pans.
3. Bake at 350°F (176°C) for about 6 minutes. Remove and cool.
4. Raise the oven temperature to 425°F (220°C).
5. In a large, deep bowl, cream the cream cheese until smooth.
6. Add the sugar, cornstarch, and salt. Mix until smooth.
7. Gradually add eggs and egg yolks, a little at a time, mixing well and scraping sides and bottom of the bowl after each addition.
8. Stir in the remaining ingredients, and blend to a smooth batter.
9. Pour filling into prepared pans and place them in a larger pan with 1 inch (3 cm) of cold water.
10. Bake at 425°F (220°C) for about 15 minutes. Remove from the oven and let cool.
11. Reduce oven temperature to 325°F (160°C).
12. Return the cheesecakes, still in the *bain marie*, to the 325°F (162°C) oven. Continue baking for about 1½ hours or until the point of a knife, when inserted through the center, comes out clean.
13. Cool in the pan for about 2 hours before removing sides of pan; then chill.

Americana Strawberry Cheesecake

YIELD:
6 lb, 14 oz (3 kg, 92 g)

	U.S.	Metric
Americana Cheesecake crust	1 recipe	
Americana Cheesecake filling	$\frac{1}{2}$ recipe	
Topping:		
Fresh strawberries	5 lb, 10 oz	2 kg, 520 g
Currant jelly	1 lb, 4 oz	562 g
Red food coloring	As needed	

1. Prepare Americana Cheesecake crust, following the instructions.
2. Make half the recipe for Americana Cheesecake. Mix and bake as instructed. Total baking time will be about 1 hour and 10 minutes.
3. Cool the pan for approximately 2 hours, and then remove the sides.
4. Hull and clean ripe strawberries, and arrange them attractively on top of the cooled cheesecakes in an upright position, stem side down and as close together as possible.
5. Boil the currant jelly gently, and then stir in a few drops of red food coloring. Remove from heat, and let stand for 5 minutes.
6. Brush the fruit with the warm glaze, and then chill the cakes.

Baked Graham Cracker Pie Shell

YIELD:
2 lb, 12 oz (1 kg, 236 g)

	U.S.	Metric
Graham cracker crumbs	1 lb, 8 oz	675 g
Granulated sugar	8 oz	225 g
Butter, softened	12 oz	336 g

1. Combine graham cracker crumbs, sugar, and butter. Blend thoroughly.
2. Press firmly into prepared pie plates.
3. Bake at 350°F (180°C) for about 10 minutes or until crust is golden brown.
4. Cool before filling.

■ Blueberry Cheesecake

Follow the recipe for Americana Strawberry Cheesecake using fresh blueberries instead of strawberries.

Cheddar Beer Cheesecake

YIELD:
19 lb, 11¹/₂ oz (8 kg, 866 g)

	U.S.	Metric
Crust:		
Graham cracker crumbs	15 oz	420 g
Butter, melted	4 oz	112 g
Granulated sugar	4 oz	112 g
Filling:		
Cream cheese, softened	10 lb	4 kg, 500 g
Cornstarch	1¹/₂ oz	42 g
Cheddar cheese, finely grated, at room temperature	1 lb, 4 oz	562 g
Granulated sugar	3 lb	1 kg, 350 g
Lemon rind, grated	¹/₂ oz	14 g
Orange rind, grated	¹/₂ oz	14 g
Eggs	2 lb	900 g
Egg yolks	10 oz	280 g
Ale (or beer)	10 oz	280 g
Heavy cream	10 oz	280 g

1. Combine the graham cracker crumbs, melted butter, and granulated sugar.
2. Firmly press mixture approximately ¹/₄ inch (6 mm) thick into the bottom of greased spring-form pans, and dust the sides with the remaining graham cracker mixture.
3. Place the pans in a cool place while preparing the filling.
4. Beat cream cheese, cornstarch, and cheddar cheese until smooth.
5. Combine the sugar and grated rinds, and add gradually to the cheese mixture.

6. Gradually add the eggs and egg yolks, beating well after each addition to prevent lumps.
7. Stir in the ale (or beer) and heavy cream.
8. Pour the cheese mixture into the prepared pans, and bake at 425°F (220°C) for 15 minutes, until the top is lightly browned. Remove cheese-cake from oven.
9. Reduce oven temperature to 225°F (105°C), leaving oven door open until temperature is reached. Return the cheesecake to the oven, close the door, and finish baking for about 1 hour and 5 minutes or until the point of a knife comes out clean.
10. Cool thoroughly before removing the sides of the pan, or chill in the refrigerator and serve cold. Cut with a sharp knife dipped in water.

Cottage Cheese Cake

YIELD:
10 lb, 1 oz (4 kg, 514 g)

	U.S.	Metric
Cottage cheese	5 lb	2 kg, 250 g
Bread flour	½ lb	225 g
Salted butter	½ lb	225 g
Eggs, separated	1 lb	450 g
Granulated sugar	1½ lb	675 g
Salt	½ oz	14 g
Vanilla extract	1 Tbsp	1 Tbsp
Milk	1½ pt	675 g

1. Cream the cheese well with the butter and flour.
2. Add the egg yolks gradually. Then add the sugar and milk.
3. Beat the egg whites until firm, and carefully fold them into the cheese mixture.
4. Line high-bordered cake pans with plain coffee cake dough, and fill with cheese mixture.
5. Bake at 375°F (190°C).

Cream Cheese Pie

YIELD:
4 lb, 6$\frac{1}{2}$ oz (1 kg, 985 g)

	U.S.	Metric
Neufchâtel, or cream cheese	1 lb	450 g
Confectioner's sugar	5 oz	140 g
Bread flour	5 oz	140 g
Eggs, separated	12 oz	350 g
Milk	1 qt	900 g
Vanilla extract	1 tsp	1 tsp

1. Press the cheese through a fine sieve into a bowl, and then add the sugar, flour, and egg yolks. Stir well.
2. Add the milk gradually.
3. Whip the egg whites to soft peaks and fold into the mixture.
4. Line a pie plate with pie crust dough and fill with the cheese mixture. Place in a 350 to 375°F (175 to 190°C) oven.
5. As soon as the filling begins to expand and a crust has formed on top, use a knife to sever the filling from the pie crust by cutting all around. This will prevent the top from cracking.
6. Let rise about $\frac{1}{2}$ inch (1 cm), and remove from oven to settle again.
7. When pie has settled to the rim, replace in the oven. Let rise again to the same height as before.
8. Repeat steps 6 and 7 three times. When settled the last time, turn pie over on a platter, then back again, and dust with powdered sugar.

Pineapple Cheesecake 1

YIELD:
1 lb, 6¹/₂ oz (632 g)

	U.S.	Metric
Americana Cheesecake crust	*1 recipe*	
Americana Cheesecake filling	*¹/₂ recipe*	

Topping:

Pineapple chunks or slices, canned	*5 lb, 10 oz*	*2 kg, 520 g*
Clear apricot jam	*1 lb, 4 oz*	*562 g*
Water	*2¹/₂ oz*	*70 g*
Maraschino cherries	*As needed*	

1. Follow the recipes for Americana Cheesecake crust and filling.
2. When the cheesecake has cooled, arrange pineapple chunks or slices on top.
3. Combine apricot jam and water in a saucepan, and bring to a boil.
4. Remove from heat and brush over fruit. Decorate with maraschino cherries.

Pineapple Cheesecake 2

YIELD:
2 lb, 1³/₄ oz (997 g)

	U.S.	Metric
Americana Cheesecake crust	*1 recipe*	
Americana Cheesecake filling	*¹/₂ recipe*	

Topping:

Clear apricot jam	*1 lb, 4oz*	*562 g*
Cornstarch	*2¹/₂ oz*	*70 g*
Granulated sugar	*5 oz*	*140 g*
Pineapple, crushed, with juice, canned	*1 lb, 9 oz*	*702 g*
Lemon juice	*1¹/₄ oz*	*35 g*
Yellow food coloring	*As needed*	

1. Follow the recipes for Americana Cheesecake crust and filling.
2. When the cheesecake has cooled, combine jam, cornstarch, sugar, crushed pineapple with juice, and lemon juice in a saucepan.
3. Bring to a boil, stirring for 1 minute or until thickened.
4. Add food coloring, and stir well.
5. Spoon hot topping over the cheesecakes.
6. Cool, and then brush with hot apricot glaze. Chill before serving.

Quick Cheesecake

YIELD:
16 lb, 4¹/₂ oz (7 kg, 321 g)

	U.S.	Metric
Crust:		
Graham cracker crumbs	12 oz	336 g
Granulated sugar	2¹/₂ oz	70 g
Butter, melted	2¹/₂ oz	70 g
Filling:		
Cottage cheese	3 lb, 12 oz	1 kg, 688 g
Cream cheese, softened	3 lb, 12 oz	1 kg, 688 g
Cornstarch	5 oz	140 g
Granulated sugar	2 lb	900 g
Lemon juice	12 oz	336 g
Eggs	2 lb, 8 oz	1 kg, 125 g
Egg yolks	4 oz	112 g
Lemon rind, grated	¹/₂ oz	14 g
Sour cream	1 lb, 14 oz	842 g

1. Combine all the ingredients for the crust, and press firmly into the bottoms of greased spring-form pans.
2. Put in a cool place while preparing the filling.
3. Press the cottage cheese through a fine sieve, and then blend with the cream cheese, cornstarch, sugar, and lemon juice in a deep bowl.
4. Add the eggs and egg yolks, a little at a time, stirring well after each addition. Scrape the sides and bottom of the bowl to ensure a lump-free batter.
5. Add the grated lemon rind and sour cream. Blend thoroughly.
6. Pour the cheese mixture into the prepared pans and bake at 350°F (180°C) for about 1 hour or until the point of a knife, when inserted through the center, comes out clean.
7. Cool overnight before removing the sides of the pan.

Refrigerator Cottage Cheese Cake

YIELD:
2 lb, 15½ oz (1 kg, 332 g)

	U.S.	Metric

Crust:

	U.S.	Metric
Graham cracker crumbs	1 lb, 6½ oz	632 g
Butter, melted	14½ oz	406 g
Granulated sugar	10 oz	280 g
Cinnamon, ground	½ oz	14 g

YIELD:
13 lb, 8¾ oz (5 kg, 643 g)

Filling:

	U.S.	Metric
Cottage cheese	5 lb, 12 oz	2 kg, 586 g
Lemon juice	5 oz	1.4 dl
Lemon rind, grated	½ oz	14 g
Salt	¾ oz	21 g
Unflavored gelatin	2½ oz	70 g
Granulated sugar	1 lb, 8 oz	675 g
Milk	1 lb, 4 oz	5.62 dl
Eggs, separated	1 lb	450 g
Heavy cream	2 lb, 8 oz	1 l, 1.25 dl

1. Combine all ingredients for crust, and spread evenly in the bottoms of greased spring-form pans. Chill in the refrigerator while preparing the filling.
2. Press the cottage cheese through a fine sieve into a deep bowl.
3. Stir in lemon juice, lemon rind, and salt.
4. Place gelatin, 1 lb (450 g) of the sugar, and milk in a saucepan over hot water and stir well. When a finger dipped into the mixture cannot tolerate the heat any longer, remove from heat, and let stand to cool a little.
5. Stir egg yolks into the cottage cheese mixture, and blend well.
6. Add gelatin mixture and beat vigorously until smooth and creamy.
7. Place in the refrigerator or over cold water, stirring occasionally to accelerate cooling, until the mixture starts to set and mounds slightly when dropped from a spoon.
8. Beat the heavy cream until stiff.
9. Beat the egg whites until stiff, but not dry, adding the remaining sugar gradually while beating.
10. Fold egg whites, alternately with the whipped cream, into the cheese mixture.
11. Pour into prepared pans, and chill for approximately 4 hours or until firm. Remove sides of pan and serve.

Refrigerator Cream Cheese Cake

YIELD:
2 lb, 15¹/₂ oz

	U.S.	Metric
Crust:		
Graham cracker crumbs	1 lb, 6½ oz	632 g
Butter, melted	14½ oz	406 g
Granulated sugar	10 oz	280 g
Cinnamon, ground	½ oz	14 g

YIELD:
18 lb, 5³/₄ oz (8 kg, 257 g)

	U.S.	Metric
Filling:		
Cream cheese, softened	7 lb, 8 oz	3 kg, 375 g
Unflavored gelatin	7½ oz	210 g
Hot water	1 lb, 4 oz	562 g
Heavy cream	3 lb, 4 oz	1 kg, 462 g
Eggs, separated	1 lb, 8 oz	675 g
Milk	1 lb, 4 oz	5.62 dl
Granulated sugar	2 lb, 9 oz	1 kg, 152 g
Salt	¾ oz	21 g
Lemon juice	7½ oz	2.1 dl
Lemon rind, grated	1 oz	28 g

1. Combine all ingredients for crust, and spread evenly in the bottoms of pre-pared spring-form pans. Chill in refrigerator while preparing the filling.
2. Cream the cheese in a deep bowl until smooth and free of lumps. Set aside.
3. Sprinkle the gelatin over hot water to dissolve.
4. Beat heavy cream until stiff, and let stand in the refrigerator.
5. Beat egg yolks with a fork, and then combine with 7 oz (196 g) of the sugar and salt.
6. Place over hot water and stir well. When finger dipped into the mixture will not tolerate heat any longer, remove from heat and stir into dissolved gelatin. Add lemon juice and grated lemon rind, and mix well.
7. Pour mixture into the cream cheese, and blend thoroughly.
8. Place in refrigerator or over cold water, stirring occasionally to accelerate cooling.
9. When the mixture starts to set and mounds slightly when dropped from a spoon, fold in the whipped cream.

10. Beat the egg whites until stiff, adding the remaining sugar gradually while beating. Quickly fold into cheese mixture.
11. Pour into prepared pans. Chill for about 4 hours or until firm, remove sides of pan, and serve.

◾ Refrigerator Cheesecake with Fruit

Combine 2 lb (900 g) of any fresh or well-drained canned fruits with the filling for either of the refrigerator cheese cakes. Add the fruit immediately after folding in the egg whites and whipped cream. Sliced strawberries, blueberries, chopped Bing cherries, sliced peaches, diced pineapple, etc. work well with these recipes.

Sour Cream Cheesecake

YIELD:
9 lb, 15 oz (4 kg, 470 g)

	U.S.	Metric
Crust:		
Americana Cheesecake crust		
Filling:		
Cream cheese, softened	5 lb	2 kg, 250 g
Eggs, separated	1 lb, 8 oz	675 g
Granulated sugar	1 lb, 9 oz	702 g
Cornstarch	5 oz	140 g
Sour cream	1 lb, 8 oz	675 g
Lemon juice	1 oz	28 g

1. Line the bottoms of greased spring-form pans with Americana Graham Cracker crust.
2. Combine cream cheese and egg yolks, and beat until smooth.
3. Add 19 oz (532 g) of sugar, cornstarch, sour cream, and lemon juice.
4. Blend all ingredients well, and beat to a very smooth, lump-free batter.
5. In a separate bowl, beat egg whites until very stiff, gradually adding remaining sugar while beating.
6. Fold egg whites gently into batter.
7. Pour into prepared pans, and place in a *bain marie* with 1 inch (3 cm) of cold water.
8. Bake at 325°F (165°C) for 1 hour or until the point of a knife, when inserted in the center, comes out clean.
9. Cool for 4 hours.
10. Remove sides of pans and serve plain or with any of the fruit toppings used with Americana Cheesecake.

Strawberry Cheese Chiffon Pie

YIELD:
10 lb, 14¹/₂ oz (4 kg, 906 g)

	U.S.	Metric
Baked Graham Cracker Pie Shell	1 recipe	
Cream cheese, softened	2¹/₂ lb	1 kg, 125 g
Egg yolks	7 oz	196 g
Unflavored gelatin	2¹/₂ oz	70 g
Hot water	5 oz	140 g
Egg whites	2 lb	900 g
Granulated sugar	1 lb	450 g
Fresh strawberries, sliced	2 lb	900 g
Heavy cream	2 lb, 8 oz	1 kg, 125 g
Fresh strawberries, whole (optional)	30	30

1. Cream the cheese until smooth.
2. Add the egg yolks, and blend well.
3. Dissolve the gelatin in hot water, and stir it into the cheese mixture.
4. Beat the egg whites until stiff, gradually adding 1 lb less 2¹/₂ oz (380 g) of sugar while beating.
5. Fold the beaten egg whites into the cheese mixture.
6. Cover the bottom of the cooled, baked pie shell with sliced strawberries.
7. Pour the cheese mixture over the strawberries, just enough to cover.
8. Drop in more strawberries, and cover with the remaining filling.
9. Place the pies in the refrigerator for at least 2 hours or until firm.
10. Whip the cream with the remaining sugar, and spread over the top of the pies. Decorate with fresh whole strawberries, if desired.

NOTE: Blueberries, diced pineapple, or cherries can be used in place of the strawberries.

❦ Gâteaux

Gâteaux, also called *tortes* or *cakes* in the United States, are a variety of very fine sponges filled with buttercreams, custard cream, aganasse cream, fruits, or jams, and are very common in France, Hungary, Belgium, and other parts of Europe, as well as in the United States. Although practically the same ingredients are used for *gâteaux* as for layer cakes, the difference in appearance and flavor is considerable. The most popular, and indeed the most dainty, are known as *gâteaux crème au beurre*, or buttercream cakes. As a rule, they are baked in iron rings on paper.

Gâteau Alcazar

Line some rings or deep layer cake pans with a sugar cookie dough, and fill three-quarters full with a mixture made from the following:

YIELD:
1 lb, 12 oz (850 g)

	U.S.	Metric
Almond paste	½ lb	225 g
Granulated sugar	½ lb	225 g
Eggs	1 lb	450 g

1. Work almond paste, sugar, and half the eggs until very smooth, then add the remaining eggs one at a time.
2. Fill the lined pans.
3. Bake at 380°F (195°C).
4. When cold, take some fancy macaroon paste and draw strips on top to form a latticework. Draw a border all around using a star tube.
5. Bake at 430°F (220°C) just to color the top of the macaroon paste.
6. When cold, fill the spaces between the latticework with apricot jam and custard cream.
7. Sprinkle finely chopped pistachio nuts on top.

■ Gâteau Alhambra

Bake an almond sponge in square-shaped molds. When cold, cut into four layers, and fill with strawberry buttercream. Frost all over with pink fondant. Decorate the top with buttercream and a few candied rose leaves.

■ Gâteau Ananas

Bake a lemon sponge in rings. When cold, cut each into three layers, and fill with buttercream and crushed pineapple mixed together. Mask the sides with buttercream, and cover all over with sliced almonds. Decorate the top with sliced pineapple, and then glaze the pineapple with a well-reduced apricot syrup.

■ Gâteau Belvilloi

Bake an almond sponge in round tins. When cold, cut each into three layers, and fill with whipped cream. Mask all over with buttercream, and then cover with finely ground, roasted filberts.

▦ Gâteau Carlos

Fill three square layers of a Progrès Cake with kirsch buttercream. Ice all over with kirsch icing. Write *Carlos* in the center with chocolate icing. Decorate with rosettes made from chocolate buttercream, and place a silver drop in the center of each rosette.

▦ Gâteau Collombies

Bake a coffee sponge in rings, and when they are cold, cut each into three layers. Fill with kirsch buttercream. Mask the sides with buttercream, and cover the top with coffee fondant. Trim the required number of *langues de chats* (cats' tongues), and line the sides of the cake so that they fit closely. Decorate the top of the cake very daintily with buttercream.

▦ Gâteau Cyrano

Bake a walnut sponge in oval molds. When they are cold, cut each into four layers, and fill with coffee buttercream. Cover all over with coffee fondant, and write *Cyrano* in the center of the cake. Decorate the top with chocolate and coffee buttercream.

▦ Gâteau Ecossais

Bake a butter sponge in square molds. When they are cold, cut each into three layers, and fill with mocha buttercream. Frost all over with a coffee fondant, and decorate the top with very small coffee éclairs and buttercream.

▦ Gâteau Fênics

Bake a walnut sponge in square molds or rings. When they are cold, cut each into four layers, and fill with vanilla buttercream. Mask the sides and top with buttercream. Cover all over with small shreds of brown nougat, and decorate the top with buttercream and a few chopped pistachios.

▰ Gâteau Fredolin

Bake four round layers of Progrès Cake, and place together with mocha buttercream. Mask the sides with the same buttercream, and ice the top with coffee fondant. Line the sides of the cake with *langues de chats* so that they fit closely. Write *Fredolin* in the center of the cake.

▰ Gâteau Javanaise

Bake a cold-process sponge in oval molds. When they are cold, cut each into three layers, and fill with coffee buttercream. Cover all over with chocolate fondant, and decorate the top with pistachio buttercream.

▰ Gâteau Marquise

Bake a chocolate sponge in rings. When they are cold, cut each into four layers. Fill and mask all over with aganasse cream. Cover the sides of the cake with chocolate shot, and decorate the top with rosettes made from aganasse cream pressed through a star tube. Sprinkle the rosettes with a few pistachios, finely chopped.

▰ Gâteau Milka

Bake a chocolate sponge in rings. When they are cold, cut each into four layers, fill with a mocha buttercream, and cover all over with chocolate fondant. Decorate the top with coffee buttercream.

▰ Gâteau Mocha

Bake a cold-process sponge in rings. When they are cold, cut each into four layers, and fill with mocha buttercream. Cover all over with chocolate fondant. Decorate the top with coffee buttercream.

❦ Gâteau Monpansée

There are two different methods of making Gâteau Monpansée. One cake is made by beating the mixture over heat, and the other is a cold mixture. Both work well. They are baked in buttered or greased angel cake pans and sprinkled with sliced almonds.

Gâteau Monpansée (Hot Process)

YIELD:
2 lb, 13 oz (1 kg, 184 g)

	U.S.	Metric
Eggs	3½ oz	100 g
Egg yolks	6 oz	160 g
Granulated sugar	11 oz	308 g
Almond powder, made from roasted almonds	5 oz	140 g
Bread flour	12 oz	336 g
Sweet butter, melted	5 oz	140 g
Lemon-flavored syrup	As needed	
Apricot jelly	As needed	

1. Beat the eggs, egg yolks, sugar, and almond powder in a pan over low heat until warm. Remove from heat, and continue to beat until cold.
2. Mix in the flour, and then add the melted butter.
3. Fill greased angel cake pans three-quarters full, and bake at 380°F (195°C).
4. When baked, turn out of pan.
5. When cold, sprinkle a light, lemon-flavored syrup over the cake, and glaze all over with apricot jelly.

Gâteau Monpansée (Cold Process)

YIELD:
7 lb, 4 oz (3 kg, 400 g)

	U.S.	Metric
Egg yolks	1 lb, 7 oz	640 g
Almond paste	1 lb	450 g
Granulated sugar	1 lb	450 g
Bread flour	1 lb	450 g
Sweet butter	1 lb	450 g
Egg whites	2 lb, 2 oz	960 g
Lemon-flavored syrup	As needed	
Apricot jelly	As needed	

1. Beat the egg yolks, almond paste, and half the sugar until very light and smooth.
2. Cut flour and butter together until very fine.
3. In a separate bowl, beat the egg whites with the remaining sugar until very light and stiff.
4. Mix the egg yolk and egg white mixtures together lightly.
5. Mix in the flour and butter.

6. Fill greased angel cake pans three-quarters full.
7. Bake at 380°F (195°C).
8. When baked, turn out of pan.
9. When cold, sprinkle a light, lemon-flavored syrup over the cake, and glaze all over with apricot jelly.

■ Gâteau Monte Carlo

Bake an almond sponge in rings. When they are cold, cut each into three layers, and fill with pistachio buttercream. Cover all over with pistachio fondant. Decorate the top with chocolate buttercream and halved pistachio nuts.

■ Gâteau Noisettes

Bake a coffee sponge in rings. When they are cold, cut each into three layers, and fill with a praline buttercream. Frost all over with coffee fondant. Decorate the top very daintily with praline buttercream pressed through a star tube and with lightly roasted hazelnuts.

Gâteau Pansée

Thinly roll out a sugar cookie dough, and line some rings or layer cake pans with it. Then prepare a frangipane from:

YIELD:
9 lb, 8 oz (4 kg, 275 g)

	U.S.	Metric
Almond paste	2 lb	900 g
Fine granulated sugar	2 lb	900 g
Sweet butter	2 lb	900 g
Eggs	2 lb	900 g
Bread flour	1/2 lb	225 g
Candied fruits, assorted	1 lb	450 g

1. Cream the almond paste, sugar, and butter.
2. Add the eggs a little at a time, and work the same as for pound cake.
3. When all the eggs have been added, mix in flour and finely chopped fruit.
4. Fill the ring about three-quarters full, and then place very thin bars across to form a latticework.
5. Bake at 380°F (195°C).
6. When cold, glaze the top with apricot jelly and then with a very thin vanilla-flavored fondant.

Gâteau Pansée Camille

Prepare the same as Gâteau Pansée, only omit the fruit from the frangipane. Instead of the bars on top, prepare a praline from:

YIELD:
1 lb, 10 oz (735 g)

	U.S.	Metric
Granulated sugar	1 lb	450 g
Egg whites	2 oz	60 g
Almonds, sliced (or other nuts)	½ lb	225 g

1. Rub ingredients well together, and sprinkle all over the cakes.
2. Bake at 380°F (195°C).
3. When cold, dust all over with 4× sugar.

▬ Gâteau Portugaise

Bake a butter sponge in rings. When they are cold, cut each into four layers, and fill with orange buttercream. Mask the sides and top with buttercream. Cover the sides with sliced almonds, and decorate the top with buttercream and orange quarters dipped in caramel sugar.

▬ Gâteau Princesse Marie

Bake a chocolate sponge in rings. When they are cold, cut each into four layers, and fill with chestnut buttercream flavored with a little kirsch. Cover all over with pink fondant. Decorate the top with chocolate buttercream and candied violets.

Progrès Cake

YIELD:
6 lb, 8 oz (2 kg, 925 g)

	U.S.	Metric
Egg whites	2 lb	900 g
Granulated sugar	2 lb	900 g
Almond powder, made from roasted almonds	2 lb	900 g
Bread flour	½ lb	225 g

1. Beat the egg whites until firm, adding the sugar slowly, as for a meringue.
2. Sift the almond powder and flour together.
3. Fold the two mixtures together gently.
4. Dress onto greased and floured pans with a plain, medium-sized tube, or spread with a palette knife. Any desired shape can be made from this mixture.
5. Bake at 325°F (165°C).

■ Gâteau Royal

Bake a round lemon sponge and cut into four layers. Spread each layer with banana jam. Assemble the layers, mask the sides with buttercream, and then cover with finely chopped, roasted almonds. Cover the top with pink fondant, and decorate with walnut halves.

■ Gâteau Suprême

Bake a plain sponge cake in rings. When they are cold, cut each into four layers, and fill with kirsch buttercream. Mask all over with the buttercream, and cover the sides with finely chopped walnuts. Decorate the top with candied fruit and buttercream.

■ Gâteau Tampouss

Roll out puff paste about 1/6 inch (4 mm) thick, and cut in a round shape. Prick with a fork, let rest, and then bake at 350°F (175°C). When cold, place three layers together with vanilla custard cream. Mask the sides with the same cream, and place sliced, roasted almonds all around. Dust the top with 4× sugar. These cakes are usually made 6 to 12 inches in diameter.

■ Gâteau Vatel

Assemble three round layers of Progrès Cake with hazelnut buttercream, about 1/2 inch (1 cm) thick between each layer. Chill in the refrigerator. When firm, ice all over with coffee icing, and write *Vatel* with royal icing in the center. Decorate all around with buttercream rosettes, and place a roasted hazelnut at the center of each rosette. This cake is sometimes finished the same as Gâteau Fredolin.

■ Gâteau de Venice

Bake a plain sponge in square pans. When they are cold, split in the middle, fill with apricot jam, and then cover all over with a well-reduced apricot jelly. Place sliced, roasted almonds all around, and decorate the top with assorted candied fruits. Using a small brush, cover the fruits with apricot jelly.

🎮 Pies

There is no doubt that pies are the best sellers, and therefore, a great deal of care should be given them. Only the best of materials should be used in the fillings and the best fruits possible. Pie crust should be flaky and always well baked. For soft pie fillings, fresh eggs and fresh milk should be used. For fruit fillings, use as little starch as possible.

When buying pie fillings, it is advisable to always buy from a good, reliable firm and to always buy the best. Also, always buy from the same house so that you will obtain the same results with your pies and uniform pies all the year round.

Experience shows that many bakeries seem unable to continually produce uniform pies and that they vary considerably from time to time. The reason for this can invariably be traced to the bakeshop, where there may be a new baker or new formulas, resulting in a different class of goods, which brings complaints from the customers that the pies are not as good as they used to be. In order to eliminate this difficulty, if you make your own fillings, you should obtain the best formulas possible and then write them down in a book. Make a list of the formulas which are used daily, and frame them under glass to hang in the shop so that when you have a new baker, your own formulas will continue to be used, resulting in the uniform quality you desire. You also will know that if the pies are not as good as they once were, the fault lies with the baker and not with the formulas or materials used.

All soft pies should be well filled and the mixture strained. Care should be taken to see that the sugar is thoroughly dissolved. Custard pies should not be overbaked, because when they are overdone, not only do they lose their good and rich flavor, but small holes form, producing a cheesy, unpalatable custard. On the other hand, if the pie is not quite done, the custard will be soft in the center and will run when cut. The public always prefers a nice full fruit pie, and yet a fruit filler made with starch becomes flat and heavy 12 hours after it is baked, and the starchy taste always remains in the filler regardless of how well it is cooked and baked. Therefore, it is advisable to use a tapioca flour in making your fruit fillers.

PIE CRUST

Pie Crust Bottom 1

YIELD:
39 lb, 12 oz (17 kg, 886 g)

	U.S.	Metric
Cake flour	20 lb	9 kg
Salted butter	6 lb	2 kg, 700 g
Shortening	6 lb	2 kg, 700 g
Salt	4 oz	112 g
Granulated sugar	8 oz	225 g
Water	3½ qt	3 kg, 150 g

1. Scale flour, butter, and shortening, and rub well together.
2. Dissolve salt and sugar in water, and add to the flour.

NOTE: Work the dough as little as possible, because a dough that is overworked will produce a tough and hard crust when baked.

Pie Crust Bottom 2

YIELD:
42 lb, 5 oz (19 kg, 40 g)

	U.S.	Metric
Cake flour	22 lb	9 kg, 900 g
Shortening	11 lb	4 kg, 950 g
Salt	5 oz	140 g
Granulated sugar	1 lb	450 g
Water	4 qt	3 kg, 600 g

Prepare as for Pie Crust Bottom 1.

Pie Crust Top 1

YIELD:
33 lb, 12 oz (15 kg, 186 g)

	U.S.	Metric
Cake flour	20 lb	9 kg
Salted butter	5 lb	2 kg, 250 g
Salt	4 oz	112 g
Granulated sugar	8 oz	224 g
Water	4 qt	3 kg, 600 g

Prepare as for Pie Crust Bottom 1.

Pie Crust Top 2

YIELD:
33 lb, 2 oz (14 kg, 905 g)

	U.S.	Metric
Cake flour	16 lb	7 kg, 200 g
Salted butter	10 lb	4 kg, 500 g
Salt	4 oz	112 g
Granulated sugar	6 oz	168 g
Water	3¼ qt	2 kg, 925 g

Prepare as for Pie Crust Bottom 1.

Pâte à Pâté (Dough for Veal and Ham Pie)

YIELD:
18 lb, 10 oz (8 kg, 384 g)

	U.S.	Metric
Bread flour	10 lb	4 kg, 500 g
Shortening	4 lb	1 kg, 800 g
Salted butter	1 lb	450 g
Salt	3 oz	84 g
Water	1½ qt	1 kg, 350 g
Egg yolks	7 oz	200 g

1. Scale the flour, shortening, and butter, and rub well together.
2. Dissolve salt in water, and add to the flour. Add the egg yolks.

NOTE: Work the dough as little as possible, because a dough that is overworked will produce a tough and hard crust when baked.

PIE FILLINGS

Blueberry Pie Filling

YIELD:
17 lb, 14 oz (8 kg, 193 g)

	U.S.	Metric
Blueberries	8 qt	6 kg, 450 g
Granulated sugar	2 lb	900 g
Cinnamon, ground	1 oz	28 g
Salt	1 oz	28 g
Lemons	2	112 g
Water	1 pt	450 g
Tapioca flour	8 oz	225 g

1. Clean the berries and bring to a boil with the sugar, cinnamon, salt, and juice of the lemons.
2. Mix the tapioca flour with the water, and add slowly to the berries.
3. Stir well, and bring to a boil again.
4. Remove from heat and place in pails to cool.

Lemon Pie Filling 1

YIELD:
7 lb, 3¹/₄ oz (3 kg, 140 g)

	U.S.	Metric
Water	2 qt	1 kg, 800 g
Salted butter	2 oz	56 g
Salt	¹/₄ oz	7 g
Granulated sugar	1 lb	450 g
Egg yolks	7 oz	200 g
Cornstarch	6 oz	168 g
Lemons	12	12

1. Bring to a boil the water, butter, salt, and half the sugar.
2. Mix in a bowl the egg yolks, the remaining sugar, and the cornstarch. Add to the boiling sugar mixture.
3. Return to a boil, stirring constantly.
4. When boiling thoroughly, remove from heat, add the juice of the lemons, and cool before using.

Lemon Pie Filling 2

YIELD:
12 lb, 8¹/₂ oz (5 kg, 639 g)

	U.S.	Metric
Water	4 qt	3 kg, 600 g
Salt	¹/₂ oz	14 g
Granulated sugar	1¹/₂ lb	675 g
Egg yolks	1 lb	450 g
Bread flour	1 lb	450 g
Lemon juice	1 pt	450 g

1. Bring to a boil the water, salt, and half the sugar.
2. Mix well together the egg yolks, flour, and the remaining sugar.
3. Slowly add some of the boiling sugar mixture to the egg yolk mixture, and then mix all together.
4. Return mixture to a boil, stirring constantly to prevent burning.
5. When thoroughly cooked, remove from heat and let cool.
6. When cold, add the lemon juice and whip.

NOTE: This recipe is used for covered and lemon meringue pies.

Mince Meat Pie Filling

YIELD:
77 lb (34 kg, 648 g)

	U.S.	Metric
Beef	24 lb	10 kg, 800 g
Suet	4 lb	1 kg, 800 g
Brown sugar	6 lb	2 kg, 700 g
Seedless raisins, no. 10	8 lb	3 kg, 600 g
Currants	12 lb	5 kg, 400 g
Apples, chopped	16 lb	7 kg, 200 g
Allspice, ground	8 oz	225 g
Cloves, ground	8 oz	225 g
Brandy	1 qt	900 g
Cider	2 qt	1 kg, 800 g

1. Boil the beef until tender. Drain off the bouillon and reserve. Remove all the stringy skins from the suet, and pass the meat and suet through a meat chopper.
2. Add the sugar, raisins, currants, apples, and spices, and mix well.
3. Add the bouillon from the beef, brandy, and cider, and mix well again.
4. Refrigerate for further use.

■ Orange Pie Filling

Prepare the same as Lemon Pie Filling 1, only use the juice of 8 oranges and 4 lemons in place of the lemon juice, and add a little orange food coloring.

Pineapple Pie Filling

YIELD:
54 lb, 12 oz (24 kg, 834 g)

	U.S.	Metric
Water	11 qt	9 kg, 900 g
Salt	4 oz	112 g
Granulated sugar	6 lb	2 kg, 700 g
Fresh pineapples, pared and cleaned	21 lb	10 kg, 886 g
Apples, peeled and cored	4 lb	1 kg, 800 g
Cornstarch	1½ lb	675 g

1. Bring to a boil 10 qt (9 kg) of water, the salt, and the sugar.
2. Pass the pineapples and the apples through a meat grinder, then add to the boiling water, and return to a boil.
3. Mix the cornstarch with the remaining quart of water, and add to the pineapple mixture. Stir well, and let boil for about 1 minute.
4. Remove from heat and set aside to cool.

Raisin Pie Filling 1

YIELD:
25 lb, 14 oz (11 kg, 600 g)

	U.S.	Metric
Water	5 qt	4 kg, 500 g
Granulated sugar	5 lb	2 kg, 250 g
Tapioca flour	6 oz	4 kg, 500 g
Large seedless raisins	10 lb	168 g
Lemons	4	4

1. Place the water, sugar, and tapioca flour in a kettle over medium heat.
2. Stir constantly until mixture comes to the boiling point, but do not allow it to boil.
3. Remove from heat, and add the raisins and the juice of the lemons.

Raisin Pie Filling 2

YIELD:
18 lb, 3 oz (8 kg, 184 g)

	U.S.	Metric
Seeded muscat raisins	7 lb	3 kg, 150 g
Granulated sugar	2 lb	900 g
Water	4½ qt	4 kg, 50 g
Tapioca flour	3 oz	84 g

Prepare as for Raisin Pie Filling 1.

Raspberry Pie Filling

YIELD:
38 lb (17 kg, 100 g)

	U.S.	Metric
Water	13 qt	11 kg, 700 g
Raspberries, dried or evaporated	5 lb	2 kg, 250 g
Granulated sugar	5 lb	2 kg, 250 g
Tapioca flour	2 lb	900 g

1. Place 12 qt (11 kg) of water, raspberries, and sugar in a kettle over medium heat.
2. Bring to a boil, and boil until raspberries are tender.
3. Mix the tapioca flour with 1 qt of water, add to the raspberry mixture, and return to a boil.
4. Remove from heat and set aside to cool.

Pie Fillings Made from Canned Fruits

When canned fruits are used for a filler, drain the fruit from the can, and place the juice in a kettle with 3 oz (84 g) of tapioca flour to each quart (900 g) of juice. Heat, but do not boil, stirring constantly until the milky appearance disappears. Remove from heat, and mix in the fruit.

For less expensive fillings, add 1 qt (900 g) of water and ½ lb (225 g) of sugar to every quart (900 g) of fruit juice and 3 oz (84 g) of tapioca flour to every quart (900 g) of liquid.

PIES

Apple Pie 1

YIELD:
16 lb, 1¹/₂ oz (7 kg, 200 g)

	U.S.	Metric
Apples	10 lb	4 kg, 500 g
Granulated sugar	3 lb	1 kg, 350 g
Salted butter	6 oz	168 g
Cinnamon, ground	¹/₂ oz	14 g
Salt	1 oz	28 g
Water	1 qt	900 g
Tapioca flour	4 oz	112 g
Lemons	3	3

1. Pare, core, and slice the apples. (Baldwin apples are preferred.)
2. Add the sugar, butter, cinnamon, salt, and 1 pt of water, and boil until the apples are soft. Remove from heat.
3. Mix the tapioca flour with 1 pt of water, add to apple mixture, and mix well. Add the juice of the lemons and let cool.
4. When cold, pour into lined pie plates and cover entirely with pie crust.
5. Brush crust with lightly beaten egg. Begin baking in a 425°F (220°C) oven.
6. When crust begins to brown, reduce heat to 350°F (175°C) and finish baking.

NOTE: If canned apples are used, add 4 lb (1 kg, 800 g) of sugar instead of 3 lb, and then continue preparation as for fresh apple pie.

Apple Pie 2

YIELD:
14 lb, ¹/₂ oz (6 kg, 314 g)

	U.S.	Metric
Apples	10 lb	4 kg, 500 g
Granulated sugar	4 lb	1 kg, 800 g
Cinnamon, ground	¹/₂ oz	14 g

1. Pare, core, and slice the apples. Mix the sugar with the cinnamon, and then mix well with the apples.
2. Place apples in lined pie plates, using about 2 lb (900 g) of apples in each 9-inch (23-cm) plate, and cover with pie crust.
3. Begin baking in a 425°F (220°C) oven. When crust begins to brown, reduce heat to 350°F (175°C) and finish baking.

■ Blueberry Pie

Line pie plates with dough, and then fill with ripe blueberries which have been carefully hulled. Mix well together 4 oz (112 g) of fine granulated sugar and a ½ oz (14 g) of cornstarch for every quart of berries. Sprinkle over berries, and cover with pie crust. Begin baking in a 425°F (220°C) oven. When crust begins to brown, reduce heat to 350°F (175°C) and finish baking. This method produces a very fine pie, with all the natural flavor of the fruit preserved.

NOTE: All berry pies may be made following this method.

■ Boston Cream Pie 1

Bake a round sponge cake in a deep pan, and then cut into three layers. Fill with custard cream mixed with one-fourth part of whipped cream. Dust the top with confectioner's sugar, or glaze with chocolate icing.

■ Boston Cream Pie 2

When a lighter cream is desired, add 1 oz (28 g) of gelatin to 1 qt (900 g) of hot custard cream. When cold, add 1 qt of cream, whipped firm. Mix well together. When set, fill the sponge cake, cut in two layers, with about 1 inch (3 cm) of cream filling.

■ Chocolate Cream Pie

Bake a pie shell, and when it is cold, fill with a hot chocolate custard cream. Refrigerate. When the cream is cold, decorate the top with vanilla-flavored whipped cream.

Chocolate Custard Pie

YIELD:
9 lb, 9 oz (4 kg, 377 g)

	U.S.	Metric
Cocoa powder	5 oz	140 g
Confectioner's sugar	1½ lb	675 g
Cornstarch	4 oz	112 g
Eggs	1 lb, 11 oz	750 g
Milk, boiling	3 qt	2 kg, 700 g
Vanilla extract	To taste	

1. Mix well together the cocoa, sugar, and cornstarch.
2. Add the eggs and stir well.
3. Add the milk and a little vanilla.
4. Fill lined pie plates, and bake at 400°F (205°C).

Coconut Custard Pie

YIELD:
2 lb, 15 oz (1 kg, 346 g)

	U.S.	Metric
Milk	1 qt	900 g
Eggs	9 oz	250 g
Granulated sugar	6 oz	168 g
Cornstarch	1 oz	28 g
Nutmeg, ground	To taste	
Coconut, finely shredded	As needed	

1. Mix milk, eggs, sugar, cornstarch, and nutmeg well together, and strain.
2. Place a layer of coconut in the bottom of lined pie plates, and then fill with custard.
3. Bake at 400°F (205°C).

Coffee Custard Pie

YIELD:
2 lb, 15 oz (1 kg, 342 g)

	U.S.	Metric
Black coffee	1 pt	450 g
Light cream	1 pt	450 g
Granulated sugar	6 oz	168 g
Eggs	9 oz	250 g
Cornstarch	1 oz	24 g
Caramel	To taste	

1. Mix all ingredients well together, and then strain.
2. Fill lined pie plates, and bake at 400°F (205°C).

Lemon Custard Pie

YIELD:
3 lb, 8 oz (1 kg, 560 g)

	U.S.	Metric
Milk	1 qt	900 g
Eggs	14 oz	400 g
Granulated sugar	8 oz	224 g
Lemons, grated rind	3	3

1. Mix well together eggs, sugar, and the grated lemon rinds.
2. Add milk, and strain.
3. Fill lined pie plates, and bake at 400°F (205°C).

Vanilla Custard Pie

YIELD:
3 lb, 6$\frac{1}{2}$ oz (1 kg, 475 g)

	U.S.	Metric
Milk	1 qt	900 g
Eggs	12 $\frac{1}{2}$ oz	350 g
Granulated sugar	$\frac{1}{2}$ lb	225 g
Vanilla extract	1 tsp	1 tsp

1. Mix all ingredients well together, and then strain.
2. Fill lined pie plates, and bake at 400°F (205°C).

Lemon Meringue Pie

YIELD:
3 lb, 7 oz (1 kg, 550 g)

	U.S.	Metric
Water	1 qt	900 g
Egg yolks	6 oz	160 g
Granulated sugar	12 oz	336 g
Cornstarch	3 oz	84 g
Lemons	4	4

1. Bring the water to a boil.
2. Mix together egg yolks, sugar, and cornstarch, and add to the water.
3. Beat briskly with an egg whip until it boils again, and then mix in the juice of the lemons. Pour into pie shells to cool.
4. When cold, finish with a stiff meringue.

Pumpkin Pie

YIELD:
20 lb, 8$^{1}/_{2}$ oz (9 kg, 239 g)

	U.S.	Metric
Brown sugar	1 lb	450 g
Granulated sugar	1 lb	450 g
Bread flour	4 oz	112 g
Cinnamon, ground	1 oz	28 g
Nutmeg, ground	$^{1}/_{4}$ oz	7 g
Ginger, ground	$^{1}/_{4}$ oz	7 g
Salt	1 oz	28 g
Pumpkin filling, canned	6 lb, 10 oz	2 kg, 980 g
Corn syrup	1$^{1}/_{2}$ lb	675 g
Milk	8 lb	3 kg, 600 g
Eggs	2 lb	900 g

1. Combine sugars, flour, spices, and salt. Mix well together.
2. Add pumpkin filling, and mix well.
3. Add corn syrup and milk. Refrigerate overnight.
4. Add eggs to pumpkin mixture, and mix well.
5. Pour filling into unbaked, fluted pie shells.
6. Bake at 430°F (205°C) until pie feels slightly firm in the center. Start checking firmness after 30 minutes.

Rhubarb Pie

YIELD:
5 lb, 2 oz (2 kg, 306 g)

	U.S.	Metric
Rhubarb	4 lb	1 kg, 800 g
Granulated sugar	1 lb	450 g
Cornstarch	2 oz	56 g

1. Remove the skin from rhubarb, and cut into small pieces. Mix in sugar and cornstarch.
2. Fill lined pie plates, and cover entirely with pie crust.
3. Bake at 400°F (205°C).

▬ Squash Pie

Prepare as for Pumpkin Pie using squash instead of pumpkin.

🍂 Biscuits, Muffins, and Scones

Most of these recipes are made without yeast and fall into the category of quick breads, aptly named since they are quick and easy to prepare. Offer some different muffins and scones on your breakfast menu, or heap a basket with various muffins on a brunch buffet. Biscuits and muffins also add an interesting, flavorful change for luncheon.

Tea Biscuits 1 (Baking Soda)

YIELD:
5 lb, 8 oz (2 kg, 474 g)

	U.S.	Metric
Shortening	4 oz	112 g
Salt	1 oz	28 g
Baking soda	1 oz	28 g
Milk	1 qt	900 g
Cake flour	3 lb	1 kg, 350 g
Cream of tartar	2 oz	56 g

1. Cream the shortening, salt, and baking soda together. Add the milk.
2. Sift together the flour and cream of tartar.
3. Combine the shortening and flour mixtures, and mix to a smooth dough.

4. Roll out the dough about ¾ inch (2 cm) thick, and cut out with a biscuit cutter.
5. Place on greased baking sheets, and bake at 410°F (210°C).

Tea Biscuits 2 (Baking Powder)

YIELD:
6 lb (2 kg, 698 g)

	U.S.	Metric
Confectioner's sugar	6 oz	168 g
Salted butter	6 oz	168 g
Salt	1 oz	28 g
Cake flour	3 lb	1 kg, 350 g
Baking powder	3 oz	84 g
Milk	1 qt	900 g

1. Cream the sugar, butter, and salt together in a mixing bowl.
2. Sift together the flour and baking powder, and add to the creamed mixture.
3. Rub together well, then add the milk, and mix very lightly.
4. Place on the table, and fold well together.
5. Roll out about ¾ inch (2 cm) thick, and cut with a biscuit cutter.
6. Place on greased baking sheets, and bake at 410°F (210°C).

Tea Biscuits 3 (Cream of Tartar)

YIELD:
15 lb, 6½ oz (6 kg, 932 g)

	U.S.	Metric
Cake flour	10 lb	4 kg, 500 g
Cream of tartar	8 oz	225 g
Salt	2½ oz	70 g
Salted butter	2 lb	900 g
Shortening	½ lb	225 g
Baking soda	4 oz	112 g
Milk	1 qt	900 g

1. Sift together the flour, cream of tartar, and salt.
2. Add the butter and shortening to the flour mixture, and rub together until all lumps have disappeared.
3. Dissolve the baking soda in the milk, and add to the mixture. Add more milk as needed to make a medium-soft dough.
4. Roll out the dough ¾ inch (2 cm) thick, and cut with a biscuit cutter.
5. Place on greased baking sheets, and bake at 410°F (210°C).

Basic Muffin Recipe

YIELD:
7 lb, 4³/₄ oz (3 kg, 281 g)

	U.S.	Metric
Cake flour, sifted	2 lb, 5 oz	1 kg, 40 g
Double-acting baking powder	2¹/₂ oz	70 g
Granulated sugar	1 lb, 5 oz	590 g
Milk	2 lb, 8 oz	1 kg, 125 g
Eggs, slightly beaten	8 oz	225 g
Butter, melted	7¹/₂ oz	210 g

1. Blend the sifted flour, baking powder, salt, and sugar. Sift together into a deep bowl.
2. Gradually stir in the milk, eggs, and butter. Blend all ingredients well. *Do not overmix.*
3. Fill greased muffin tins two-thirds full.
4. Bake at 400°F (205°C) for approximately 20 minutes or until golden brown.

■ Blueberry Muffins

Stir 1 lb, 14 oz (842 g) of fresh blueberries into the Basic Muffin Recipe. Frozen blueberries, thawed and drained, or drained canned blueberries may be substituted for fresh.

Bran Muffins

YIELD:
4 lb, 6 oz (1 kg, 983 g)

	U.S.	Metric
Confectioner's sugar	8 oz	225 g
Salted butter	4 oz	112 g
Salt	¹/₂ oz	14 g
Eggs	3¹/₂ oz	100 g
Light molasses	¹/₄ pt	112 g
Milk	1¹/₂ pt	675 g
Bran flour	¹/₂ lb	225 g
Bread flour	1 lb	450 g
Baking soda	¹/₂ oz	14 g
Sultana raisins	2 oz	56 g

1. Cream well together the sugar, butter, and salt.
2. Add the eggs, and mix in the molasses and milk.
3. Sift together the flours and baking soda, and fold into the egg mixture.
4. Add the raisins.
5. Fill greased muffins tins about three-fourths full, and bake at 425°F (220°C).

■ Cheese Corn Muffins

Substitute 1 lb, 11 oz (758 g) of yellow corn meal for half the cake flour in the Basic Muffin Recipe. Add 1 lb, 3 oz (392 g) of shredded sharp cheese to the dry ingredients before adding the liquid.

Corn Muffins 1

YIELD:
14 lb, 6 oz (6 kg, 468 g)

	U.S.	Metric
Salted butter	1 lb	450 g
Confectioner's sugar	2 lb	900 g
Salt	2 oz	56 g
Eggs	1 lb	450 g
Milk	2 qt	1 kg, 800 g
Yellow corn meal	2 lb	900 g
Cake flour	4 lb	1 kg, 800 g
Baking powder	4 oz	112 g

1. Cream well together the butter, sugar, and salt.
2. Add the eggs gradually, and then mix in the milk and corn meal.
3. Sift together the cake flour and baking powder, and fold into egg mixture.
4. Fill greased muffin tins about three-quarters full, and bake at 400°F (205°C).

Corn Muffins 2

YIELD:
5 lb, 13 oz (2 kg, 634 g)

	U.S.	Metric
Confectioner's sugar	1/2 lb	225 g
Salted butter	1/2 lb	225 g
Salt	1 oz	28 g
Eggs	11 oz	300 g
Milk	1 qt	900 g
White corn meal	1 lb	450 g
Cake flour	1 lb	450 g
Baking powder	2 oz	56 g

1. Cream together the sugar, butter, and salt.
2. Add the eggs gradually, and then mix in the milk and corn meal.
3. Sift together the cake flour and baking powder, and fold into egg mixture.
4. Fill greased muffin tins three-quarters full, and bake at 400°F (205°C).

■ Date Muffins

Add 1 lb, 3 oz (534 g) of finely chopped dates to the dry ingredients in the Basic Muffin Recipe.

Graham Muffins

YIELD:
10 lb, 15 oz (4 kg, 936 g)

	U.S.	Metric
Confectioner's sugar	20 oz	560 g
Shortening	12 oz	336 g
Salt	1 oz	28 g
Eggs	11 oz	300 g
Milk	2 qt	1 kg, 800 g
Cake flour	3 lb	1 kg, 350 g
Graham flour	1 lb	450 g
Baking powder	4 oz	112 g

1. Cream together the sugar, shortening, and salt.
2. Add the eggs gradually, and then mix in the milk.
3. Sift together the flours, and baking powder, and fold into egg mixture.
4. Place a few raisins in the bottom of greased muffin tins and fill three-quarters full with batter. Bake at 400°F (205°C).

◼ Lemon Muffins

Add the grated rind of five lemons to the dry ingredients in the Basic Muffin Recipe. Use only 10 oz (2.8 dl) of milk, and add 10 oz (2.8 dl) of lemon juice.

◼ Orange Muffins

Add the grated rind of five oranges to the dry ingredients in the Basic Muffin Recipe. Use only 10 oz (2.8 dl) of milk, and add 10 oz (2.8 dl) of orange juice.

◼ Raisin Muffins

Add 1 lb, 3 oz (534 g) of seedless raisins to the dry ingredients in the Basic Muffin Recipe.

Rye Muffins

YIELD:
9 lb, 11¹/₄ oz (4 kg, 316 g)

	U.S.	Metric
Confectioner's sugar	¹/₂ lb	225 g
Salted butter	¹/₂ lb	225 g
Salt	¹/₄ oz	7 g
Eggs	14 oz	400 g
Milk	2 qt	1 kg, 800 g
White corn meal	¹/₂ lb	225 g
Rye flour	2 lb	900 g
Bread flour	1 lb	450 g
Baking powder	3 oz	84 g

1. Cream together the sugar, butter, and salt.
2. Add the eggs gradually, and then mix in the milk and corn meal.
3. Sift together the flours and baking powder, and fold into egg mixture.
4. Fill greased muffin tins three-quarters full, and bake at 400°F (205°C).

Raised Whole Wheat Muffins

YIELD:
6 lb, 3¹/₂ oz (2 kg, 797 g)

	U.S.	Metric
Yeast, compressed	1¹/₂ oz	42 g
Milk, lukewarm	1 qt	900 g
Shortening	6 oz	168 g
Confectioner's sugar	2 oz	56 g
Salt	1 oz	28 g
Malt	1 oz	28 g
Whole wheat flour	3 lb	1 kg, 350 g
Sultana raisins	¹/₂ lb	225 g

1. Dissolve the yeast in the milk.
2. Cream the shortening, sugar, salt, and malt.
3. Add the milk with the dissolved yeast. Then add the flour and raisins, and mix to make a smooth dough.
4. Let proof twice. Divide into small rolls, place in greased muffin tins, and then place in proof box.
5. When ready, bake at 400°F (205°C).

NOTE: The dough can be used to make excellent whole wheat rolls.

English Muffins

YIELD:
5 lb, 10 oz (2 kg, 531 g)

	U.S.	Metric
Yeast, compressed	1 oz	28 g
Milk, lukewarm	3 lb	1 kg, 350 g
Salt	1 oz	28 g
Bread flour	2¹/₂ lb	1 kg, 125 g

1. Dissolve the yeast in the milk. Add the salt and flour, and mix to make a smooth batter. Let rise.
2. When batter has risen to about twice its original size, bake on a hot griddle. When partly colored, turn over and finish baking.

NOTE: When portioning the batter, do not mix, but take from the top lightly with a ladle to keep the batter raised.

Scotch Scones 1

YIELD:
4 lb, 13¹/₂ oz (2 kg, 178 g)

	U.S.	Metric
Bread flour	1 lb	450 g
Cake flour	1 lb	450 g
Cream of tartar	1 oz	28 g
Salted butter	6 oz	168 g
Confectioner's sugar	6 oz	168 g
Baking soda	¹/₂ oz	14 g
Milk	1¹/₂ pt	675 g
Lemon extract	1 drop	1 drop
Sultana raisins	8 oz	225 g

1. Place in a mixing bowl the flours, cream of tartar, and butter. Rub between your hands until all lumps have disappeared.
2. Dissolve the sugar and baking soda in the milk. Add to the flour mixture, and mix into a smooth dough. Add the extract and raisins.
3. Scale into 12-oz (336-g) pieces and flatten round with hand or roll out and cut into six pieces. Bake on greased baking sheets at 400°F (205°C).
4. When half baked, turn over and finish baking on the other side.

Scotch Scones 2

YIELD:
16 lb, 14 oz (7 kg, 593 g)

	U.S.	Metric
Salted butter	1 lb	450 g
Confectioner's sugar	¹/₂ lb	225 g
Baking soda	2 oz	56 g
Eggs	1 lb	450 g
Milk	3 qt	2 kg, 700 g
Cake flour	8 lb	3 kg, 600 g
Cream of tartar	4 oz	112 g

1. Cream the butter, sugar, and baking soda.
2. Add the eggs gradually, and then add the milk.
3. Sift together the flour and cream of tartar, and mix into egg mixture.
4. Scale into 12-oz (336-g) pieces, and flatten round with hand or roll out and cut into six pieces. Bake on greased baking sheets at 400°F (205°C).
5. When half baked, turn over and finish baking on the other side.

Graham Scotch Scones

YIELD:
4 lb, 7¹/₂ oz (2 kg, 10 g)

	U.S.	Metric
Graham flour	2 lb	900 g
Cream of tartar	1 oz	28 g
Salted butter	8 oz	225 g
Confectioner's sugar	6 oz	168 g
Baking soda	¹/₂ oz	14 g
Milk	1¹/₂ pt	675 g

1. Place in a mixing bowl the flour, cream of tartar, and butter, and rub between your hands until all lumps have disappeared.
2. Dissolve the sugar and baking soda in the milk. Add to the flour mixture, and mix into a smooth dough.
3. Scale into 12-oz (336-g) pieces, and flatten round with hand or roll out and cut into six pieces. Bake on greased baking sheets at 400°F (205°C).
4. When half baked, turn over and finish baking on the other side.

Popovers 1

YIELD:
7 lb, 8¹/₂ oz (3 kg, 389 g)

	U.S.	Metric
Bread flour	2 lb	900 g
Milk	1³/₄ qt	1 kg, 675 g
Salt	¹/₂ oz	14 g
Eggs	1 lb, 12 oz	800 g

1. Make a smooth batter from the flour, milk, and salt.
2. Beat the eggs slightly with a whip, and add to the batter.
3. Mix all together, then fill greased muffin tins about three-quarters full with the mixture, and bake at 425°F (220°C).

Popovers 2

YIELD:
3 lb, 13¼ oz (1 kg, 685 g)

	U.S.	Metric
Bread flour	1 lb	450 g
Confectioner's sugar	1 oz	28 g
Milk	1 qt	900 g
Salt	¼ oz	7 g
Eggs	11 oz	300 g

1. Make a smooth batter from the flour, sugar, milk, and salt.
2. Beat the eggs slightly with a whip, and add to the batter.
3. Mix all together, then fill greased muffin tins about three-quarters full with the mixture, and bake at 425°F (220°C).

🦃 Doughnuts and Crullers

In order to make good doughnuts, care must be taken to have the fat the proper temperature. A too-hot fat will make the doughnuts small, while a too-cold fat will produce a grease-soaked doughnut. Always clean the fat daily. Otherwise, the flour will form a crust on the bottom of the kettle. This will act as an insulation, and you will have trouble obtaining the proper temperature. Consequently, the doughnuts will be gray in color.

Handmade Doughnuts 1

YIELD:
8 lb, 3 oz (3 kg, 646 g)

	U.S.	Metric
Granulated sugar	1 lb, 2 oz	506 g
Salt	1 oz	28 g
Shortening	2 oz	56 g
Eggs	11 oz	300 g
Milk	1 qt	900 g
Cake flour	4 lb	1 kg, 800 g
Baking powder	2 oz	56 g

1. Cream together the sugar, salt, and shortening.
2. Slightly rub in the eggs, and then add the milk.
3. Sift together the flour and baking powder, and fold into mixture.
4. Roll out on the bench, cut with a doughnut cutter, and fry in deep fat at 375°F (190°C).

Handmade Doughnuts 2

YIELD:
8 lb (3 kg, 606 g)

	U.S.	Metric
Confectioner's sugar	1 lb	450 g
Salted butter	5 oz	140 g
Salt	1/2 oz	14 g
Eggs	9 oz	250 g
Milk	1 qt	900 g
Bread flour	2 lb	900 g
Cake flour	2 lb	900 g
Baking powder	1 1/2 oz	52 g

1. Cream the sugar, butter, and salt. Add the eggs and milk.
2. Sift together the flours and baking powder, and fold into the mixture.
3. Roll out and cut with a doughnut cutter. Fry in deep fat at 375°F (190°C).

Machine Doughnuts 1

YIELD:
73 lb (32 kg, 849 g)

	U.S.	Metric
Bread flour	32 lb	14 kg 400 g
Confectioner's sugar	11 lb	4 kg, 950 g
Shortening	1 1/2 lb	675 g
Eggs	2 lb	900 g
Baking soda	8 oz	225 g
Cream of tartar	8 oz	225 g
Nutmeg, ground	4 oz	112 g
Salt	4 oz	112 g
Milk	12 1/2 qt	11 kg 250 g

Fry at 375°F (190°C).

Machine Doughnuts 2

YIELD:
6 lb, 11¹/₂ oz (3 kg, 4 g)

	U.S.	Metric
Confectioner's sugar	1 lb	450 g
Salted butter	4 oz	112 g
Baking soda	¹/₂ oz	14 g
Eggs	5 ¹/₂ oz	150 g
Milk	1 qt	900 g
Cake flour	3 lb	1 kg, 350 g
Cream of tartar	1 oz	28 g

1. Cream the sugar, butter, and baking soda.
2. Add the eggs and milk.
3. Sift together the flour and cream of tartar, and then mix with batter.
4. Fry at 375°F (190°C).

■ Raised Doughnuts

Use any of the sweet doughs, and add some milk to make the dough softer. Then roll out ³/₄ inch (2 cm) thick, cut with a doughnut cutter, and set to rise on cloth. When proofed, fry in deep fat at 375°F (190°C).

■ Crullers

Use any of the sweet doughs, and add some milk to make the dough softer. Roll out, cut in long strips, and then double the strips and twist into a corkscrew shape. Fry in deep fat at 375°F (190°C).

■ French Crullers

Make a cream puff paste. Dress in rings with a bag and star tube onto a sinker or paper. When deep fat is hot, put the sinker into the fat and fry. If paper is used, turn paper and rings into hot fat. Leave until the paper loosens from the paste, and then take off the paper and finish frying. When done, dip one side in a soft icing flavored with rum.

❦ Waffles and Griddle Cakes

Waffles and griddle cakes have long served as satisfying staples of most breakfast menus. Here we offer a variety of griddle cakes that meet today's demand for high nutrition and low fat, while appealing to the trend toward comfort foods.

Waffle Batter 1

YIELD:
3 lb, 11 oz (1 kg, 734 g)

	U.S.	Metric
Eggs	11 oz	300 g
Salt	1/2 oz	14 g
Milk	1 1/2 pt	675 g
Bread flour	1 1/2 lb	675 g
Baking powder	2 1/2 oz	70 g

1. Mix well together the eggs, salt, and milk.
2. Sift together the flour and baking powder, and add to mixture.
3. Bake in hot irons, greasing the irons well each time before using.
4. Serve hot, with warm maple syrup on the side.

Waffle Batter 2

YIELD:
14 lb, 10 1/2 oz (6 kg, 594 g)

	U.S.	Metric
Granulated sugar	4 oz	112 g
Salted butter	1 lb	450 g
Eggs	2 lb	900 g
Salt	1 1/2 oz	42 g
Milk	2 1/2 qt	2 kg, 250 g
Bread flour	6 lb	2 kg, 700 g
Baking powder	5 oz	140 g

1. Cream well together the sugar and butter. Gradually add the eggs, salt, and milk.
2. Sift together the flour and baking powder, and add to the mixture.
3. Pour the batter into hot irons in a thin stream, and bake, greasing the irons well each time before using.
4. Serve hot, with warm maple syrup on the side.

Waffles with Sour Cream

YIELD:
4 lb, 7¹/₂ oz (1 kg, 948 g)

	U.S.	Metric
Eggs	1 lb, 2 oz	500 g
Salt	1 oz	28 g
Granulated sugar	2 oz	56 g
Sour cream	1 pt	450 g
Baking soda	¹/₂ oz	14 g
Bread flour	2 lb	900 g

1. Mix all ingredients well together. Add enough sweet milk to make a soft batter.
2. Pour the batter into hot irons in a thin stream, and bake, greasing the irons well each time before using.
3. Serve hot, with warm maple syrup on the side.

Wheat Cakes

YIELD:
5 lb, 5¹/₂ oz (2 kg, 354 g)

	U.S.	Metric
Eggs	14 oz	400 g
Granulated sugar	3 oz	84 g
Salt	¹/₂ oz	14 g
Milk	1 qt	900 g
Bread flour	1¹/₂ lb	675 g
Whole wheat flour	¹/₂ lb	225 g
Baking powder	2 oz	56 g

1. Mix all ingredients well together.
2. Add milk to make a soft batter, and then add 4 oz (112 g) of melted butter.
3. Bake on a greased hot griddle.
4. Serve hot, with warm maple syrup on the side.

Johnny Cakes

YIELD:
8 lb (3 kg, 563 g)

	U.S.	Metric
Eggs, separated	14 oz	400 g
Granulated sugar	6 oz	168 g
Salt	To taste	
Milk	3 pt	1 kg, 350 g
Yellow corn meal	1 lb	450 g
Whole wheat flour	1 lb	450 g
Bread flour	1 lb	450 g
Baking powder	2½ oz	70 g
Salted butter, melted	½ lb	225 g

1. Mix together the egg yolks, sugar, and salt, and then add a little of the milk to form a smooth batter.
2. Add the cornmeal. Sift together the flours and baking powder, and add to the mixture.
3. Add the remaining milk.
4. Beat the egg whites until firm, and fold into batter.
5. Mix in the butter, and then bake on a greased hot griddle.
6. Serve hot, with warm maple syrup on the side.

Buckwheat Cakes

YIELD:
2 lb, 15½ oz (1 kg, 360 g)

	U.S.	Metric
Buckwheat flour	2 lb	900 g
Eggs	9 oz	250 g
Granulated sugar	2 oz	56 g
Salted butter, melted	3 oz	84 g
Milk	1½ oz	42
Salt	To taste	
Baking powder	1 oz	28 g

1. Mix together the flour, eggs, sugar, butter, milk, and salt.
2. Add the baking powder, and then add more milk to make a soft batter.
3. Bake on a greased hot griddle.
4. Serve hot, with warm maple syrup on the side.

Corn Cakes

YIELD:
3 lb, 12¹/₂ oz (1 kg, 663 g)

	U.S.	Metric
White corn meal	1 lb	450 g
Cake flour	1 lb	450 g
Eggs	11 oz	300 g
Granulated sugar	4 oz	112 g
Salted butter, melted	¹/₂ lb	225 g
Milk	1¹/₂ oz	42 g
Salt	1 oz	28 g
Baking powder	2 oz	56 g

1. Mix together the corn meal, flour, eggs, sugar, butter, milk, and salt.
2. Add the baking powder, and then add more milk to make a soft batter.
3. Bake on a greased hot griddle.
4. Serve hot, with warm maple syrup on the side.

Flannel Cakes

YIELD:
5 lb, 14 oz (2 kg, 653 g)

	U.S.	Metric
Corn meal	4 oz	112 g
Cake flour	3 lb	1 kg, 350 g
Eggs	1 lb, 2 oz	400 g
Granulated sugar	6 oz	168 g
Salted butter, melted	3 oz	84 g
Sour milk	1 pt	450 g
Salt	1 tsp	1 tsp
Baking powder	3 oz	84 g

1. Mix together corn meal, flour, eggs, sugar, butter, milk, and salt.
2. Add the baking powder, and then add more milk to make a soft batter.
3. Bake on a greased hot griddle.
4. Serve hot, with warm maple syrup on the side.

6

Ice Creams,
Water Ices,
and Sherbets

❦ Frozen Desserts

Making ice cream is not difficult, and the principal reason for failure is carelessness in the scaling and measuring of ingredients. When making ice cream, use the best eggs available. Always use fresh fruit when possible, and avoid the use of essences and essential oils.

There are two kinds of ice creams: *French ice cream* and *American ice cream,* which is sometimes called *Philadelphia ice cream.* French ice cream is the richer of the two, but American ice cream is, generally speaking, the more popular in the United States.

French ice cream is made from cream, milk, sugar, eggs, fruit, and other flavors. It is always cooked, or rather heated to certain degrees, which will be explained later.

American ice cream is uncooked, and no eggs are used. It is usually made by mixing medium heavy cream, sugar, vanilla extract, and fruits together, and then the mixture is frozen.

Water ices, often called *sorbets,* are made from water, sugar, and the juice, rind, or pulp of fruits. When ices are made, the syrup scale or sugar scale should be used to assure quality. A syrup scale is very inexpensive, and the trouble saved and results obtained by its use will fully repay you many times over for its purchase. All the sugar and syrup temperatures given in the following formulas are on the Baumé sugar scale. This scale is an industry standard and is highly recommended.

The object of freezing is to reduce the temperature and to make the ice cream or water ice more fairly solid. For this, ice and salt are needed. The best results are obtained by using cracked ice and rock salt (or freezing salt), and 1 lb (450 g) of salt to 6 lb (2.7 kg) of ice is considered the correct proportion to use.

❦ French Ice Creams

French ice creams, sometimes called *boiled custard creams,* are made from cream, milk, eggs, sugar, and flavors. The cream or milk is boiled with half the sugar, and the eggs are beaten with the rest of the sugar. The cream or milk is added slowly to the eggs to obtain a perfect mixture without cooking the eggs. The mixture is then heated in a steam kettle until it thickens, but it must not be allowed to boil. When there is no steam kettle, the cream or milk mixture is boiled over an open flame, and the boiling and heating is the same as by steam.

The cooking of French ice cream requires special care and attention, because when it is overheated, the mixture becomes grainy and short, producing an ice cream that lacks the velvety smoothness so necessary to French ice cream. If not heated enough, on the other hand, the mixture is thin, the ice cream short, and the flavor not fully developed. When your ice cream is a little overheated, you may obtain a smooth mixture by removing it from the kettle and adding 1 oz (28 g) of sweet butter to every quart (liter), then straining at once, and placing on ice in a flat pan so that it cools as quickly as possible. If the mixture has been allowed to boil, however, then it should not be used, because it will produce a very poor and unsatisfactory ice cream. For this reason, it is always best to use a thermometer, heating the mixture to exactly 180°F (82°C), so that you will always obtain good and uniform results.

It is also very important that the cooling be done as quickly as possible. If the cream is allowed to stand in containers without stirring from time to time, the mixture will continue heating, and before it is cool, the results will be the same as from an overheated mixture.

When a thermometer is not available, the cream or milk is boiled with three-quarters of the sugar, and the eggs are beaten with the remaining sugar. When the cream or milk boils, shut off the steam or remove from heat, and let stand for 2 minutes. Then add the eggs slowly, stirring constantly. As soon as well mixed, pour the mixture into 10-qt (10-liter) pails, stirring from time to time to ensure a perfect mixture and to aid the cooling. If these directions are carefully followed, the result should be a perfect, smooth, and velvety ice cream.

French Banana Ice Cream

YIELD:
16 lb, 2 oz (5 kg, 670 g)

	U.S.	Metric
Cream, 20 percent	*3 qt*	*2 liters, 7 dl*
Milk	*2 qt*	*9 dl*
Granulated sugar	*2 lb, 4 oz*	*1 kg, 12 g*
Egg yolks	*1 lb*	*450 g*
Banana pulp	*4 lb, 12 oz*	*2 kg, 135 g*
Lemons	*4*	*4*

1. Bring to a boil the cream, milk, and 1 lb, 6 oz (618 g) of the sugar.
2. Beat together the egg yolks and the remaining sugar.
3. When the cream is boiling, shut off the steam, and add the egg yolk mixture slowly, stirring constantly.
4. When well mixed, remove from the steam kettle, strain, and place in pails to cool.
5. When cold, mix in the banana pulp and the juice of the lemons.
6. Strain through a fine sieve, and freeze.

French Chocolate Ice Cream

YIELD:
15 lb, 13 oz (7 kg, 115 g)

	U.S.	Metric
Sweet chocolate	1 lb, 4 oz	562 g
Bitter chocolate	8 oz	225 g
Granulated sugar	3 lb	1 kg, 350 g
Cream, 20 percent	5 qt	4 liters, 5 dl
Vanilla beans, split	10	10
Egg yolks	1 pt	450 g

1. Melt the chocolates in a kettle or double boiler with 1 lb (450 g) of the sugar.
2. Boil the cream, 1 lb (450 g) of the sugar, and the vanilla beans.
3. Slowly add the cream to the melted chocolate, working the chocolate well with a whip to obtain a smooth mixture.
4. When well mixed, return to the kettle, bring to a second boil, then remove from the kettle.
5. Beat the egg yolks and the remaining sugar together well, and slowly add to the mixture.
6. When well mixed, strain, and let cool. Freeze when cold.

NOTE: When a thermometer is used, boil the cream or cream and milk together. When boiling, shut off the steam, add the beaten egg yolks with the rest of the sugar, and stir well. Then hang a thermometer into the mixture, and heat to 180°F (82°C), stirring continually. When the proper temperature is reached, shut off the steam, and pour the mixture from the kettle as soon as possible into 10-qt (9-liter) pails so that it cools quickly. The temperature given is for 40% cream. When 20% cream is used, heat to 190°F (87°C), and when milk is used, heat to 200°F (93°C). Heat one degree less for every thousand feet above sea level.

French Coffee Ice Cream

YIELD:
13 lb, 12 oz (6 kg, 187 g)

	U.S.	Metric
Cream, 20 percent	3 qt	2 liters, 7 dl
Milk	2 qt	1 liter, 8 dl
Coffee, ground	8 oz	225 g
Granulated sugar	2 lb, 4 oz	1 kg, 12 g
Egg yolks	1 lb	450 g

1. Boil the milk and the coffee together, and then let stand for about 15 minutes in a closed jar or a covered pail.
2. Boil the cream with two-thirds of the sugar, and then beat the egg yolks with the remaining sugar.
3. Strain the coffee solution, then add it to the cream, and let boil together.
4. Shut off the steam, and let stand for a few seconds. Then add the egg yolk mixture slowly, stirring constantly.
5. When well mixed, remove from the kettle and place in pails to cool. Freeze when cold. If a deeper color is desired, add a little coffee extract.

NOTE: Coffee ice cream may be made from any of the vanilla ice cream mixtures by adding coffee extract and leaving out the vanilla beans. A very good coffee ice cream may be made by using the preceding coffee ice cream formula, but instead of using 3 qt (2 liters, 7 dl) of cream and 2 qt (1 liter, 8 dl) of milk, use 3¾ qt (3 liters, 3.5 dl) of cream, 1¼ qt (900 dl) of black coffee, and a little coffee extract.

French Peach Ice Cream

YIELD:
13 lb, 4 oz (5 kg, 964 g)

	U.S.	Metric
Peach pulp	2 qt	1 kg, 800 g
Granulated sugar	2 lb, 8 oz	1 kg, 125 g
Peach extract	⅛ oz	3 g
Cream, 20 percent	3 qt	2 liters, 7 dl
Egg yolks	12 oz	336 g
Red food coloring	As needed	

1. Strain enough very ripe peaches through a sieve to make 2 qt (1.8 liters) of pulp, add half the sugar, and mix well together. Mix in the peach extract.
2. Boil the cream with the remaining sugar.
3. When the cream boils, shut off the steam, and add the egg yolks slowly, stirring constantly.
4. When well mixed, remove from the kettle and strain. Place in pails to cool.
5. When cold, add the peaches and the coloring, and freeze.

French Pistachio Ice Cream

YIELD:
14 lb, ³/₄ oz (6 kg, 309 g)

	U.S.	Metric
Cream, 20 percent	7 lb, 8 oz	3 liters, 375 ml
Milk	2 lb, 8 oz	1 liter, 325 ml
Granulated sugar	3 lb	1 kg, 350 g
Almond paste	8 oz	225 g
Egg yolks	8 oz	225 g
Rose water	¹/₈ oz	3 g
Pistachio extract	¹/₈ oz	3 g
Kirsch extract		
[or 2 oz (50 g) kirsch]	¹/₈ oz	3 g
Almond extract	To taste	
Green and yellow food coloring	As needed	

1. Boil together the cream, milk, and two-thirds of the sugar.
2. When boiling, add the almond paste, and stir well. Let boil again, and then shut off the steam.
3. Beat the egg yolks and the remaining sugar together, and add to the cream mixture.
4. When well mixed, remove from the steam kettle, and strain. Place in pails to cool.
5. When cold, add the rose water, extracts, and coloring, and freeze.

NOTE: If pistachio nuts are used, omit the almond paste, and use 8 oz (225 g) of nuts. Crush them fine, and then simmer in the milk. Use all the other flavoring extracts mentioned, however, since the pistachio nut has a very mild and delicate flavor and when used alone is not sufficiently strong to produce a good flavored ice cream.

French Praline Ice Cream

YIELD:
12 lb, 12³⁄₄ oz (5 kg, 755 g)

	U.S.	Metric
Cream, 20 percent	3 qt	2 liters, 7 dl
Milk	1¹⁄₂ qt	1 liter, 3.5 dl
Granulated sugar	1 lb, 12 oz	784 g
Vanilla bean, split	¹⁄₂	¹⁄₂
Coffee extract	¹⁄₄ oz	7 g
Bitter chocolate	¹⁄₂ oz	14 g
Egg yolks	8 oz	225 g
Praline Paste (directions follow)	1¹⁄₂ lb	675 g

1. Boil together the cream, milk, 1 lb (450 g) of the sugar, and the vanilla beans. Add the coffee extract and the chocolate, boil again, and then shut off the steam.
2. Beat the egg yolks with the remaining sugar, and add slowly to the cream mixture, stirring constantly.
3. When well mixed, remove from the kettle, add the praline, and strain. Let cool, and freeze when cold.

Praline Paste

YIELD:
6 lb (2 kg, 700 g)

	U.S.	Metric
Granulated sugar	3 lb	1 kg, 350 g
Almonds, roasted	1¹⁄₂ lb	675 g
Filberts, roasted	1¹⁄₂ lb	675 g

1. Gradually place the sugar in a kettle and melt.
2. When the sugar turns golden brown, add almonds and filberts.
3. Remove from heat, and place in greased pans.
4. When cold, grind fine with a rolling pin.

NOTE: Good-quality praline paste also may be purchased commercially.

French Strawberry Ice Cream

YIELD:
12 lb, 10¹/₂ oz (5 kg, 695 g)

	U.S.	Metric
Strawberry juice	2¹/₂ qt	2 liters, 2.5 dl
Granulated sugar	2 lb, 2 oz	956 g
Lemon juice	¹/₂ oz	14 g
Cream, 40 percent	2¹/₂ qt	2 liters, 2.5 dl
Egg yolks	8 oz	225 g
Red food coloring	As needed	

1. Hull and wash thoroughly enough very ripe strawberries to produce 2¹/₂ qt (2 liters, 2.5 dl) of juice and strain. Add 1 lb (450 g) of the sugar and the lemon juice.
2. Boil the cream with 12 oz (336 g) of the sugar, and then shut off the steam.
3. Beat the egg yolks with the remaining sugar, and add slowly to the cream mixture, stirring constantly.
4. When well mixed, remove from the kettle, strain, and let cool.
5. When cold, add the strawberry juice and the coloring, and freeze.

French Vanilla Ice Cream 1

YIELD:
14 lb (6 kg, 300 g)

	U.S.	Metric
Cream, 20 percent	5 qt	4 liters, 5 dl
Granulated sugar	2¹/₂ lb	1 kg, 125 g
Vanilla beans, split	2¹/₂	2¹/₂
Egg yolks	1¹/₂ lb	675 g

1. Bring to a boil the cream, three-quarters of the sugar, and the vanilla beans.
2. Beat the egg yolks with the remaining sugar.
3. When the cream comes to a boil, shut off the steam and let rest for a few seconds, and then add the egg yolk mixture slowly, stirring constantly.
4. When the mixing is complete, remove the mixture from the kettle and pour into pails to cool.
5. When cold, put the mixture through a sieve, and freeze.

NOTE: If vanilla extract is used, choose the very best quality, and use 2 oz (56 g) for the recipe given. When a lighter ice cream is desired, boil half the cream, and then add the other half when ready to freeze.

French Vanilla Ice Cream 2

YIELD:
14 lb (6 kg, 294 g)

	U.S.	Metric
Cream, 20 percent	3½ qt	3 liters, 1.5 dl
Milk	1½ qt	1 liter, 3.5 dl
Granulated sugar	2 lb, 12 oz	1 kg, 232 g
Vanilla beans, split	2½	
Egg yolks	1 lb, 4 oz	562 g

1. Boil half the cream, the milk, three-quarters of the sugar, and the vanilla beans.
2. Beat the egg yolks with the remaining sugar.
3. When the cream comes to a boil, shut off the steam and let rest for a few seconds. Then add the egg yolk mixture slowly, stirring constantly.
4. When the mixing is complete, remove the mixture from the kettle and pour into pails to cool.
5. When cold, add the remaining cream, strain, and freeze.

French Walnut Ice Cream

YIELD:
13 lb, 8¼ oz (6 kg, 81 g)

	U.S.	Metric
Milk	2½ qt	2 liters, 2.5 dl
Granulated sugar	2 lb, 4 oz	1 kg, 12 g
Egg yolks	1 lb	450 g
Walnut Brittle (directions follow)	1 lb	450 g
Cream, 40 percent	2 qt	1 liter, 8 dl
Coffee extract	½ oz	14 g
Walnuts, chopped fine	4 oz	112 g

1. Boil the milk with two-thirds of the sugar.
2. Beat the egg yolks and the remaining sugar.
3. When the milk boils, shut off the steam, and add the egg yolk mixture slowly, stirring constantly. Mix well, then remove from the kettle, and strain.
4. Add the walnut brittle, and let cool.
5. When cold, add the cream, the coffee extract, and the walnut meats, and freeze.

Walnut Brittle

YIELD:
5 lb (2 kg, 250 g)

	U.S.	Metric
Granulated sugar	2 lb	900 g
Water	1 pt	450 g
Walnut meats, lightly roasted	2 lb	900 g

1. Boil sugar with water to a light caramel color, about 328°F (165°C).
2. Mix in walnut meats, then pour on a greased slab or pan, and let cool.
3. When cold, crush fine with a rolling pin or put through a fine meat chopper.

❦ American (or Philadelphia) Ice Cream

When making American ice cream, a better product will result if the cream is mixed with the rest of the ingredients and refrigerated for 24 hours rather than frozen the same day. American ice cream should be watched carefully during the freezing process and be taken out just on time. When the cream remains too long in the freezer, it becomes too light and often forms butter lumps when a rich cream is used. If removed from the freezer too soon, you will find hard ice shells all through the cream. For this reason, it is important to watch your cream carefully while freezing, and as soon as it forms a running, creamy mass, remove at once—if left only 1 minute past this point, the ice cream will lack flavor and smoothness.

Because American ice cream is the best liked by the American public, special care should be taken to produce as uniform and as excellent a product as possible, since there is plenty of competition in this line. The firm that supplies the best American ice cream is the one that will have the largest amount of business.

Vanilla ice cream is the general favorite, so it is advisable to use the best materials available in its manufacture. It is especially important to select a good grade of cream and a high grade of vanilla extract. You will find it worthwhile in the long run to pay more for a good brand.

As vanilla is the queen of ice creams, so strawberry is the prime favorite among fruit ice creams. If you are able to produce a very good vanilla and a very good strawberry ice cream, these two alone will bring you many customers.

From 4 to 8 oz (100 to 225 g) of gelatin dissolved in water may be added to ice cream mixture before freezing. This will keep the ice cream from getting soft for a greater length of time, which is desirable for caterers or for shipping, when ice cream must travel long distances before being used. When ice cream is made and served in the same place, however, it is better made without gelatin.

American Banana Ice Cream

YIELD:
16 lb, 2 oz (7 kg, 256 g)

	U.S.	Metric
Banana pulp	2 qt	2 kg, 475 g
Granulated sugar	2½ lb	1 kg, 125 g
Orange	1	1
Cream, 20 percent	4 qt	3 liters, 6 dl

1. Peel enough ripe bananas to make 2 qt (2 kg, 475 g) of pulp, and then strain the pulp through a sieve.
2. Add half the sugar, and the juice of the orange.
3. Mix the cream with the remaining sugar until the sugar has dissolved. Mix together with the banana mixture and freeze at once.

NOTE: Although the banana is rich and luscious, it is entirely devoid of acid. For this reason, it is necessary to add a little lemon or orange juice in order to give the ice cream a fine flavor.

If the banana pulp is allowed to stand for any length of time, it darkens in color, and the ice cream, when frozen, will be dull and muddy in color rather than clear and bright.

American Chocolate Ice Cream 1

YIELD:
14 lb, 2 oz (6 kg, 354 g)

	U.S.	Metric
Cream, 20 percent	3 qt	2 liters, 7 dl
Cream, 40 percent	2 qt	1 liter, 8 dl
Granulated sugar	3 lb, 4 oz	1 kg, 462 g
Bitter chocolate	12 oz	336 g
Vanilla extract	2 oz	56 g

1. Boil together half the 20% cream and 10 oz (280 g) of sugar. When boiling, add the chocolate, cut up in very small pieces, and stir with a whip until very smooth.
2. Dissolve the remaining sugar in the remaining 20% cream, and add the vanilla.

3. Mix slowly the 40% cream with the chocolate mixture.
4. Mix all together and freeze.

NOTE: By boiling the chocolate with part of the sugar and cream, you obtain a smoother, darker mixture than when the chocolate is boiled with water, resulting in better flavor.

American Chocolate Ice Cream 2

YIELD:
14 lb, 7¹/₂ oz (6 kg, 509 g)

	U.S.	Metric
Cream, 20 percent	5 qt	4 liters, 5 dl
Granulated sugar	3¹/₂ lb	1 kg, 575 g
Bitter chocolate	14 oz	392 g
Vanilla extract	1¹/₂ oz	42 g

Prepare the same as American Chocolate Ice Cream 1.

American Coffee Ice Cream

YIELD:
14 lb (6 kg, 300 g)

	U.S.	Metric
Coffee, ground fine	8 oz	225 g
Milk	1 qt	9 dl
Granulated sugar	2¹/₂ lb	1 kg, 125 g
Cream, 20 percent	4¹/₂ qt	4 liters, 0.5 dl

1. Boil the coffee and the milk together. As soon as they are boiling, remove from heat. Place in a covered jar for at least 1 hour.
2. Dissolve the sugar in the cream, and then add the coffee mixture, well strained through a cloth.
3. Mix well together, and freeze. A little coffee extract or burned sugar for deeper color.

American Peach Ice Cream 1

YIELD:
12 lb, 8 oz (5 kg, 628 g)

	U.S.	Metric
Peach pulp	5 lb	2 kg, 250 g
Granulated sugar	2½ lb	1 kg, 125 g
Peach extract	⅛ oz	3 g
Cream, 20 percent	2½ qt	2 liters, 2.5 dl

1. Select very ripe peaches, and put a sufficient amount through a sieve to make 5 lb (2 kg, 250 g) of pulp.
2. Add the sugar and the extract to the peach pulp, and mix well together.
3. Add the cream, mix thoroughly, and let stand for 2 hours before freezing. A little red coloring may be added, if desired.

NOTE: One-quarter of the peaches may be chopped fine and added to the ice cream when nearly frozen, if desired. When this is done, 6 oz (168 g) of sugar should be added to every quart (900 g) of chopped peaches used to prevent the peaches from becoming hard. When the ice cream is nearly frozen, add the peaches together with the syrup, and finish freezing.

American Peach Ice Cream 2

YIELD:
14 lb, 8 oz (6 kg, 525 g)

	U.S.	Metric
Peach pulp	5 lb	2 kg, 250 g
Granulated sugar	2½ lb	1 kg, 125 g
Cream, 20 percent	2 qt	1 liter, 8 dl
Milk	1½ qt	1 liter, 3.5 dl

Prepare the same as American Peach Ice Cream 1.

American Strawberry Ice Cream 1

YIELD:
_14 lb (6 kg, 298 g)_

	U.S.	Metric
Strawberry pulp	6 lb, 12 oz	3 kg, 36 g
Granulated sugar	2 lb, 4 oz	1 kg, 12 g
Cream, 20 percent	2½ qt	2 liters, 2.5 dl
Red food coloring	As needed	

1. Hull and wash thoroughly a sufficient amount of very ripe strawberries to make 5 lb (3 kg, 36 g) of pulp.
2. Add the sugar to the strawberries and let stand for awhile. Add the cream and the coloring, and freeze.

NOTE: If desired, about one-quarter of the fruit may be chopped and mixed with sugar, using 6 oz (168 g) of sugar to every quart (900 g) of berries. Add the fruit to the ice cream when nearly frozen, then finish freezing.

In using canned fruits, when the berries are preserved in water, take sufficient strawberries and water to make 2½ qt (1 liter, 2.5 dl), and add to this 4 oz (112 g) more of sugar than the formula calls for. Cold-pack strawberries are usually preserved with 8 oz (224 g) of sugar to every pound (450 g) of berries, and when strawberries are preserved in syrup, 1 lb (450 g) of sugar is generally used to the quart (9 dl). When using these kinds of preserved fruits, the sugar must be decreased accordingly.

American Strawberry Ice Cream 2

YIELD:
_13 lb, 10 oz (6 kg, 129 g)_

	U.S.	Metric
Strawberry pulp	3 lb, 12 oz	1 kg, 686 g
Granulated sugar	2 lb, 6 oz	1 kg, 68 g
Cream, 20 percent	3¾ qt	3 liters, 375 ml

Prepare the same as American Strawberry Ice Cream 1.

American Vanilla Ice Cream 1

YIELD:
12 lb, 10 oz (5 kg, 681 g)

	U.S.	Metric
Cream, 40 percent	1½ qt	1 liter, 3.5 dl
Cream, 20 percent	3½ qt	3 liters, 1.5 dl
Granulated sugar	2½ lb	1 kg, 125 g
Vanilla extract	2 oz	56 g

1. Mix together well all ingredients.
2. Let stand for 24 hours before freezing.

American Vanilla Ice Cream 2

YIELD:
12 lb, 10½ oz (5 kg, 695 g)

	U.S.	Metric
Cream, 20 percent	5 qt	4 liters, 5 dl
Granulated sugar	2½ lb	1 kg, 125 g
Vanilla extract	2½ oz	70 g

1. Mix together well all ingredients.
2. Let stand for 24 hours before freezing.

❧ Water Ices and Sherbets

Water ices, perhaps better known as *sorbets,* are made from water, sugar, and fruits. Some of the fruit ices are very fine when blended with a meringue, while others are better when mixed with a little ice cream. Water ices should be as smooth as ice cream, never hard or lumpy, and should never separate. That is, the syrup should never separate from the rest of the ingredients. When an ice is too hard, there is not enough sugar in it, and when it is too soft, there is too much sugar. Therefore, it is very important to use a sugar scale to produce uniformly good results.

The glucose or corn syrup used prevents the ices from graining and also aids in keeping the frozen mixture smooth. Meringue or cream is used to obtain lightness.

For those who never use a sugar scale, some of the following formulas indicate approximate degrees, and very satisfactory results may be obtained by their use. However, anyone who once uses a sugar scale will never do without one thereafter and also will be more than pleased with the results obtained.

Sherbets and water ices are two different articles, though often confused and generally regarded as one and the same thing. Water ices are made from sugar, water, fruit juice or pulp, and different flavorings and are frozen firmly (as an ice cream). They are served as a dessert at the end of a meal, either plain or in various fancy forms. Sherbets are made from ices as a base but with the addition of wines, champagnes, or spirits and are semifrozen. They should only be served in the middle of a dinner, just before the roast.

To make ices of the same consistency and quality day after day, it is absolutely necessary to use a sugar scale, which can be purchased very inexpensively. Again, the Baumé scale is recommended. The proper degrees will vary from 16 to 19°, according to the kind of fruit used, because some fruit juices are heavy and others are thin and sharply acidic. Weighing and measuring of all ingredients used are also essential to achieve quality ices. In all formulas for ices, 1 lb (450 g) of the sugar may be replaced by $1\frac{1}{2}$ lb (675 g) of glucose or corn syrup.

To obtain a smooth and velvety consistency, ices made from strawberries, raspberries, apricots, pears, bananas, and cantaloupe are better with an addition of whipped cream. Those made from lemons, oranges, pineapples, and tangerines are better with an addition of meringue.

The quality of the syrup has a great deal to do with the flavor of an ice. Because a syrup that is boiled always gives a slightly cooked taste to the ice, a syrup made without boiling is suggested.

WATER ICES

Apricot Water Ice

YIELD:
7 lb, 14 oz (3 kg, 537 g)

	U.S.	Metric
Granulated sugar [or 1 lb, 12 oz (786 g) of sugar and 6 oz (168 g) melted glucose]	2 !lb	900 g
Water	1¼ qt	1 liter, 1.25 dl
Lemon	1	1
Apricot pulp	3 lb, 9 oz	1 kg, 406 g
Cream, 40 percent	2 oz	0.5 dl
Red food coloring	As needed	

1. Dissolve the sugar in the water. Add the juice of the lemon, and the apricot pulp, and strain.
2. Bring the syrup to 17° on the Baumé scale. If it is above 17°, add more water, and if below, add more sugar.
3. When regulated to exactly 17°, freeze.
4. Whip the cream with a little sugar. When the mixture is nearly frozen, add the whipped cream, and finish freezing.

NOTE: If the cream is not sweetened, it will form small icy lumps and will not mix properly. If canned apricots are used, use the juice and the fruit, and reduce the sugar to 8 oz (225 g).

Black Currant Water Ice

YIELD:
7 lb, 11 oz (3 kg, 453 g)

	U.S.	Metric
Granulated sugar	2 lb	900 g
Water	1½ qt	1 liter, 3.5 dl
Lemon	½	½
Black currant juice	1½ qt	1 liter, 1.25 dl
Cream, 40 percent	2 oz	0.5 dl

1. Dissolve the sugar in the water. Add the juice of the lemon and the currant juice, and strain.

2. Bring the syrup to 16° on the Baumé scale. If it is above 16°, add more water, and if below, add more sugar.
3. When regulated to exactly 16°, freeze.
4. Whip the cream with a little sugar. When the mixture is nearly frozen, add the whipped cream, and finish freezing.

Lemon Water Ice

YIELD:
8 lb, 11 oz (3 kg, 906 g)

	U.S.	Metric
Granulated sugar	3 lb	1 kg, 350 g
Water	2¼ qt	2 liters, 0.2 dl
Lemons	1 lb, 2 oz	506 g
Egg whites	1 oz	30 g

1. Dissolve the sugar in the water, and add the grated rind of one-third of the lemons and all the lemon juice. Let stand for ½ hour so that the sugar becomes thoroughly dissolved and the lemon flavor infused in the syrup.
2. Strain the syrup, regulate to 19° on the Baumé scale, and freeze.
3. Whip the egg whites with a little sugar to make a meringue.
4. When nearly frozen, add the meringue to the mixture, and finish freezing.

Melon Water Ice

YIELD:
10 lb, 2¾ oz (4 kg, 571 g)

	U.S.	Metric
Granulated sugar	3 lb	1 kg, 350 g
Water	2¼ qt	2 liters, 0.2 dl
Lemons	2 oz	56 g
Oranges	¼ oz	7 g
Melon, grated	12 lb, 8 oz	1 kg, 124 g
Egg whites	½ oz	14 g

1. Dissolve the sugar in the water. Add the grated rind and juice of the lemons and oranges and the grated melon.
2. Strain the syrup, regulate to 18° on the Baumé scale, and freeze.
3. Make a meringue by beating the egg whites with a little sugar.
4. When nearly frozen, add the meringue to the mixture, and finish freezing.

NOTE: Any firm flesh melon is suitable for this formula. Try cantaloupe or honeydew.

Orange Water Ice

YIELD:
9 lb, 12 oz (4 kg, 386 g)

	U.S.	Metric
Granulated sugar	3½ lb	1 kg, 574 g
Water	2½ qt	2 liters, 2.5 dl
Oranges	8	8
Lemons	2	2
Egg whites	1 oz	28 g
Orange food coloring	As needed	

1. Dissolve the sugar in the water. Add the grated rind of 3 oranges and 1 lemon and the juice of all the fruit.
2. Strain the syrup, regulate to 19° on the Baumé scale, and freeze.
3. Whip the egg whites with a little sugar to make a meringue.
4. When nearly frozen, add the meringue to the mixture, and finish freezing.

Peach Water Ice

YIELD:
15 lb, 3 oz (6 kg, 826 g)

	U.S.	Metric
Granulated sugar	3 lb, 12 oz	1 kg, 686 g
Water	2½ qt	2 liters, 2.5 dl
Lemon	½	½
Peach pulp	6 lb, 4 oz	2 kg, 812 g
Cream, 40 percent	2 oz	0.5 dl
Red food coloring	As needed	

1. Dissolve the sugar in the water. Add the juice of the lemon and the peach pulp, and strain.
2. Bring the syrup to 17° on the Baumé scale. If it is above 17°, add more water, and if below, add more sugar.
3. When regulated to exactly 17°, freeze.
4. Whip the cream with a little sugar. When the mixture is nearly frozen, add the whipped cream, and finish freezing.

Pear Water Ice

YIELD:
6 lb, 3 oz (2 kg, 778 g)

	U.S.	Metric
Granulated sugar	1$\frac{1}{2}$ lb	675 g
Water	1 qt	9 dl
Lemons	1 oz	28 g
Pear pulp	2 lb, 8 oz	1 kg, 125 g
Cream, 40 percent	2 oz	0.5 dl

1. Dissolve the sugar in the water. Add the juice of the lemons and the pear pulp, and strain.
2. Bring the syrup to 16° on the Baumé scale. If it is above 16°, add more water, and if below, add more sugar.
3. When regulated to exactly 16°, freeze.
4. Whip the cream with a little sugar. When the mixture is nearly frozen, add the whipped cream, and finish freezing.

Pineapple Water Ice

YIELD:
10 lb, 3 oz (4 kg, 578 g)

	U.S.	Metric
Water	2$\frac{1}{4}$ qt	2 liters, 0.25 dl
Granulated sugar	3 lb	1 kg, 350 g
Lemon	1	
Orange	$\frac{1}{4}$	
Pineapple, grated	2 lb, 8 oz	1 kg, 125 g
Egg whites	$\frac{1}{2}$ oz	15 g

1. Dissolve the sugar in the water. Add the grated rind and juice of the lemon and orange and the grated pineapple.
2. Strain the syrup, regulate to 18° on the Baumé scale, and freeze.
3. Whip the egg whites with a little sugar to make a meringue.
4. When nearly frozen, add the meringue to the mixture, and finish freezing.

Raspberry Water Ice

YIELD:
15 lb, 6 oz (6 kg, 913 g)

	U.S.	Metric
Granulated sugar	3 lb, 12 oz	1 kg, 686 g
Water	2½ qt	2 liters, 2.5 dl
Lemons	2	2
Raspberry pulp	6 lb, 4 oz	2 kg, 815 g
Cream, 40 percent	2 oz	0.5 dl

1. Dissolve the sugar in the water. Add the juice of the lemons and the raspberry pulp, and strain.
2. Bring the syrup to 17° on the Baumé scale. If it is above 17°, add more water, and if below, add more sugar.
3. When regulated to exactly 17°, freeze.
4. Whip the cream with a little sugar. When the mixture is nearly frozen, add the whipped cream, and finish freezing.

Strawberry Water Ice

YIELD:
15 lb, 11 oz (7 kg, 55 g)

	U.S.	Metric
Granulated sugar	4 lb	1 kg, 800 g
Water	2½ qt	2 liters, 2.5 dl
Strawberry pulp	6 lb, 4 oz	2 kg, 815 g
Raspberry pulp	5 oz	140 g
Cream, 40 percent	2 oz	0.5 dl
Red food coloring	As needed	

1. Dissolve the sugar in the water. Add the strawberry and raspberry pulp, and strain.
2. Bring the syrup to 18° on the Baumé scale. If it is above 18°, add more water, and if below, add more sugar.
3. When regulated to exactly 18°, freeze.
4. Whip the cream with a little sugar. When the mixture is nearly frozen, add the whipped cream, and finish freezing.

Tangerine Water Ice

YIELD:
9 lb, 6 oz (4 kg, 220 g)

	U.S.	Metric
Granulated sugar	3 lb, 2 oz	1 kg, 406 g
Water	2¼ qt	2 liters, 0.25 dl
Tangerines	12	
Lemons	1½	
Egg whites	1 oz	30 g
Orange food coloring	As needed	

1. Add to the dissolved sugar and water the grated rind of 6 tangerines and 1 lemon and the juice of all the fruit.
2. Bring to 18° on the Baumé scale.
3. When regulated to exactly 18°, freeze.
4. Whip the cream with a little sugar. When the mixture is nearly frozen, add the whipped cream, and finish freezing.

SHERBETS

■ Champagne Sherbet

Champagne Sherbet is prepared by mixing together 1 qt (9 dl) of frozen lemon ice and ½ pt (2.25 dl) of champagne. When well mixed, return to the freezer and let stand for awhile, until of proper consistency. Serve in sherbet glasses, with a little *vin de champagne* poured over the top. If desired, orange ice may be used instead of the lemon ice.

■ Sherbet au Kirsch

Sherbet with kirsch is prepared by mixing together 1 qt (9 dl) of frozen lemon ice, 4 oz (1.1 dl) of wine (chablis is preferred), and 4 oz (1.1 dl) of kirsch liqueur. Treat the same as Champagne Sherbet. Before serving, pour a little kirsch over the top of each sherbet.

NOTE: Brandy, Kummel, Chartreuse, Benedictine, or other liqueurs are used in the same proportions as for Kirsch Sherbet.

■ Maraschino Sherbet

Maraschino Sherbet is prepared by mixing 1 qt (9 dl) of lemon ice with 4 oz (1.1 dl) of white wine and 4 oz (1.1 dl) of maraschino liqueur. Treat the same as Champagne Sherbet, and serve with a little maraschino liqueur poured over each sherbet.

■ Marquise au Champagne Sherbet

Marquise au Champagne Sherbet is prepared by mixing 1 pt (4.5 dl) of pineapple ice with 1 pt (4.5 dl) of lemon ice and then adding ½ pt (2.25 dl) of champagne. When well mixed together, return to the freezer and let stand for awhile, until of the proper consistency. Serve in champagne glasses with a little *vin de champagne* poured over the top.

NOTE: Marquise Sherbets of all flavors may be prepared in the same way by using half lemon and half pineapple ice and any wine or liqueur desired.

■ Port Sherbet

Port Sherbet is prepared by mixing 1 qt (9 dl) of frozen orange ice with ½ pt (2.25 dl) of port wine. Treat the same as Champagne Sherbet, and pour a little port wine over each sherbet just before serving.

NOTE: Madeira, Samos, Xeres, Marsala, Frontignan, and other wines are served the same way as port in the Port Sherbet.

■ Rum Sherbet

Rum Sherbet is prepared in the same way and proportions as the Kirsch Sherbet, only rum is used instead of kirsch.

■ Soyer au Champagne

Soyer au Champagne is simply orange ice served in sherbet glasses filled three-quarters with the ice and with plenty of champagne poured over the top.

❦ Chocolate Appareil and Appareils au Pâte à Bombe

Chocolate appareils, or pastes, for ice cream desserts are made by boiling milk, cream, sugar, and bitter chocolate together and then setting aside to cool. When cold, it is used in the preparation of *biscuits glacés*, *soufflés glacés*, mousses, parfaits, etc. It is a very practical and useful mixture, always ready, and very easy to incorporate into any frozen dessert.

Chocolate Appareil

YIELD:
13 lb (5 kg, 850 g)

	U.S.	Metric
Milk	2 qt	1 liter, 8 dl
Heavy cream	2 qt	1 liter, 8 dl
Granulated sugar	2 lb	900 g
Bitter chocolate	3 lb	1 kg, 350 g

1. Bring to a boil the milk, cream, and the sugar.
2. Add the chocolate, and strain. Refrigerate until needed.

APPAREILS AU PÂTE À BOMBE

Appareils au Pâte à Bombe, or pastes for bombes, are bisque pastes made from egg yolks, sugar, and water. They are used in the center of bombes and to make biscuits *glacés*, mousses, etc. There are two methods of preparing this paste. One is by the syrup process, cooking over heat, and is very difficult. It requires experience to prepare the paste correctly and calls for much labor and attention. The second method, which is the better as well as the more practical, is by boiling the sugar. The formulas for both methods follow.

Pâte à Bombe (Syrup Process)

YIELD:
9 lb (4 kg, 50 g)

	U.S.	Metric
Sugar syrup	2 qt	1 liter, 8 dl
Egg yolks	4 lb	1 liter, 8 dl

1. Prepare 2 qt of sugar syrup at 30° on the Baumé scale.
2. Beat the egg yolks with a whip.
3. When the syrup is cold, pour it over the beaten egg yolks, beating constantly so that it becomes well mixed.
4. When well mixed, strain through a fine sieve. Place in a *bain marie* or double boiler, and cook until it is thick and creamy.
5. Remove from heat and place in mixer. Beat at medium speed until cold.
6. When cold, remove from bowl and place in refrigerator until needed. This paste will keep for 1 week or longer.

Pâte à Bombe (Boiled Sugar Process)

YIELD:
10 lb (4 kg, 500 g)

	U.S.	Metric
Granulated sugar	4 lb	1 kg, 800 g
Glucose or corn syrup	1 lb	450 g
Water	1 qt	9 dl
Egg yolks	3 lb	1 kg, 350 g

1. Place sugar, glucose or corn syrup, and water in a pan. Cook to 250°F (121°C).
2. Place egg yolks in mixer and beat at medium speed.
3. When the sugar is ready, pour it slowly over the beaten egg yolks while the machine is running, and beat until cold and of creamy consistency.
4. Remove from bowl, place in a jar, and refrigerate for further use. This paste will keep for 1 week or longer.

🐦 Whipped Cream

A 40% butterfat cream is generally used for whipping and should be kept at a temperature of 40°F (4°C) during the beating process. A 30% butterfat cream, when fully rendered viscous by age, also will whip perfectly if kept at a temperature of 40°F (4°C).

Many creams containing the same percentage of butterfat are not of the same consistency or thickness, and this is due to the difference in viscosity or resistance of the fluid to a portion of its particles which is brought about by age. The older a cream becomes, the more thoroughly viscous, or thickened, it will be. Thick cream always whips better than thin cream, and for this reason, a cream that has aged 48 hours will whip better than a fresh cream, though both contain the same percentage of butterfat. When cream is to be used for whipping or for freezing in ice cream, it should be allowed to age for 2 or 3 days before using. Cream should always be refrigerated.

When cream is whipped to be mixed with other mixtures, it should never be whipped until firm, since when mixed with other mixtures it often becomes overwhipped during the mixing and in this way loses much of its richness, smoothness, and flavor. Cream whipped for decorating or serving should be sweetened in the proportion of 4 oz (112 g) of 4× sugar to a quart (9 dl) of cream.

It is better to whip cream by machine than by hand. When cream is whipped by a machine running at medium speed, the yield will be 25% greater than if the same amount and quality of cream were whipped by hand. Cream should be whipped by a continuously even and steady motion, and the machine is able to do this perfectly, while it is practically impossible by hand. The changing of hands or motion with the whip breaks down a part of the air cells formed during the beating process and retards the whipping. The yield is consequently not as great as when whipped by machine.

🐦 Frozen Sweets

Frozen sweets are ice cream deserts made from ice cream, ices, cake, fruits, etc. and are served decorated with whipped cream or with a separate sauce. The less elaborate ones are well adapted for serving in tea rooms, ice cream parlors, etc., as well as in hotels and restaurants.

Many frozen sweets are made in ice cream molds. When the dessert is frozen, remove it from the mold by dipping first into lukewarm water for a moment. Then turn over onto a platter with a folded napkin underneath, or serve in individual portions. Always accompany with an appropriate sauce.

■ Caracas Ice Cream

Fill a brick mold half full with chocolate ice cream, then fill the rest of the mold with vanilla ice cream, and freeze. Serve with a hot or cold chocolate sauce.

■ Charlotte Glacé Panache

Trim enough lady fingers to line the sides of individual Charlotte molds. Fill the molds with vanilla and strawberry ice creams in equal portions, freeze, and then turn out into glass dishes. Decorate with whipped cream and serve. This Charlotte may be made with any desired flavors of ice creams and also may be frozen and served in large forms (from 4 to 12 covers).

■ Harlequin Ice Cream

Fill a brick mold with layers of vanilla ice cream, raspberry ice, pistachio ice cream, and orange ice, and freeze. When frozen, remove from the mold and cut into slices. Place a spoonful of apricot sauce or marmalade in glass dishes, and place over this a slice of the ice cream. Decorate with whipped cream, and serve.

Macaroon Bisque

YIELD:
6 lb, 12 oz (3 kg, 37 g)

	U.S.	Metric
Confectioner's sugar	1 lb, 4 oz	562 g
Cream, 40 percent	2½ lb	1 liter, 1.25 dl
Milk	2½ lb	1 liter, 1.25 dl
Macaroons, finely crushed	8 oz	225 g
Rum flavoring	To taste	

1. Mix all ingredients well together, and then let stand for 1 hour, stirring occasionally. Then freeze the same as ice cream.
2. When frozen, put into brick form, and place in a hardening room for 12 hours.
3. Remove from the molds, cut each into eight portions, and serve in glass dishes with a rum-flavored mousseline sauce. For large parties, serve the brick on a platter with a folded napkin underneath and the sauce in a separate sauce bowl.

■ Marcelline Ice Cream

Fill a brick mold half full with banana ice cream, place on top a layer of chopped walnuts, then fill the mold with vanilla ice cream, and freeze. Serve with maple syrup on the side, or cut into slices and serve in glass dishes with a spoonful of syrup on top.

■ Melon Glacé en Surprise

Select a ripe cantaloupe and cut a piece from the top (stalk end). With a spoon, scoop out the interior, and fill with melon ice mixed with a macédoine of fruit flavored with kirsch. Replace the top piece, and decorate with a stalk and leaf made from sugar. Place a round mold or form of vanilla ice cream on a platter with a folded napkin underneath, and position the melon on top.

■ Neapolitan Brick Ice Cream

Fill brick molds with strawberry, vanilla, and chocolate ice creams, and freeze. Serve with strawberry sauce.

Nesselrode Ice Cream

YIELD:
7 lb, 3 oz (3 kg, 233 g)

	U.S.	Metric
Confectioner's sugar	1 lb, 4 oz	562 g
Cream, 40 percent	1 qt	9 dl
Milk	1 qt	9 dl
Tutti-Frutti mixture		
(see Tutti-Frutti Ice Cream)	5 oz	140 g
Chestnuts, broken	8 oz	225 g
4× sugar	2 oz	56 g
Heavy cream, whipped	1 pt	450 g

1. Mix well together the confectioner's sugar, cream, milk, and tutti-frutti mixture, and freeze.
2. When half frozen, add the chestnuts, 4× sugar, and whipped cream. Finish freezing.
3. When frozen, serve loose or in brick form.

■ Oyster Bay Ice Cream

Mix vanilla ice cream with broken chestnuts, crushed macaroons, and maraschino cherries. Flavor with brandy, and freeze in brick molds. Serve with coffee mousseline sauce.

■ Pineapple Glacé à la Reine

Select a large ripe pineapple, and cut off the top portion. Carefully scoop out the whole of the interior, and fill the shell with a pineapple ice. When filled, replace the top. Place a round mold or form of vanilla ice cream which has been frozen very hard on a platter with a folded napkin underneath, and position the pineapple on top.

■ Snowball Ice Cream

Roll a portion of vanilla ice cream in shredded coconut, dust all over with 4× sugar, and serve in paper cups.

■ Spoom à la Romaine

Fill a brick mold half full with orange water ice, then fill the rest of the way with macaroon bisque, and freeze. Serve with orange marmalade, or cut into slices and serve in glass dishes with a spoonful of orange marmalade on top of each.

Tutti-Frutti Ice Cream

YIELD:
7 lb, 11¹/₂ oz (3 kg, 468 g)

	U.S.	Metric
Confectioner's sugar	1 lb, 4 oz	562 g
Cream, 20 percent	2¹/₂ qt	2 liters, 2.5 dl
Rum, or rum flavor	2 oz	56 g
Tutti-Frutti mixture (directions follow)	1 lb, 5¹/₂ oz	600 g

1. Combine all ingredients, mix well, and freeze.
2. When frozen, mold in brick forms or serve loose.

Tutti-Frutti Mixture

YIELD:
7 lb, 12 oz (3 kg, 487 g)

	U.S.	Metric
Candied fruits, assorted	3 lb	1 kg, 350 g
Candied cherries	1 lb	450 g
Preserved pineapple	1 lb	450 g
Sugar syrup	1 lb, 8 oz	675 g
Rum, or rum flavoring	4 oz	112 g
Sultana raisins	1 lb	450 g

1. Chop the fruits into fine pieces.
2. Make sugar syrup of 30° on the Baumé sugar scale.
3. Mix the fruit with the syrup, rum, and raisins. Place in jar for further use.

🐦 Frozen Puddings

Frozen puddings are traditional sweets prepared with a mixture of ice cream, preserved fruit, and nuts. The result is a rich dessert that should be served in small portions and garnished with an appropriate sauce and whipped cream.

■ Frozen Pudding 1

To every quart of vanilla ice cream used, add $\frac{1}{2}$ lb (225 g) of tutti-frutti mixture and $\frac{1}{2}$ lb (225 g) of blanched, chopped almonds. Fill dariole molds, pudding molds, or pudding cups with the mixture, place in the freezer, and freeze firm. When frozen, remove from the molds, place in deep dishes, decorate with whipped cream, and serve.

Frozen Pudding 2

YIELD:
6 lb, 15 oz (3 kg, 120 g)

	U.S.	Metric
Confectioner's sugar	1 lb, 4 oz	562 g
Cream, 20 percent	1½ qt	1 liter, 3.5 dl
Milk	1 qt	9 dl
Tutti-Frutti mixture	5 oz	140 g
Walnuts, finely chopped	2 oz	56 g
Macaroons, finely chopped	2 oz	56 g
Pecans, chopped	2 oz	56 g

1. Combine all ingredients, mix well, and freeze.
2. When frozen, mold in pudding molds, and serve with rum-flavored mousseline sauce.

■ Marquisette Pudding

To every quart (9 dl) of chocolate ice cream used, add 1 lb (450 g) of preserved cherries, ½ lb (225 g) of chopped walnut meats, and 1 pt (4.5 dl) of whipped cream sweetened with ½ lb (225 g) of sugar. Freeze the same as Nesslerode Pudding, and serve with hot chocolate sauce on the side.

■ Tutti-Frutti Pudding

To every 2 qt (1 liter, 8 dl) of vanilla ice cream used, add 1 pt (4.5 dl) of tutti-frutti mixture and 1 pt (4.5 dl) of sweetened whipped cream, and freeze the same as Nesslerode Pudding. Serve with an apricot sauce flavored with kirsch.

🍒 Bombes

Bombes are one of the oldest and best-known frozen desserts served in hotels and by catering places. They are made in cylindrical forms and are usually coated with ice cream or ices of different flavors, while the center is filled with a mousse mixture, fruits, jams, etc. When frozen, the bombe is removed from the form, placed on a platter with a folded napkin underneath, and then decorated with whipped cream, various sauces, fruits, nuts, etc.

When bombe molds are masked with ice cream, the molds should be placed on ice beforehand so that they become thoroughly chilled. Better still, place them standing up in fine ice—this method makes it much easier to mask the mold and keeps the ice cream from sinking to the bottom of the mold while masking.

When a bombe is made from two or more kinds of ice cream, the mold should be masked very evenly with a firm ice cream not more than ½ inch (2 cm) thick, then the center should be filled with a mousse or other flavors of ice cream, and then it should be frozen. When frozen, the bombe is removed from the mold by dipping into lukewarm water for a moment and then given a sharp jerk with the hand, and the bombe will slide out.

The general directions for making a bombe are to mask the mold with about ½ inch (2 cm) of ice cream, fill the center, place a cover on top, and freeze. When frozen, remove from the mold, garnish, and decorate. The following are some classic ideas for bombes:

Name	Mask	Center	Garnish
Alhambra	Vanilla ice cream	Strawberry mousse	Chopped roasted almonds, 4× sugar
Alsacienne	Pistachio ice cream	Chocolate mousse	Chocolate leaves
Andalouse	Coffee ice cream	Vanilla mouse mixed with sliced bananas and Malaga grapes saturated with kirsch	Malagra grapes, whipped cream
Carmen	Vanilla ice cream	Raspberry mousse	Raspberries
Comtesse		Alternate layers of vanilla mousse and red currant jelly	Walnuts, finely chopped
Comtesse-Marie	Strawberry ice cream	Vanilla mousse mixed with previously soaked macaroons	Whipped cream
Créole		Banana mousse mixed with chopped walnuts	Mousseline
Cyrano	Banana ice cream	Strawberry mousse	Whipped cream
Duchesse	Orange ice	Alternate layers of vanilla mousse and red currant jelly	Sliced oranges
Elysée	Orange ice	Strawberry mousse mixed with red currant jelly	Whipped cream
Espagnole	Strawberry ice cream	Banana mousse mixed with crushed nougat and a few candied cherries	Chocolate sauce
Fédora	Apricot ice	Alternate layers of peach mousse and apricot jam	Roasted hazelnuts, finely chopped
Fleurettes	Pineapple ice	Strawberry mousse mixed with sliced stewed peaches	Melba sauce (on the side)
Gloria Swanson	Pistachio and strawberry ice cream	Pear mousse mixed with sliced stewed pears	Red currant sauce (on the side)
Grand-Duc		Praline mousse flavored with rum	Cocoa powder
Grand-Duchesse	Vanilla ice cream	Alternate layers of vanilla mousse and sliced stewed pears	Whipped cream

Name	Mask	Center	Garnish
Havanaise	Coffee ice cream	Rum-flavored mousse	Whipped cream, chocolate-coated coffee beans
Hélène		Vanilla mousse	Hot chocolate sauce
Jeanette		Vanilla mousse; when nearly frozen scoop out some of the soft part of the mousse from center, and fill with cocoa powder; cover with vanilla ice cream and finish freezing	Cocoa powder
Livadia	Pineapple ice	Banana mousse flavored with chartreuse	Whipped cream, sliced bananas
Lucette	Raspberry ice	Strawberry mousse	Whipped cream, strawberries
Manon	Praline ice cream	Alternate layers of kirsch-flavored mousse and apricot jam	Whipped cream, apricot and kirsch-flavored sauce (on the side)
Marie-Louise	Strawberry ice cream	Alternate layers of banana mousse and red currant jelly	Whipped cream, Melba sauce (on the side)
Mary Pickford	Strawberry ice cream	Banana mousse mixed with candied fruit flavored with kummel	Whipped cream, apricot sauce (on the side)
Mireille	Coffee ice cream	Praline mousse	Whipped cream and macaroons
Nélusko	Chocolate ice cream	Rum-flavored praline mousse	Chocolate leaves, whipped cream
Ninon	Banana ice cream	Chocolate mousse	Candied violets, whipped cream
Olga	Strawberry ice cream	Praline mousse	Powdered roasted almonds
Pacifique	Pistachio ice cream	Praline mousse	Whipped cream
Petit Duc	Coffee ice cream	Alternate layers of vanilla mousse and red currant jelly	
Richelieu	Raspberry ice	Alternate layers of strawberry mousse and red currant jelly	Whipped cream
Santiago	Banana ice cream	Coffee mousse	Sliced bananas, whipped cream, rum-flavored custard sauce (on the side)
Sapho	Chocolate ice cream	Rum-flavored mousse mixed with candied fruits	Hot mousseline sauce (on the side)
Sarah Bernhardt	Strawberry ice cream	Mousse marron	Chestnuts, whipped cream
Succès	Orange ice	Chestnut mousse	Sliced oranges and chestnuts
Victoria	Apricot ice	Alternate layers of vanilla mousse and strawberry jam	Whipped cream and apricot halves

SPUMONI ICE CREAM

Spumoni Ice Cream is made in bombe-shaped molds that are a little shorter and wider than the usual bombe mold. The mold is first masked with a layer of vanilla ice cream, and then with a coating of chocolate ice cream. The center is filled with a tutti-frutti ice cream or with vanilla mousse mixed with an assortment of chopped candied fruits. It is then placed in a hardening room, and when firm, it is unmolded and served the same as bombes.

🐦 Coupes (Sundaes)

Coupes are made from ice creams, ices, fruits, spirits, whipped cream, and sauces of various kinds. The spirits may be replaced by syrups flavored with extracts. They are usually served in tall champagne glasses and are classed as a luxury among desserts. High prices are charged for them, and for this reason, special care should be taken to see that they are made right. They are very simple and easily made, however, and the less elaborate ones are appropriate for serving in tea rooms and ice cream parlors.

The basic method for preparing a coupe is as follows:
1. Fill a glass one-half to three-quarters full with a base item (usually fruit).
2. Cover with a little liquid, jelly, or sauce for color and flavor.
3. Add a layer of ice cream, ice, and/or fruit.
4. Decorate with whipped cream and/or garnish with fruit, sprinkles, or a sauce.

Although the number and combination of items assembled to create a coupe are guided by the preference of the guest, some classic ideas for coupes are suggested on pages 268–269.

🐦 Mousses (Glacés)

Mousses are frozen desserts of different flavors, usually frozen in brick form and cut into slices or served in large services uncut. They are decorated with whipped cream or fruits or served with a sauce. When served in individual portions, each brick is cut into eight pieces, and each slice is placed in a glass dish and decorated. The mousse mixture is used extensively in the preparation of bombes.

Name	Base	Layers	Garnishes
Antigny	¾-full peaches, fresh or canned	Peach brandy, strawberry ice cream	Whipped cream through star tube, cream rosette
Aremberg	¾-full pears, fresh, very ripe, or stewed	Kirsch, pineapple ice	Whipped cream through star tube, pear slice
Beau-Rivage	½-full strawberry Bavarian cream	To ¾ full raspberry ice, Port wine, banana ice cream	Banana slices, Port wine
Coeur-de-Jeannette	½-full vanilla ice cream	Red currant jelly, strawberry ice cream	Melba sauce, macaroons
Comtesse	½-full sliced peaches	1 Tbsp Melba sauce, vanilla ice cream, pistachio ice cream	Sliced peaches
Comtesse-Marie	½-full sliced peaches	To ¾-full orange ice, curaçao, peach ice cream	Sliced peaches
Cyrano	½-full diced pineapple	Raspberry ice, vanilla ice cream	Candied violet
Dijonnaise	½-full sliced bananas	Black currant ice, strawberry ice cream	Sliced bananas, Benedictine
Espérance	¾-full sliced pears and bananas	Pistachio ice cream	Whipped cream
Eve	½-full sliced, stewed apples	Lemon ice, pistachio ice cream	Cherry
Havanaise	½-full sliced bananas	Melba sauce	Kirsch-flavored mousseline sauce
Hilda	½-full thinly sliced bananas and pineapple	Pineapple ice, banana ice cream	Whipped cream
Manon	½-full thinly sliced bananas	Pineapple ice, banana ice cream	Melba sauce flavored with Chartreuse, broken candied violets
Marie-Louise	½-full fresh strawberries sprinkled with sugar and curaçao	Strawberry ice cream	Whipped cream, large strawberry
Medicis	½-full macedoine of fruit: sliced bananas, diced apples, pears, and pineapple	Kirsch, apricot ice, lemon ice, apricot marmalade	Chopped pistachios
Merveilleux	½-full grated chocolate	Vanilla ice cream, 4 chocolate leaves	Whipped cream between the leaves, through star tube, cream rosette
Mireille	½-full sliced peaches	Peach brandy, banana ice cream, vanilla ice cream	Sliced peaches
Mona Lisa	¾-full sliced pears and bananas	Melba sauce, banana ice cream	Whipped cream, candied violet
Monte Carlo	¾-full sliced pineapples and oranges	Kirsch orange ice, strawberry ice cream	Orange slices
Montmorency	½-full fresh cherries	Kirsch and Melba sauces (mixed together), vanilla ice cream, raspberry ice	Cherries, whipped cream
Orientale	¾-full diced figs, dates, and pineapple	Strawberry ice cream, Kummel	Whipped cream, dates, cover with veil of spun sugar

Name	Base	Layers	Garnishes
St. Jacques	¾-full fruit macedoine: sliced oranges and bananas and diced apples and pineapples	Lemon ice, strawberry ice cream	Sliced oranges
St. Martin	½-full fruit macedoine: sliced bananas, almonds, and Benedictine	Raspberry ice, lemon ice	Large strawberry
Sarah Bernhardt	½-full fruit macedoine: sliced bananas and oranges, diced pears, apples and pineapple	Banana ice cream, strawberry ice cream	Whole marron glacé, 2 cream rosettes
Solange	½-full fresh strawberries sprinkled with confectioner's sugar	Port wine, vanilla ice cream, gourmet sauce	Candied violet
Thaïs	¾-full fruit macedoine: sliced bananas and oranges, and diced pears, apples, and pineapple, flavored with kirsch	Lemon ice	Whipped cream
Valencia	¾-full sliced oranges	Banana ice cream, orange ice, curaçao	Sliced oranges
Voltaire	½-full sliced pears, sprinkled with confectioner's sugar	Kirsch, orange ice, strawberry ice cream	Sliced pears
Yvette	¾-full fruit macedoine: sliced bananas and oranges, diced pears, apples, and pineapple, flavored with Crème Yvette	Lemon ice, strawberry ice cream	Candied violets, Crème Yvette

Banana Mousse

YIELD:
4 lb, 2 oz (1 kg, 855 g)

	U.S.	Metric
Banana pulp	1 lb	450 g
Pâte à bombe	10 oz	280 g
Confectioner's sugar	½ lb	225 g
Cream, 40 percent, whipped firm	1 qt	9 dl
Yellow food coloring	As needed	

1. Select sufficient thoroughly ripe bananas to make 1 lb (450 g) of banana pulp. Pass through a sieve, and combine with remaining ingredients.
2. Mix well together, fill into brick molds, and freeze.
3. When frozen, remove from the mold by first dipping it into lukewarm water for a moment, and then turn over onto a platter.
4. Decorate the top with sliced bananas and whipped cream.

Chocolate Mousse

YIELD:
4 lb (1 kg, 800 g)

	U.S.	Metric
Chocolate paste (appareil)	1 pt	675 g
Cream, 40 percent, whipped firm	1 qt	9 dl
Confectioner's sugar	8 oz	225 g

1. Mix all ingredients well together; then fill into brick molds and freeze.
2. When frozen, remove from the mold and place on a platter.
3. Decorate with whipped cream.

■ Mousse Hélène

Prepare the same as Vanilla Mousse, and serve with a hot chocolate sauce on the side.

■ Mousse Hericart

Prepare the same as Strawberry Mousse, and serve with a Melba sauce.

Mousse Marron

YIELD:
3 lb, 8 oz (1 kg, 573 g)

	U.S.	Metric
Pâte à bombe	10 oz	280 g
Chestnut syrup	6 oz	168 g
Cream, 40 percent, whipped firm	1 qt	9 dl
Chestnuts, broken	½ lb	225 g

1. Mix all ingredients together. Fill into brick molds, and freeze.
2. When frozen, remove from mold by first dipping it into lukewarm water for a moment, and then turn over onto a platter. Decorate the top with chestnut halves and whipped cream.

Mousse Mikado

YIELD:
3 lb, 4 oz (1 kg, 460 g)

	U.S.	Metric
Chocolate paste (appareil)	12 oz	336 g
Cream, 40 percent, whipped firm	1 qt	9 dl
Chestnuts, broken	8 oz	225 g

1. Mix all ingredients together. Fill into brick molds, and freeze.
2. When frozen, remove from mold by first dipping it into lukewarm water for a moment. Then turn over onto a platter, and serve with a hot chocolate sauce on the side.

■ Mousse Mon Désir

Prepare the same as Strawberry Mousse, but serve with a sauce composed of crushed strawberries, port wine, and whipped cream mixed together.

Mousse Montélimar

YIELD:
7 lb, 9 oz (3 kg, 402 g)

	U.S.	Metric
Chocolate paste (appareil)	1 pt	675 g
Chocolate ice cream	5 oz	140 g
Pâte à bombe	8 oz	225 g
Maraschino cherries	8 oz	225 g
Cream, 40 percent, whipped firm	2 qt	1 liter, 8 dl
Almonds	8 oz	225 g
Walnuts, broken	4 oz	112 g

1. Soak whole almonds in liqueur or water until soft and add to other ingredients. Mix well together; then fill into brick molds, and freeze.
2. When frozen, remove from the mold by first dipping it into lukewarm water for a moment, and then turn over onto a platter. Decorate with whipped cream.

Mousse Montreuil

YIELD:
3 lb, 12 oz (1 kg, 687 g)

	U.S.	Metric
Peach pulp	1 lb, 4 oz	562 g
4× sugar	½ lb	225 g
Cream, 40 percent, whipped firm	1 qt	9 dl
Peach brandy	To taste	

1. Mix fruit, sugar, and whipped cream together. Add a few sliced peaches soaked in peach brandy and a little coloring. Fill into brick molds, and freeze.
2. When frozen, remove from mold by dipping it into lukewarm water for a moment, and then turn over onto a platter. Decorate the top with sliced peaches and whipped cream.

■ Peach Mousse

Prepare the same as Mousse Montreuil but without the sliced peaches.

Praline Mousse

YIELD:
5 lb, 10 oz (2 kg, 531 g)

	U.S.	Metric
Pâte à bombe	8 oz	225 g
Praline	1 lb	450 g
Cream, 40 percent, whipped firm	2 qt	1 liter, 8 dl
4× sugar	2 oz	56 g

1. Mix the pâte à bombe and praline together until very smooth.
2. Add cream and sugar to praline mixture.
3. Fill into brick molds, and freeze.
4. When frozen, remove from the mold by dipping into lukewarm water for a moment. Turn over onto a platter, and decorate the top with whipped cream and roasted hazelnuts.

Raspberry Mousse

YIELD:
3 lb, 15 oz (1 lb, 771 g)

	U.S.	Metric
Raspberries	1 lb, 7oz	646 g
Confectioner's sugar	1/2 lb	225 g
Cream, 40 percent, whipped firm	1 qt	9 dl
Port wine	To taste	
Red food coloring	As needed	

1. Press 1 lb (450 g) of the raspberries through a sieve, and chop the rest. Mix together with the sugar and whipped cream, flavor with wine, and add coloring.
2. Fill into brick molds, and freeze.
3. When frozen, remove from mold by first dipping it into lukewarm water for a moment. Turn over onto a platter, and decorate the top with whipped cream and fresh raspberries.

■ Strawberry Mousse

Prepare the same as Raspberry Mousse, only use strawberries instead of raspberries and curaçao instead of port wine.

Vanilla Mousse

YIELD:
3 lb (1 kg, 350 g)

	U.S.	Metric
Cream, 40 percent, whipped firm	1 qt	9 dl
Pâte à bombe	8 oz	225 g
4× sugar	8 oz	225 g
Vanilla extract	To taste	

1. Mix all ingredients together. Fill into brick molds, and freeze.
2. When frozen, remove from the mold by first dipping into lukewarm water for a moment. Turn over onto a platter, and decorate the top and sides with whipped cream.

NOTE: Any spirit flavor or liqueur may be used instead of the vanilla extract, if desired.

❦ Biscuits Glacés

Biscuits glacés are frozen desserts of various forms and colors that are frozen in paper cups or cases and served in the same cups. When served at large parties or services of eight covers or more, they are frozen in brick forms, then removed from the forms, and placed in paper boxes. The top of the *glacé* is then decorated to correspond with its flavor or in harmony with the decorations for the occasion. Pulled sugar flowers make an appropriate and attractive decoration for *biscuits glacés*. *Biscuit Glacé au Fraise* is only one example of the elegant dessert.

Biscuit Glacé au Fraise

YIELD:
3 lb, 12 oz (1 kg, 685 g)

	U.S.	Metric
Strawberries, crushed	14 oz	392 g
Pâte à bombe	8 oz	225 g
Cream, 40 percent, whipped firm	1 qt	9 dl
4× sugar	6 oz	168 g

1. Mix all ingredients together, and when well mixed, fill into biscuit cases or cups.
2. Add a little more whipped cream to the mixture. Decorate the top with whipped cream through a star tube, and freeze.
3. When frozen, decorate with a large ripe strawberry.

❦ Soufflés Glacés

Soufflés glacés are very attractive desserts that are simple to make. When served in individual forms, double soufflé cases, consisting of a plain case that fits inside a fancy one, should be used. Place paper bands around the plain cases, about 1 inch (2.5 cm) higher than the case itself, and secure with rubber bands. Fill to the top of the paper bands with the soufflé mixture, and place in the freezer. When frozen, remove the paper bands, mark the tops with a knife in squares or in a diamond pattern, place inside of the fancy cases, and serve on dessert plates with paper doilies underneath. The soufflé will then have the appearance of a high soufflé which has risen above the form or mold. For larger services, use a soufflé dish, and butter the inside along the top. Then line with a paper band about 2½ inches (6 cm) wide so that 1½ inches (4 cm) extend above the soufflé dish. Fill the dish with the soufflé mixture to the top of the paper rim, and place in the freezer. When frozen, dip the dish into hot water just long enough to remove the paper band, mark the top with a knife, and serve on a platter. When made in this way, these soufflés have the appearance of hot soufflés.

Chocolate Soufflé Glacé

YIELD:
3 lb, 8¹/₂ oz (1 kg, 580 g)

	U.S.	Metric
Cream, 40 percent	1 qt	9 dl
4× sugar	4 oz	112 g
Chocolate ice cream	8 oz	225 g
Chocolate paste (appareil)	12 oz	336 g
Vanilla extract	¹/₄ oz	7 g

1. Whip the cream with the sugar until firm.
2. Mix together the chocolate ice cream, chocolate paste, whipped cream, and vanilla.
3. Fill into prepared soufflé cases and freeze.
4. When frozen, prepare according to general instructions. Dust the tops with cocoa powder.

Soufflé Glacé Hericart

YIELD:
3 lb, 4 oz (1 kg, 460 g)

	U.S.	Metric
Strawberry ice cream	5 oz	140 g
Strawberries, crushed	9 oz	252 g
4× sugar	6 oz	168 g
Cream, 40 percent, whipped firm	1 qt	9 dl
Curaçao	To taste	

1. Mix all ingredients together. Fill into prepared soufflé cases, and freeze.
2. When frozen, prepare according to general instructions. Decorate the top with strawberries.

Soufflé Glacé Montreuil

YIELD:
4 lb, 7 oz (1 kg, 995 g)

	U.S.	Metric
Peach ice cream	5 oz	140 g
Peach pulp	1 lb, 4 oz	562 g
4× sugar	½ lb	225 g
Peaches, crushed	2	168 g
Cream, 40 percent, whipped firm	1 qt	9 dl
Peach brandy	To taste	

1. Mix all ingredients together. Fill prepared soufflé cases with the mixture, and freeze.
2. When frozen, prepare according to general instructions. Decorate the top with sliced peaches.

Soufflé Glacé Praline

YIELD:
3 lb, 3 oz (1 kg, 433 g)

	U.S.	Metric
Coffee ice cream	5 oz	140 g
Pâte à bombe	8 oz	225 g
Cream, 40 percent, whipped firm	1 qt	9 dl
Praline	6 oz	168 g

1. Mix all ingredients together. Fill into prepared soufflé cases, and freeze.
2. When frozen, prepare according to general instructions. Dust the tops with praline powder or macaroon dust.

Vanilla Soufflé Glacé

YIELD:
3 lb, 6¹⁄₄ oz (1 kg, 526 g)

	U.S.	Metric
Vanilla ice cream	10 oz	280 g
Pâte à bombe	8 oz	225 g
Confectioner's sugar	4 oz	112 g
Cream, 40 percent, whipped firm	1 qt	9 dl
Vanilla extract	¹⁄₄ oz	7 g

1. Mix together, then fill into prepared soufflé cases, and freeze.
2. When frozen, mark the tops with a knife, remove the paper bands, and place inside fancy paper cases.

NOTE: Any other flavor may be used instead of the vanilla, if desired. The best flavors are chartreuse, kirsch, benedictine, kummel, curaçao, and crème de menthe.

❦ Floating Hearts

Floating Hearts are desserts frozen in heart-shaped forms and served with a sauce. Most of them are decorated with sliced stewed or fresh fruits, with fruit served in the sauce. They are very attractive and may be served either in large forms or small, individual forms, but the latter are more popular.

Floating Hearts are all made the same way—it is only the sauce or the garnish that varies. When served in individual portions, the accompanying sauce is placed in a deep glass dish with the heart at the center, served on a dessert plate with a paper doily underneath. For large services, place the glass dish in another, larger bowl filled with fine cracked ice. Then place this double service on a platter.

Floating Heart

YIELD:
3 lb, 4 oz (1 kg, 461 g)

	U.S.	Metric
Pâte à bombe	*12 oz*	*336 g*
4× sugar	*8 oz*	*225 g*
Cream, 40 percent, whipped firm	*1 qt*	*9 dl*
Vanilla extract	*To taste*	
Macaroons	*1 lb*	*450 g*
Vanilla or kirsch-flavored syrup	*As needed*	

1. Soak the macaroons in the syrup. Mix the pâte à bombe with the sugar, whipped cream, and vanilla.
2. Fill heart-shaped molds in alternating layers of the cream mixture and macaroons, and freeze.
3. When frozen, serve with any desired sauce or garnish.

❦ Parfaits

Parfaits are made from a combination of different colored and flavored ice creams, fruits, sauces, and jams and are usually served in very tall, narrow glasses. The parfait originally was a very rich, semifrozen mousse, but today it is simply a combination of different ice creams and/or fruits served in a tall glass and decorated on top with whipped cream.

Café Parfait

YIELD:
1 lb, 13 oz (815 g)

	U.S.	Metric
Coffee ice cream	*5 oz*	*140 g*
4× sugar	*8 oz*	*225 g*
Cream, 40 percent, whipped firm	*1 pt*	*4.5 dl*
Coffee extract	*To taste*	

1. Mix all ingredients together.
2. Freeze in parfait glasses, and serve with whipped cream on top.

Chocolate Parfait

YIELD:
2 lb, 14 oz (1 kg, 291 g)

	U.S.	Metric
Chocolate ice cream	10 oz	280 g
Chocolate paste (appareil)	12 oz	336 g
Cream, 40 percent, whipped firm	1 pt	4.5 dl
Confectioner's sugar	8 oz	225 g

1. Mix all ingredients together.
2. Freeze in parfait glasses, and serve with whipped cream and chocolate powder on top.

Strawberry Parfait

YIELD:
3 lb, 4 oz (1 kg, 461 g)

	U.S.	Metric
Strawberry ice cream	10 oz	280 g
Strawberries, crushed	1 lb, 2 oz	506 g
Cream, 40 percent, whipped firm	1 pt	4.5 dl
4× sugar	½ lb	225 g

1. Mix all ingredients together.
2. Freeze in parfait glasses, and serve with whipped cream on top.

The following are some classic parfaits, which are assembled in a similar manner. If a syrup or sauce is used, 1 to 2 Tbsp should be placed at the bottom of the parfait glass and then swirled so that the syrup coats the sides. Alternate layers of the ice cream, ice, and/or fruit are then placed in the glass, and whipped cream and garnish are added.

Syrup	Layers	Garnish
Red currant jelly	Vanilla ice cream, red currant jelly, macedoine of fruit	
	Vanilla ice cream, strawberry ice cream, macedoine of fruit	
Melba sauce	Vanilla ice cream	
	Vanilla ice cream rolled in finely crushed nougat or peanut brittle	Crushed nougat
Orange blossom syrup	Vanilla ice cream	Orange blossom syrup, cream rosette, candied rose leaf

Name	Syrup	Layers	Garnish
St. Martin		Vanilla ice cream, strawberry ice cream, fruit macedoine	Fruit macedoine
Voltaire		Lemon sherbet, sliced bananas, soaked in curaçao, strawberry ice cream	

🐾 Fruits Served with Ice Cream

There are many different ways of serving fruits with ice cream, ices, sauces, and jams of different flavors. A small portion of ice cream, a half peach, a pear, or a few berries and a little sauce make a very appetizing and delicious combination for a dessert at a very moderate cost. When properly made and served, fruit and ice cream desserts are very attractive and can be a novel addition to a menu.

The fruit used should be drained of all juice or syrup and should be very cold before being placed on the ice cream. The sauce should then be poured over the fruit so that it covers it completely. When berries are served, the ice cream should be placed on top of the berries and completely covered with the sauce.

Fruits with ice cream are usually served in individual portions using a deep glass dish or an ice cream dish for each. When made for large services, they are placed in glass or silver bowls, set inside of larger bowls half filled with fine cracked ice, and then served on a prepared silver tray or platter.

The possible combinations of fruits served with ice cream are endless. Try varying the flavor of ice or ice cream, the type of fruit, the sauce, and garnish to create a signature dessert. A few examples follow.

■ Banana Fraisette

Fill a glass dish half full with sliced bananas mixed with Melba sauce. Place on top a portion of strawberry ice cream, and cover all over with strawberry sauce.

■ Peach Diane

Place a portion of banana ice cream in a dish with a small stewed peach on top. Cover with apricot sauce, and decorate with chestnuts and whipped cream.

■ Strawberry des Gourmets

Fill a dish half full with prepared strawberries. Place on top a portion of pineapple ice, and cover all over with gourmet sauce. Sprinkle small profiterolles on top.

CHAPTER 7

Bread and Rolls

The art of making raised bread is thought to have originated in Egypt, and has since been considered the most widely eaten and most important food in the world. Virtually all households, bakeshops, and successful restaurants serve excellent bread. The unique characteristics of flour, when combined with water and mixed or kneaded, develop gluten to form a dough, which is the basis of production of all types of yeast leavened breads, including wheat, French, whole wheat, and rye.

If you are making bread, however, make it right. Formulate your dough, learn how to use a thermometer, study flour and fermentation as well as temperature, and keep the bake shop perfectly clean.

It is not possible to give exact formulas for bread, since flour is not always the same, and therefore, either more or less water has to be used. The baker must exercise discretion and judgment in the use of the following formulas. The recipes given here are especially good for the hotel and restaurant baker or the small baker lacking a knowledge of the technical end of the business, and good results will be obtained by their use.

In many cases where poor bread is obtained, the reason is that the dough was not mixed long enough. If the mixing of the dough is hurried, the gluten in the dough is not fully developed, and the bread is a grayish tint, instead of being a fresh creamy white color. When bread is grayish in color, nine times out of ten it is from a dough run short. On the other hand, a dough can be overworked, and the result of this is a bread that is tough and dry.

Select a strong spring flour. Throughout the formulas, this is called *bread flour*. All bread flours are good, but some bakers seem to prefer one kind, while others will think an entirely different flour is the best. Often, the formula good for one flour may be unsatisfactory when used with another brand of flour, but by making a slight change in the formula, this difficulty can be overcome. Some flours absorb more liquid than others, and one flour may contain much more protein than another. Gluten is one of the most important factors to be considered in the use of flour. It is not the percentage of protein or the gluten in flour that counts, however, but the quality.

The baking of French bread, Vienna bread, and rolls should be done by steam. Steam is used to produce a high glaze and a crisp crust. Thirty to 90 seconds of steam should be used. The oven should be filled with steam before the goods are put in, and when the oven is filled with bread or rolls, more steam should be turned on and left on until they are three-quarters baked.

Bread and rolls should be proofed in a steambox to keep the goods moist, and the temperature of the box should be 90 to 96°F (33 to 35°C) at 80% humidity. The steam keeps the bread and rolls moist on top, which also helps to produce a finer glaze and a nicer general appearance when baked.

There are two doughs known to the baker—the sponge dough and the straight dough. The sponge dough is generally used in Europe, while in America the straight dough is preferred. The straight dough is best for bread that is consumed fresh, because it is sweeter. This method also saves much time and labor. Bread made from a sponge dough, however, will keep moist and fresh longer.

It is always better to use a dough that is rather young than one that is overproofed. The first punch should be given just before the dough is fully proofed and the second punch when a little over three-quarters proofed. This will produce a loaf of bread with a nice soft crust. It will also be sweeter, whiter in color, and keep longer.

To make a loaf of bread, follow these simple steps:

1. Use a one pound piece of dough. Punch out all the gases and press the dough flat.
2. Roll the dough toward you, locking out all air pockets.
3. Seal the seam, which is the weakest point in the loaf, and place it on the underside of the loaf. Otherwise, the heat and steam produced during baking will cause the loaf to crack or burst at the seam.

Frequent Causes of Poor Bread

When the crust of your bread is tough, it may be caused by under-mixing the dough, not enough shortening, incorrect percentage of water, incorrect fermentation, too much steam in the proof box, too much steam in the oven, or an overworked dough.

A cracked crust is often caused by cooling the bread too rapidly or by a dough that has crusted before baking. Thick crust is caused by an overfermented dough, a dough that has crusted while proofing, a too cool oven, baking for longer periods of time, or insufficient sweetening in the dough.

Dark crumb may be caused by improper mixing, too much salt, a young dough, too much steam in the proofing box, crusting of dough during fermentation, or by dough mixed too warm. Bad color or lack of color in the crust may be caused by a cool oven, overfermentation of the dough, or not enough sweetening in the dough.

Lumps, streaks, or poor grain may be caused by improper mixing, using a pan too small for the weight of the dough, lumpy flour, damp flour, too high a temperature in the dough, a cool oven, or a chilled dough.

Holes in bread may be caused by improper punching of dough, poor molding, old dough, or a too soft dough. Poor flavor may be caused by an unbalanced formula, lack of proper ingredients, poor quality of ingredients, a dough mixed too warm, or incorrect fermentation.

A dough can be compared to the human system with regard to the effect that different and especially extreme degrees of temperature have on it. When overheated or too cold, it lacks its usual life and vitality and for this reason becomes more or less unproductive.

Rope in Bread

Rope is one of the most feared bread diseases. It is caused by bacteria and is more likely to develop during warm weather than during the winter months.

Bread infected with rope has a sickly odor. The crumb in the center of the infected loaf becomes sticky and dark in color, and when the loaf is broken open, the center is often stringy, which is the reason for its being called *rope*.

Whole wheat bread is more susceptible than white bread to the disease, and high humidity and underbaking contribute to its growth.

To prevent rope, wash all utensils, mixers, troughs, etc. with a 25% solution of vinegar from time to time. Rope cannot grow in acid media.

The Functions of Bread Ingredients

The functions of bread ingredients are as follows:

Flour: The master constituent and the foundation of bread and rolls.

Water: Determines the consistency of the dough, makes possible the formation of gluten, dissolves the salts, makes bread palatable, and wets and swells the starch, which renders it more digestible.

Milk: Gives food value, supplies vitamins, improves flavor and keeping qualities, and tightens the dough.

Malt: Improves crust color, gives better flavor, aids in keeping the loaf moist, and adds nutrition.

Shortening: Produces a soft, velvety crumb, a finer texture, and a more tender crust and also gives a better color to the crust.

Yeast: Raises the dough, develops flavor, and supplies vitamins.

Sugar: Aids food value, gives color to the crust, and sweetens the bread.

Salt: Whitens the crumb, retards fermentation, develops bread aroma, and accentuates the taste. Salt also makes bread digestible.

🐦 Breads

There is an old saying that "who has baked a good batch of bread has done a good day's work." Bread making should stand at the head of the baker's accomplishments, since the health and happiness of the family depends immeasurably upon good bread. There comes a time in the experience of all true professional bakers when they are proud of their ability to make a nice loaf of bread.

White Bread (Three-Hour Straight Dough)

YIELD:
46 lb, 12 oz (21 kg, 34 g)

	U.S.	Metric
Yeast	6 oz	168 g
Water	15 lb	6 liters, 7.5 dl
Granulated sugar	6 oz	168 g
Malt	4 oz	112 g
Salt	6 oz	168 g
Bread flour	30 lb	13 kg, 500 g
Shortening	6 oz	168 g

1. Dissolve the yeast in part of the water.
2. Mix well together the remaining water, sugar, malt, salt, and part of the flour.
3. Add the yeast solution, and then slowly add the remaining flour.
4. Finally, add the shortening, and mix in a slow speed mixer for 25 minutes. If the temperature of the mixing room is 80°F (26°C), the fermentation time will be approximately 1½ hours to first punch, 1 hour to second punch, and 30 minutes to bench.
5. Bake at 430 to 450°F (220 to 230°C).

White Bread (Five-Hour Straight Dough)

YIELD:
46 lb, 7¹/₂ oz (20 kg, 908 g)

	U.S.	Metric
Yeast	5 oz	140 g
Water	7¹/₂ qt	6 liters, 7.5 dl
Granulated sugar	2¹/₂ oz	70 g
Malt	4 oz	112 g
Salt	6 oz	168 g
Bread flour	30 lb	13 kg, 500 g
Shortening	6 oz	168 g

Treat the same as the Three-Hour Straight Dough and set the dough at 78°F (25°C).

NOTE: If a richer dough is desired, half milk and half water may be used or all milk. If milk is used, add 2 qt (1.8 liters) more than the water used in each formula.

White Bread (Sponge Dough)

YIELD:
46 lb, 13¹/₂ oz (21 kg, 76 g)

	U.S.	Metric
Bread flour	30 lb	13 kg, 500 g
Water	7¹/₂ qt	6 liters, 7.5 dl
Yeast	6 oz	168 g
Malt	4 oz	112 g
Granulated sugar	6 oz	168 g
Shortening	6 oz	168 g
Salt	7¹/₂ oz	210 g

1. Make a sponge from 6 lb (2 kg, 700 g) of flour, 4¹/₂ qt (4 liters) of water, the yeast, and the malt. Set in a temperature of 76°F (24°C).
2. When the sponge drops, add a solution made from the salt, sugar, and the remaining water.
3. Mix in a slow speed mixer.
4. Add the remaining flour, and mix for 25 minutes.
5. Proof and bake the same as a straight dough.

Boston Brown Bread

YIELD:
18 lb, 10 oz (8 kg, 352 g)

	U.S.	Metric
Bread flour	2 lb	900 g
White rye flour	2 lb	900 g
Graham flour	2 lb	900 g
Fine corn meal	2 lb	900 g
Cream of tartar	2 oz	56 g
Baking soda	4 oz	112 g
Milk	4 qt	3 liters, 6 dl
Molasses	1 pt	672 g
Salt	4 oz	112 g
Eggs	4	200 g

1. Mix well together the flours, corn meal, and cream of tartar.
2. Dissolve the soda in 1 pt (4.5 dl) of milk.
3. Mix well the remaining milk, molasses, salt, and eggs, and add the dissolved soda.
4. Add the flour, and mix well.
5. Fill milk bread pans about three-quarters full, cover, and proof for 3 hours.

■ Raisin Brown Bread

Add to the Boston Brown Bread mixture 2 lb (900 g) of seeded muscat raisins.

Corn Bread

YIELD:
15 lb, 6 oz (7 kg, 354 g)

	U.S.	Metric
Eggs	2 lb, 4 oz	1 kg
Salt	2 oz	56 g
Granulated sugar	12 oz	336 g
Milk	3 qt	2 liters, 7 dl
Bread flour	3 lb	1 kg, 350 g
Yellow corn meal	3 lb	1 kg, 350 g
Baking powder	4 oz	112 g
Salted butter, melted	1 lb	450 g

1. Beat together the eggs, salt, and sugar.
2. Add the milk.
3. Sift together the flour, corn meal, and baking powder, and add to mixture.
4. Mix thoroughly, and then mix in the butter.
5. Fill in greased cast iron pre-formed corn bread pans with rims, and bake at 450°F (230°C).

French Bread

YIELD:
20 lb, 8 oz (9 kg, 224 g)

	U.S.	Metric
Water	4 qt	3 liters, 6 dl
Yeast	4 oz	112 g
Salt	4 oz	112 g
Bread flour	12 lb	5 kg, 400 g

1. Make a dough from these ingredients, the same as a straight bread dough. Let proof twice.
2. Scale 15 oz for a 2-ft (60 cm) mold. Form loaves, proof in cloth, cut, and bake the same as Vienna bread.

Graham Bread

YIELD:
23 lb, 14 oz (10 kg, 742 g)

	U.S.	Metric
Yeast	4 oz	112 g
Water	4 qt	3 liters, 6 dl
Salt	4 oz	112 g
Molasses	6 oz	168 g
Graham flour	8 lb	3 kg, 600 g
Bread flour	7 lb	3 kg, 150 g

1. Dissolve the yeast in half the water.
2. Mix salt, molasses, and the remaining water.
3. Add the yeast and the flour slowly to the molasses mixture.
4. Mix thoroughly.
5. Make up into loaves, and bake at 400°F (205°C).

Milk Bread 1

YIELD:
50 lb, 10 oz (22 kg, 776 g)

	U.S.	Metric
Yeast	6 oz	168 g
Water	2 gal	7 liters, 2 dl
Milk powder	14 oz	392 g
Granulated sugar	6 oz	168 g
Salt	6 oz	168 g
Malt	2 oz	56 g
Shortening	8 oz	225 g
Bread flour	32 lb	14 kg, 400 g

1. Dissolve the yeast in half the water and the milk powder in the other half.
2. Mix the sugar, salt, malt, and shortening.
3. Add the milk solution and then the yeast dissolved in water.
4. Add the flour, a small amount at a time, and mix thoroughly, letting the mixer run for about 25 minutes before removing. If the temperature of the mixing room is 80°F (26°C), the fermentation time will be approximately 1 hour and 40 minutes to first rising, 1 hour to second rising, and ½ hour to bench.

NOTE: Any rolls made from milk dough will be fine in flavor and in appearance. The addition of milk powder is not costly, and of course, good looking as well as good tasting rolls always attract more customers.

Milk Bread 2

YIELD:
46 lb, 14 oz (21 kg, 90 g)

	U.S.	Metric
Yeast	6 oz	168 g
Water	4 qt	3 liters, 6 dl
Granulated sugar	8 oz	225 g
Salt	6 oz	168 g
Shortening	10 oz	280 g
Milk	3½ qt	3 liters, 1.5 dl
Bread flour	30 lb	13 kg, 500 g

Treat the same as Milk Bread 1.

Pumpernickel Bread

YIELD:
21 lb, 14 oz (9 kg, 842 g)

	U.S.	Metric
Yeast	6 oz	168 g
Water	4 qt	3 liters, 6 dl
Salt	4 oz	112 g
Granulated sugar	4 oz	112 g
Dark rye flour	7 lb	3 kg, 150 g
Graham flour	3 lb	1 kg, 350 g
Bread flour	3 lb	1 kg, 350 g

Treat and bake the same as Graham Bread.

❦ Rye Bread

Rye bread is a healthful and very tasty bread. Traditionally, the Jewish population has been the largest consumer of white rye flour and Germans of the dark rye flour, while the American population in general has preferred a medium rye flour and a light, spongy loaf. The baker should conform production to the tastes of the local customers.

Swedish rye bread is made the same way as the medium rye bread, with the addition of 3 pt (1 liter, 3.5 dl) of molasses, and sometimes 1 lb (450 g) of raisins is added to every gallon (3 liters, 6 dl) of water.

White Rye (Straight Dough)

YIELD:
41 lb, 2 oz (18 kg, 503 g)

	U.S.	Metric
Yeast	6 oz	168 g
Water	14 lb, 8 oz	6 liters, 5.25 dl
Salt	8 oz	225 g
Malt	4 oz	112 g
Bread flour	16 lb, 4 oz	7 kg, 312 g
White rye flour	9 lb, 4 oz	4 kg, 162 g

1. Prepare the dough the same as any straight dough.
2. In a temperature of 80°F (26°C), the fermentation time will be approximately 1½ hours to first punch, 50 minutes to second punch, and 20 minutes to bench.
3. Make up, slashing top 3 or 4 times. Place in boxes to proof, and put up in cloths.
4. When fully proofed, bake at 400°F (205°C).

Medium Dark Rye Bread (Straight Dough)

YIELD:
40 lb, 11¹/₂ oz (18 kg, 320 g)

	U.S.	Metric
Yeast	6¹/₂ oz	182 g
Water	15 lb	6 liters, 7.5 dl
Salt	8 oz	225 g
Malt	4 oz	112 g
Caraway seeds	1 oz	28 g
Bread flour	16 lb, 4 oz	7 kg, 312 g
Medium rye flour	8 lb, 4 oz	3 kg, 712 g

Prepare and treat the dough the same as for White Rye Bread.

Dark Rye Bread (Straight Dough)

YIELD:
41 lb, 9 oz (18 kg, 700 g)

	U.S.	Metric
Yeast	1 lb	450 g
Water	15 lb	6 liters, 7.5 dl
Salt	8 oz	225 g
Malt	4 oz	112 g
Caraway seeds	1 oz	28 g
Bread flour	18 lb, 8 oz	8 kg, 324 g
Dark rye flour	6 lb, 4 oz	2 kg, 812 g

Prepare and treat the dough the same as for White Rye Bread.

Dark Rye Bread (Sponge Dough)

YIELD:
40 lb, 12 oz (18 kg, 332 g)

	U.S.	Metric
Dark rye flour	3 lb, 12 oz	1 kg, 686 g
Water	3½ qt	3 liters, 1.5 dl
Yeast	6 oz	168 g
Water	4 qt	3 liters, 6 dl
Salt	8 oz	225 g
Malt	6 oz	168 g
Bread flour	20 lb, 12 oz	9 kg, 336 g

1. Make a sponge dough from the rye flour, water, and yeast. When sponge is ready, add the remaining ingredients.
2. Set the dough in a temperature of 80°F (26°C), and let rise fully (approximately 70 minutes).
3. Punch down, let stand for 20 minutes, and then make up in the usual way.

NOTE: Medium and white rye sponge dough breads are made the same way, by changing the proportions and types of flour as for straight doughs.

🍎 Sandwich Bread

Sandwich bread, sometimes called *Pullman bread* or *toast bread,* is best when made from milk bread dough. It must be molded very tight and should not be proofed much. When 4 × 12 inch (10 × 30 cm) pans are used, scale 1 lb, 6 oz (600 g), and for 5 × 18 inch (12.5 × 45 cm) pans, scale 1 lb, 12 oz (800 g). Bake at 400°F (205°C).

Vienna Bread

YIELD:
27 lb, 10 oz (12 kg, 376 g)

	U.S.	Metric
Water	2½ qt	2 liters, 2.5 dl
Yeast	4 oz	112 g
Malt	1 oz	28 g
Bread flour	6 lb, 4 oz	2 kg, 812 g
Milk	2½ qt	2 liters, 2.5 dl
Granulated sugar	2 oz	56 g
Shortening	6 oz	168 g
Bread flour	10 lb	4 kg, 500 g
Salt	5 oz	140 g

1. Make a sponge from the water, yeast, malt, and 6 lb, 4 oz of flour. Ferment in a temperature of 76°F (24°C) for 2 to 4 hours.
2. When the sponge drops, add the remaining ingredients, along with the rest of the flour.
3. Let rise once. Scale in 1 lb loaves, round up, and set in a box to proof until doubled in size. Then mold very tightly into oblong loaves, wide in the center, and with sharp-pointed ends. Place on flour-dusted cloths. The cloth is then drawn up on the sides of each loaf, with the seam on top, to prevent them from sticking together while proofing.
4. When ready, place on an oven peel or baking sheet sprinkled with white corn meal. Then take a sharp knife or razor blade and cut three small gashes across the loaf to sever the crust.
5. Quickly place in a steam-filled oven, and bake at 450°F (230°C).

NOTE: An *oven peel* is a long-handled paddle used to put a loaf of bread into a deck oven and to remove the bread when finished. It is an old method of making hearth bread still used by many bakers.

Whole Wheat Bread 1

YIELD:
50 lb, 6 oz (22 kg, 666 g)

	U.S.	Metric
Yeast	8 oz	225 g
Water	2 gal	7 liters, 2 dl
Granulated sugar	4 oz	112 g
Malt	2 oz	56 g
Salt	8 oz	225 g
Shortening	1 lb	450 g
Whole wheat flour	32 lb	14 kg, 400 g

1. Dissolve the yeast in half the water.
2. Mix the sugar, malt, salt, and shortening.
3. Add the remaining water, then the yeast solution, and then the flour. Let the mixer run at medium speed for 30 minutes. A well-mixed, cool dough will produce a very good whole wheat bread.
4. When the dough is set in a temperature of 76°F (24°C), the fermentation time will be approximately 1½ hours to first punch, 45 minutes to second punch, and 20 minutes to bench.
5. Use 1-lb (450-g) pans for 1½-lb (675 g) loaves. Bake thoroughly at 400°F (205°C) with relatively short proof and with no steam in the oven.

Whole Wheat Bread 2

YIELD:
53 lb, 14¹/₂ oz (24 kg, 254 g)

	U.S.	Metric
Yeast	6¹/₂ oz	182 g
Water	8¹/₂ qt	7 liters, 6.5 dl
Granulated sugar	4 oz	112 g
Salt	8 oz	225 g
Shortening	8 oz	225 g
Sweetened condensed milk	1 lb, 4 oz	562 g
Whole wheat flour	34 lb	15 kg, 300 g

1. Dissolve the yeast in half the water.
2. Mix the sugar, salt, and shortening.
3. Add the remaining water, the milk, and then the yeast mixture.
4. Mix in the flour. Good results will be obtained if the dough is mixed in a cake mixer run at medium speed for 30 minutes.
5. When the dough is set in a temperature of 76 to 78°F (24 to 25°C) the fermentation time will be approximatley 1¹/₂ hours to first punch, ¹/₂ hour to second punch, and ¹/₂ hour to bench.
6. Use 1-lb (450-g) pans for 1¹/₂-lb (675-g) loaves, and bake the same as for Whole Wheat Bread 1.

❦ Rolls

There are many different fancy rolls made from bread dough, milk bread dough, and sweet dough, and it would take too long to describe them all here. However, directions are given for making a few of the best-known and most popular rolls that are generally made daily.

To obtain a nice glaze for sweet rolls, prepare a wash from 2 qt (1 liter, 8 dl) water and 1¹/₂ oz (42 g) cornstarch. Boil the water, then add the cornstarch dissolved in a little water, and boil together. Set aside for use when needed. When the rolls are baked, wash them over with this preparation, and return to the oven for a few seconds.

■ Bread Sticks

Make a French Bread Dough, and roll out into long and very thin sticks. Place on pans to proof. When ready, wash with egg, and bake at 450°F (230°C).

■ Finger Rolls

Shape small rolls in finger shapes of about $1\frac{1}{2}$ oz (14 g) each from the Vienna Bread Dough. Roll very tightly, and place on greased pans (not too close together). When ready, wash with an egg wash made from equal parts of egg and milk, and bake at 450°F (230°C).

■ French (or Spanish) Rolls

Treat the same as Split Rolls, but instead of using butter for splitting, dust the rolls with wheat flour and bake without steam.

■ French Dinner Rolls

Cut French Bread Dough in pieces and roll out about $\frac{1}{2}$ inch (1 cm) thick in long strips. Place them in a box covered with a cloth, and sprinkle with dusting flour. When half proofed, cut into pieces about 3 inches (7 cm) long with a scraper dipped in lard. Cover with a cloth and let proof. When ready, place the rolls on a peel dusted with flour, then cut the top of each roll with a sharp knife (the same as for French bread), and bake in a steam-filled oven at 450°F (230°C).

■ Pan Rolls

Use any of the bread doughs, and divide into small pieces of about 1 oz (28 g) each. Roll up and place them on pans side by side. Place in the proof box with steam, and bake when ready at 450°F (230°C).

■ Split Rolls (Pistolets)

Make a Vienna Bread Dough, and divide into small pieces of 1 oz (28 g) each. Roll them into rounds, and place on a dusted cloth far enough apart that they will not stick together. Draw the cloth out on the sides of the rolls to prevent them from sticking together. When half proofed, dip a small rolling pin into melted butter and press across the center of each roll, creating a split. Turn them over, split face down, cover, and let proof. When ready, turn over on a peel dusted with fine white corn meal, split face up, and place in the oven. Bake with steam, the same as for French bread, at 450°F (232°C).

■ Tea Rolls (Turnover Rolls)

Use a Milk Bread Dough, and divide into pieces of 1 oz (28 g) each. Roll them into rounds, then set on the bench, and let proof for awhile. Then place two of them side by side, and roll out in the middle with one stroke of the rolling pin. Wash the top with melted butter, and then fold one end of the roll on top of the other. Place on pans so that they touch each other, and proof in the steam box. When ready, bake at 450°F (230°C), and wash with butter while hot.

■ Vienna Rolls

Make a Vienna Bread Dough and divide into 1-oz (28-g) pieces. Roll into round shapes, let stand for a few minutes, and then mold into small shapes like Vienna Bread. Place on slightly greased pans, and proof in a wet steam box. When ready, wash the tops with milk, cut a sharp gash across each roll, and bake in a steam-filled oven at 450°F (230°C).

❦ Sweet Dough

Sweet dough products make up one of the most profitable lines of merchandise carried by the baker. Therefore, special care should be given to their production, and they should be attractively displayed and well advertised. Instruct your salespeople to tell all your customers how really delicious they are, and see that they are made the same week after week. No line of merchandise will gain popularity unless its quality and attractive appearance remain uniform. It is important to give the public what it demands, and that is thoroughly good and wholesome materials, careful workmanship, and attractive appearance—both in the product and in the manner of its display.

To produce a uniform product, it is absolutely essential that the amounts of all ingredients called for in a recipe be weighed and measured exactly. Accurate weighing and measuring require a little more time, but you will find that you are more than repaid for your trouble by the uniformly satisfactory results obtained.

Sweet Dough

YIELD:
14 lb, 10 oz (6 kg, 579 g)

	U.S.	Metric
Granulated sugar	1 lb, 4 oz	562 g
Salt	1¾ oz	49 g
Salted butter (or shortening)	1 lb	450 g
Malt	2 oz	56 g
Mace, ground	¼ oz	7 g
Lemon rind, grated	2 oz	56 g
Eggs	8 oz	225 g
Yeast	4 oz	112 g
Bread flour	7 lb, 4 oz	3 kg, 262 g
Milk	2 qt	1 kg, 800 g

1. Cream the sugar, salt, butter, malt, mace, and grated lemon rind.
2. Add the eggs gradually.
3. Dissolve the yeast in 1 pt of the milk.
4. Add the remaining milk to the creamed mixture, and stir thoroughly.
5. Add half the flour, and begin mixing.
6. Pour in the yeast solution, add the remaining flour, and continue mixing until the dough is smooth.
7. Allow the dough to rise twice, the same as bread dough, before taking to the bench to be worked up. Bake at 375°F (190°C).

Glossary

à la After the style or fashion of, such as *à la Française,* "French style"; *à l'imperatrice,* "empress' style"; *à l'Anglaise,* "English style"; etc.

Ananas The French word for pineapple.

Aremberg A dessert made from pears, named after Count Aremberg, who grew the highest grade of pears in his gardens.

Arlequin (or Harlequin) An ice cream of four different colors and flavors.

Baba A very light sweet dough dessert.

Bain marie A double boiler or open vessel that has a loose bottom for the reception of hot water and which is used to keep sauces at a boiling point.

Batter A thin mixture of flour with some liquid.

Bande au pomme A French pastry, long in shape, and made with sliced apples.

Bavaroise (or Bavarian cream) A cream dessert made with gelatin.

Beignets Fritters.

Beurre The French word for butter.

Beurre noisette Butter melted until brown.

Biscuit glacé A frozen dessert consisting of a mixture of whipped cream, pâte à bombe, and flavoring.

Bisque A paste or purée.

Blanch To remove the skins from various nuts, etc. by scalding.

Bouchées Very small puff paste patties, small enough to be a mouthful only.

Bombe A cylindrical or bomb-shaped form consisting of ice cream with a mousse center or made entirely of plain mousse, decorated, and sometimes served with a sauce separate.

Brioche A light, sweet dough baked in molds.

Bun A sweet roll.

Caramel Sugar boiled until it becomes light brown in color.

Casis The French word for black currants.

Chafing dish A dish, usually silver, set within another dish that contains hot water, with a small lamp underneath, used for keeping foods hot until served.

Charlotte A sweet dessert lined with lady fingers, cake, or bread.

Choux chantilly A cream puff filled with whipped cream.

Choux paste Puff paste.

Clarify To clear any liquid, such as butter, fruit juices, jellies, etc.

Crème à la glace Ice cream.

Compote Fruit stewed in syrup or a mixture of different stewed fruits.

Condé (or à la condé) Named after Prince Louis de Condé, a famous seventeenth-century epicure.

Confiture A very sweet preserve or jam.

Corbeille A basket of any form or material, sometimes made from sugar or cut out of ice, and used as a table decoration, filled with fancy cakes, candy, fruit, flowers, etc.

Coupe A dessert served in a champagne glass and usually made of fresh fruit and ice cream.

Couronne (en) To serve any article of food on a dish arranged in the shape of a crown.

Cream aganasse A Hungarian chocolate cream.

Crème au beurre (or buttercream) A light buttercream used for cake fillings, etc.

Crêpes French pancakes.

Cuisine The French word for kitchen or cooking.

Culinaire Culinary. This word is applied to anything connected with the art of cooking or baking.

Darioles Molds made from tin or copper which are the size of a glass tumbler.

Divorson A French pastry of two different colors.

Drying room A ventilated room heated by steam (or other means) to a temperature ranging from 100 to 128°F and used for drying starch goods, fruits, liqueur bonbons, etc.

Éclair A long finger-shaped puff pastry filled with cream.

Entremets Sweet or vegetable dishes served as a second course or dessert.

Etufe A drying room.

Fecule A fine flour used for binding sauces.

Feuilletage Puff paste.

Flamande (à la) Flemish style.

Flan A French custard tart or fruit tart.

Fleurons Garnitures made from light puff paste cut into oval, diamond, or crescent shapes and served with meat, fish, or soup.

Floating heart A frozen dessert in the shape of a heart, served with a sauce and a garnish.

Française (à la) French style.

Frangipanne A light almond sponge cream.

Friandises Very small, dainty cakes made from sponges, buttercreams, and jams.

French pancake A very thin, sweet pancake, either served plain or rolled and filled with jelly or jam, etc. and served as a dessert.

Gâteaux Layer or sponge cakes filled and masked with buttercream.

Glacé (or glacéd) Frozen or iced.

Gourmand One who eats to excess—a glutton.

Gourmet A connoisseur in fine foods—an epicure.

Goût Taste, flavor.

Gugelhupf A very light sweet dough cake.

Hericart Signifying a dessert made from strawberries or served with strawberries.

Icing A frosting or coating of liquid sugar for pies, cakes, etc., made by mixing confectioner's sugar with water, egg whites, etc.

Imperatrice Signifying a dessert named after an empress.

Italienne (à la) Italian style.

Jalstroff Signifying a dessert made from raspberries or served with raspberries.

l'Ambassadrice Signifying a dessert named after the wife of an ambassador.

Line To place paste, pie crust, lady fingers, etc. around the inside edge or bottom of molds, rings, plates, etc.

Maçedoine A mixture of fruits or vegetables.

Marrons The French word for chestnuts.

Mask To cover cakes with any cream, sauce, or icing.

Melba (à la) Signifying a dessert served with Melba sauce.

Mignardise Another name for *petits fours*.

Millefeuilles Meaning a thousand leaves; the name given to pastries made from puff paste.

Montmorency Signifying a dessert made with cherries.

Montreuil Signifying a dessert made with peaches; a section of France where the finest peaches are grown.

Mousse A light frozen dessert consisting of whipped cream, pâte à bombe, and flavoring.

Napolitaine (à la) In the style of Naples.

Nesselrode An iced pudding flavored with chestnuts.

Noisette The French word for hazelnut.

Normande Signifying a dessert made from apples.

Nougat A confection made from almonds, pistachio nuts, sugar, and paste.

Oven peel A long-handled paddle used to put a loaf of bread into a deck oven and to remove the bread when finished.

Pain The French word for bread.

Pain à la meque A cream puff in the shape of a small loaf, filled with cream.

Panache A term signifying a mixture of two or more kinds or flavors of fruit or ice cream.

Parfait A frozen sweet made from mousse and ice cream and served in tall glasses.

Paste pincers Small pincers used for indenting the edges or borders of French tarts, pies, etc.

Pâte Paste.

Pâte à bombe A sponge made from egg yolks and boiled sugar and used in ice creams, buttercream, etc.

Pàtisserie Pastry.

Petits fours Small cakes of various shapes and flavors.

Petits pains Rolls.

Pomme The French word for apples.

Pompadour Signifying a dessert (always of a reddish color) names after Madame Pompadour, who was very fond of, and always wore, red.

Pote crème A custard baked and served in a cup.

Praline A paste made from sugar, almonds, and other nuts and used in pastries, creams, candies, etc.

Profiterolles Small cream puffs filled with cream and covered with a sauce. They are sometimes made very small and served with soup.

Puit d'Amoure A baked tartlet shell filled with boiled custard cream, with a little burned sugar on top.

Purée Mashed ingredients.

Reine The French word for queen.

Rimgo-Janji Signifying a dish named after a musical genius.

Sabayon A foaming sauce made from eggs, sugar, and spirits.

Sacher torte A chocolate cake invented by Sacher, a pastry cook and proprietor of a famous pastry shop in Vienna.

Score To make incisions forming a pattern on cakes or pies, etc.

Shrink To roll out paste and allow it to rest before baking in order to prevent shrinking.

Sorbet A well-flavored semifrozen ice.

Soufflé A very light, baked or steamed pudding or dessert.

Soufflé glacé A light and well-flavored dessert made from ice cream, pâte à bombe, and whipped cream, and frozen in soufflé dishes.

Suprême A dessert or pastry composed of the best parts of the sweet line.

Surprise (or en surprise) A culinary expression for any dessert that presents an appearance which is contrary to its actual nature.

Tourte A tart baked in a shallow ring or hoop.

Turban A dish made in a turban-shaped mold.

Turn When puff paste is mixed, to "give a turn" means to roll it out to a length of 4 ft, then fold over one-third, and fold the other third over this.

Tutti-frutti A term signifying a mixture of various kinds of chopped candied fruits or a mixture of fruit ice cream.

Valencia Signifying a dessert made from oranges or served with oranges.

Vol-au-vent A light puff paste cut either round or oval and usually filled with meat or fish.

Whip To beat eggs or cream, etc. with a whip or whisk.

Work To beat a mixture of eggs, cream, butter, flour, water, etc. with a spatula. Various pastes are also worked on the bench or in bowls.

Index

Adul, 66
Africaine, 66
Aganasse, 47
    marquise roll, 32
Algériennes, 66
Alice, 66
Allumettes, 13, 72
Almond
    bars, 72
    biscuit caprice, 62
    biscuit progrès, 63
    bread cookies, 91
    cyrano, 75
    gâteau alcazar, 199
    kisses, 92
    mercédes pudding, 125
    pastry cream, 53
    pâte à biscuit, 64-65
    pâte à caraques, 65
    slices, 35
    soufflé, 88
    sponge cake, 22
    tart, 55
Americana
    brownies, 113
    cheesecake, 188
Americus, 67
Angel cake, 186-187
Anise
    cookies, 94
    sponge cookies, 95
Anita, 67
Apple
    bande au pomme, 13
    Canadian pudding, 123
    charlotte, 148
    compote, 171
    condé, 149
    crêpes normande, 160
    fritters, 159
    meringue, 149
    normande pudding, 137
    pie, 213
    rice pudding, 121
    soufflé normandy, 156
    tapioca pudding, 122
    tart, 55

turnovers, 18
Apricot
    Bavarian cream, 141
    charlotte, 143
    compote, 172
    condé, 149
    delna sauce, 165
    gâteau de venice, 206
    mignon, 13
    sauce, 164-165
    savarin nesselrode, 147
    soufflé
        palmyre, 157
        pudding, 132
    tart, 56
        à la crème, 56
    water ice, 250
Arlequins, 67

Baba rum, 60, 150
Baked Alaska, 151
    jubilee, 152
    milady, 152
    milord, 152
Baking soda biscuits, 218-219
Banana
    Bavarian
        cream, 139
        pudding, 128
    carlos cake, 184
    fraisette, 280
    fritters, 159
    ice cream, 236, 244
    mousse, 269
    soufflé, 153
        new ocean, 147
    white mountain cake, 178
Bar le duc tart, 67
Barquette melba, 20
Bavarian
    cream, 139-142
        charlotte, 143-144
        pudding, 128-131
Beignets with cherries, 73
Belloca, 67
Biarritz, 72
Biscuit, 218-219

arlequins, 62
caprice, 62
glacé au fraise, 274
manque, 63
pâte à, 64
    with almonds, 64
progrès, 63
Black and white squares, 114
Black currant water ice, 250
Blackberry tart, 56
Blueberry
    cake, 183
    cheesecake, 190
    muffins, 220
    pie, 214
        filling, 209
    pudding, 136
Bombes, 264-266
    fruits with pistachio, 68
Boston brown bread, 286
Boston cream pie, 214
Boules
    au chocolate, 68
    with pistachio nuts, 68
Bran muffins, 220
Brandy snaps, 96
Bread, 284-294
    and butter pudding, 122
    normande pudding, 137
    sticks, 294
Breton, 60
Brioche
    Flammande, 59
    Parisian, 58
Brownies, 113-116
    icing, 117
Buckwheat cakes, 232
Buffalo, 68
Butter sponge cake, 23
Buttercreams, 45-48

Cabinet pudding, 122
Cakes
    Bohemian, 41
    Crème d'or, 41
    Vienna, 41-45

Canadian pudding, 123
Caprice, 68
Caramel custard, 163
Carlos
    cake, 184
    gâteau, 200
Cat's tongues, 73, 96
Cendrillon, 68
Champagne sherbet, 256
Charlottes, 143–144
    glacé panache, 260
    puddings, 131
Cheddar beer cheesecake, 190
Cheese
    cheddar beer cheesecake, 190
    corn muffins, 221
    cottage cheese cake, 191
    soufflé, 154
    sticks, 13
Cheesecake, 188–198
Cherry
Baked Alaska jubilee, 152
    beignets with, 73
    cake, 179
    compote, 172
    jubilee, 152
    kisses, pecan, 108
    maraschino sherbet, 256
    montmorency soufflé pudding, 133
    oxford cake, 177
    oyster bay ice cream, 262
    savarin flambé montmorency, 153
    tart, 56
Chestnut
    marron mixture, 147
    mousse marron, 270
    mousse mikado, 271
    nesselrode ice cream, 261
    oyster bay ice cream, 262
    savarin mont blanc, 146
Chiffon
    strawberry cheese pie, 198
Chocolate
    angel cake, 187
    appareil, 257
    Bavarian cream, 140
    Bavarian pudding, 128
    biscuit arlequins, 62
    black and white squares, 114
    blidak, 36
    bohemian cake, 41
    boules, 68
    brownies, 113–116
    buttercream, 48
    charlotte, 143
    chip cookies, 97

chocolate chip cookies, 98
    cream pie, 214
    custard, 161
    custard pie, 15
    ice box cookies, 98
    ice cream, 237, 244–245
    icing, 117
    layer cake, 181
    logs, 74
    macaroon, 80
    manqué, 69
    marquisette Bavarian cream, 141
    mousse, 270
    mousse mikado, 271
    parfait, 279
    pastry cream, 53
    pinwheels, 99
    profiterole, 150
    roll, 31
    sauce, 166
    soufflé, 154
    soufflé glacé, 275
    soufflé pudding, 132
    sponge cake, 23
    tips, 74
    Vienna sponge, 33
Choux
    chantilly, 21
    paste, 19
        pastry, 20–21
        profiteroles, 150
    petits, 70
Cigarettes, 75, 100
Clairettes, 69
Coconut
    custard pie, 215
    delight, 100
    ice box cookies, 101
    macaroons, 80
    pudding, 136
    snowball ice cream, 262
Coffee
    Bavarian
        cream, 140
        pudding, 129
    bettina, 36
    buttercream, 46
    café parfait, 278
    charlotte, 143
    custard, 162
        pie, 216
        sauce, 170
    ice cream, 238, 245
    java, 38
    pastry cream, 53
    soufflé, 155
    sponge cake, 24
    Vienna sponge, 34
Cold sweets, 138–148
Compote, fruit, 171–173

Cookies, 91–112
Corn
    bread, 286
    cakes, 233
    flannel cakes, 233
    muffins, 221–222
        with cheese, 221
Coupes, 267–269
Cream
    envelopes, 14
    horns, 14
    pastry, 51–54
    puff
        paste, 19
        pastry, 20–21
    whipped, 259
        ginger snaps, 112
Crème pâtissière, 51–54
Crêpes, 160
Crullers, 229
Crust
    pie, 207–208
        graham cracker, 189
    short, 54
Cupcakes, 184
Custard cream, 161, 163
    Boston cream pie, 214
Cyrano, 75
    gâteau, 200

Danswan, 69
Dartois, 14
Date
    brownies, raisin and, 116
    ice box cookies, 102
    muffins, 222
    soufflé pudding, 133
Delna sauce, 165
Devil's food cake, 185
Diplomat pudding, 123
Divorson, 21
Dobos torte, 42
Doughnuts, 227–229
Duchesses, 76
Dundee cake, 180

Eclairs, 20–21
English muffins, 224

Farina pudding, 124
Favorites, 76
Fédora, 42
Fig
    border à la condé, 151
    condé, 149
    soufflé pudding, 133
Filbert
    Bavarian cream, 142
    charlotte, 144
    duchesse, 76
Finger rolls, 295

Flannel cakes, 233
Floating hearts, 277-278
Florentine, 102
Frangipane, 48-49
  gâteau pansée, 203
French
  bread, 287
  rolls, 295
Fritters, 159
Frozen sweets, 259-264
Fruit
  cake, 180
    dundee cake, 180
    light, 179
    riche cake, 177
  compotes, 171-173
  kisses, 102
  pastry cream, 53
  pudding cake, 65
  refrigerator cheesecake
    with, 197
  served with ice cream, 280
  tartlet, 14
  tarts, 55-57

Gâteaux, 198-206
Ginger
  cake, 186
  Canadian pudding, 123
  snaps with whipped cream,
    112
Gooseberry tart, 57
Graham
  bread, 287
  cracker crust, 189
  muffins, 222
  scotch scones, 226
Gourmet sauce, 166
Griddle cakes, 231-233
Gugelhupf, 60

Half-and-half's, 99
Hard sauce, 161, 167
Harlequin ice cream, 260
Hermits, 103
Hot sweets, 148-158

Ice box cookies, 109
  chocolate, 99
  coconut, 101
  date, 102
Ice cream
  American, 243-248
  French, 236-242
Indian pudding, 124

Jan hagel, 77
Jelly, 145
  crêpes mirette, 160
  envelopes, 14
  roll, 31

Jocunde, 14

Kisses
  almond, 92
  fancy, 77
  fruit, 102
  lace cookies, 92
  pecan cherry, 108

Lady fingers, 78-79
Langues des Chats, 73, 96
  gâteau collombies, 200
  gâteau fredolin, 201
Layer cake, 181-182
Leckerli, 104
Lemon
  custard sauce, 167
  jelly, 145
  macaroons, 81
  muffins, 223
  pie
    custard, 216
    filling, 209-210
    meringue, 217
  pudding soufflé saxon, 134
  soufflé, 155
  sponge cake, 24
  water ice, 251
Linzer torte, 43
Logs, chocolate, 74

Macaroon, 79-83
  bisque, 260
  oyster bay ice cream, 262
  pudding, 137
  soufflé royale, 159
  spoom à la reine, 262
  tartlet, 15
Madeleines, 105
Manque, 63
  with rum, 69
Maple
  layer cake, 181
  pound cake, 176
Marguerite cake, 44
Marquise, 69
  au champagne sherbet,
    256
Marquisette
  Bavarian cream, 141
  pudding, 264
Marron. *See also* chestnut
Marshmallow layer cake, 182
Melba
  Bavarian cream, 141
  delna sauce, 165
  gourmet sauce, 166
  sauce, 168
Melon
  glacé en surprise, 261
  water ice, 251

Meringue, 50-51
  kisses, 77
  lemon pie, 217
  rocher, 87
Merliton, 15
Merveilleuses, 38
Mignon, 39
  apricot, 13
Milk bread, 288-89
Millefeuilles, 16
Mince meat pie filling, 210
Mocha
  cake, 44
  gâteau, 201
  marguerite roll, 32
  roll, 32
  squares, 29
Mokke
  anversoise, 83
  hollandaise, 84
Monpansée, gâteau, 202
Montmorency
  savarin flambé, 153
  soufflé pudding, 133
Moscovites, 16
Mousse, frozen, 269-273
Mousseline
  apricot, 165
  foundation, 170
  poudrés, 84
  sauce
    cold, 169
    hot, 168
Muffins, 220-224

Napoleon, 16
Neapolitan brick ice cream,
  261
Nesselrode
  ice cream, 261
  savarin, 147
Néva wafers, 39

Omelette soufflé, 156
Orange
  custard, 163
  jelly, 145
  macaroons, 82
  muffins, 223
  pie filling, 211
  soufflé, 157
    pudding, 134
  soyer au champagne, 257
  spoom à la romaine, 262
  water ice, 252
Oxford cake, 177
Oyster bay ice cream, 262

Pains
  à la meque, 21
  d'Amande, 85

Palais des dames, 106
Palets
    de dames, 85
    fourrées, 86
    glacés, 86
Palmyres
    leaves, 16
    soufflé, 157
Pan rolls, 295
Pancakes. *See also* crêpes
Papillon, 17
Parfait, 278-280
Parisian, 69
    macaroons, 82
Parisienne, 86
Pastry cream, 51-54
Pâte
    à biscuit, 64
        with almonds, 64
    à bombe, 258
    à caraques, 65
    à choux, 19
        petits choux, 70
    à pâté, 208
Patty shells, 17
Peach
    à l'ambassadrice, 146
    baked Alaska milady, 152
    Bavarian cream, 141
    charlotte, 143
    compote, 172
    condé, 149
    diane, 280
    ice cream, 238, 246
    meringue, 149
    mousse, 272
        montreuil, 272
    sauce, 169
    soufflé glacé montreuil,
        276
    tart, 57
    water ice, 252
Peanut butter spritz cookies,
    107
Pear
    baked Alaska milord, 152
    compote, 172
    condé, 149
    fritters, 159
    meringue, 149
    tart, 56
    water ice, 253
Pecan
    cherry kisses, 108
    drops, 93
    fudge brownies, 115
    oxford cake, 177
    southern lace cookies, 110
Petits fours
    glacés, 66-71

sec, 72-90
    sponges, 62-65
Pie, 213-218
    cream cheese, 192
    crust, 207-209
        graham cracker, 189
    filling, 209-212
Pineapple
    cheesecake, 193
    delna sauce, 165
    fritters, 159
    gâteau ananas, 199
    glacé à la reine, 262
    pie filling, 211
    tart, 57
    water ice, 253
Pisinger cake, 44
Pistachio
    Bavarian cream, 142
    bombes fruits with, 28
    boules with, 68
    charlotte, 144
    fédora roll, 31
    gâteau Monte Carlo, 203
    ice cream, 239
    squares, 29
Plum
    compote, 172
    pudding, 138
Polka, 21
Pontneuf, 21
Popovers, 226-227
Port sherbet, 257
Pound cake, 176
Praline
    bars, 17
    Bavarian pudding, 129
    Bavarian cream, 142
    charlotte, 144
    gâteau pansée camille, 204
    ice cream, 240
    mousse, 240
    paste, 240
    pastry cream, 54
    soufflé glacé, 276
Profiterole, 150
Progres, 63, 204
    gâteau carlos, 200
    gâteau fredolin, 201
    gâteau vatel, 205
Pudding
    baked, 120-127
    chilled, 128-131
    frozen, 263-264
    soufflé, 132-135
    steamed, 136-138
Puff paste, 12
    gâteau tampouss, 205
    millefeuilles, 16
    pastry, 13-18

Puits d'amoures, 18
Pumpernickel bread, 289
Pumpkin pie, 217

Quick cheesecake, 194

Raisin
    brown bread, 286
    date brownies, 116
    drops, 108
    hermits, 103
    muffins, 223
    pie filling, 211-212
    plum pudding, 138
Raspberry
    Bavarian cream, 141
    charlotte, 143
    compote, 173
    jellied, 145
    mousse, 273
    pie filling, 212
    sauce, 169
    Washington layer cake,
        182
    water ice, 254
Refrigerator
    cookies, 109
    cottage cheese cake, 195
    cream cheese cake, 196
Religieux, 18
Rhubarb
    compote, 173
    pie, 218
Rice
    à l'imperatrice, 144
    apricot condé, 149
    pudding, 125
        apple, 120-121
Riche cake, 177
Rimgo-Janji cake, 44
Rolls, 294-296
    filled, 30-32
    milk bread, 288
Rum
    flavored syrup, 150
    sherbet, 257
Russie, 70
Rye
    bread, 290-92
    muffins, 223

Sabayon, 171
Sacher torte, 44
Sago pudding, 127
Saint honoré, 21
Sandwich bread, 292
Sauces, 164-171
    hard, 161
Savarin
    cake, 59

chantilly, 146
glacé, 146
flambé montmorency, 153
kirsch, 153
mont-blanc, 146
nesselrode, 146
Savory sponge, 26
Scones, 225-226
Shanzy, 70
Sherbet, 256-257
Short crust, 54
Snow balls, 70
Soufflé, 153-158
  almond, 87
  glacé, 274-277
  new ocean, 147
  puddings, 132-135
  walnut, 88
Sour cream
  cheesecake, 197
  waffles with, 231
Southern lace cookies, 110
Split rolls, 295
Sponge cakes, 22-26
  petits fours, 62-65
  Vienna, 33-34
Spritz cookies, 110
  peanut butter, 107
Spumoni, 267
Squash pie, 218
Strawberry
  banana fraisette, 280
  Bavarian
    cream, 141
    pudding, 130
  biscuit glacé au fraise, 274
  charlotte, 143
  cheese chiffon pie, 198
  cheesecake, 189
  compote, 173
  des gourmets, 280
  gâteau Alhambra, 199
  ice cream, 241, 247
  Marie Antoinette, 38
  mousse, 273
    mon désir, 271
  parfait, 279
  sauce, 169
  shortcake, 148
  soufflé, 158

glacé hericart, 275
  pudding, 130
  water ice, 254
Sundaes. *See also* coupes
Suprême, 71
Sweet dough, 296-297
  French, 57-60
Sweets
  cold, 138-148
  hot, 148-163
Swiss roll, 32

Tangerine water ice, 255
Tapioca
  apple pudding, 121
  Canadian pudding, 123
  minute pudding, 125
Tarts
  French fruit, 54-57
  Brésiliennes, 88
Tea
  biscuits, 218-219
  drops, 111
  rolls, 296
Tortes. *See also* large Vienna
    cakes
  dobos, 42
  linzer, 43
  sacher, 44
Truffles
  loïe fuller, 38
Tuiles
  French, 89
  Belgian, 89
Turinos, 18, 71
Turnovers, 18
  rolls, 296
Tutti-frutti
  ice cream, 262
    nesselrode, 261
  mixture, 263
  pudding, 264

Vanilla
  Bavarian
    cream, 142
    pudding, 130
  charlotte, 144
  custard, 162
    pie, 216

sauce, 170
  French sauce, 170
ice cream, 241-242, 248
layer cake, 182
mousse, 273
pastry cream, 52
soufflé, 158
  glacé, 277
  pudding, 135
Vienna
  bread, 292
  cookie dough, 35
  pastry, 36-40
  rolls, 296
  sponge, 32-34
  wafers, 90
Vol-au-vents, 17

Wafers
  curled, 101
  Vienna, 90
Waffles, 230-231
Walnut
  Americana cookies, 94
  Bavarian
    cream, 142
    pudding, 131
  biscuit manqué, 63
  bohemian cake, 41
  branika, 36
  brittle, 243
  charlotte, 144
    romaine, 143
  ice cream, 242
  soufflé, 88
  sponge, 26
    Vienna, 34
Washington layer cake, 192
Water ice, 250-255
Wheat
  bread, 293-294
  cakes, 231
  muffins, 224
White bread, 284-285
White mountain cake, 178
Wine
  cake, 178
  sabayon, 171